Eduardo De Filippo

FOUR PLAYS

A Smith and Kraus Book
Published by Smith and Kraus, Inc.
177 Lyme Road, Hanover, NH 03755
www.smithkraus.com

First Edition: May 2002
10 9 8 7 6 5 4 3 2 1

Cover and Text Design by Julia Hill Gignoux, Freedom Hill Design
Cover: Maria Tucci as Filumena, Williamstown Theatre Festival.
Photo by Richard Feldman.

THE LIBRARY OF CONGRESS CATALOGING-IN-PUBLICATION DATA
De Filippo, Eduardo, 1900–
[Plays. English. Selections]
Eduardo de Filippo : four plays / Eduardo de Filippo ; translated by Maria Tucci.
p. cm. — (Great translations series)
Contents: Filumena-a marriage Italian style (Filumena marturano) — Christmas in Naples (Natale in casa Cupiello) — Those damned ghosts (Questi fantasmi) — Naples gets rich (Napoli milionaria).
ISBN 1-57525-229-5
1. De Filippo, Eduardo, 1900– —Translations into English. I. Tucci, Maria. II. Title.
III. Great translations for actors series.

Eduardo De Filippo

FOUR PLAYS

Translated by Maria Tucci

Introduction by Ronald Harwood

Great Translations Series

SK
A SMITH AND KRAUS BOOK

To my husband, Bob Gottlieb, who insisted,
and my daughter, Elizabeth Gottlieb Young, who supported

Contents

Introduction by Ronald Harwood vii

Translator's Note xiii

Filumena — A Marriage Italian Style
(*Filumena Marturano*) 1

Christmas in Naples *(Natale in Casa Cupiello)* 41

Those Damned Ghosts *(Questi Fantasmi)* 87

Naples Gets Rich *(Napoli Milionaria)* 123

Introduction

In the late summer of 1899 a renowned Italian actor-manager and playwright, Eduardo Scarpetta, seduced his niece Luisa De Filippo. Fortunately, this happened in Naples and even more fortunately, although Luisa may not have thought so at the time, she fell pregnant. The following year, on 24th May, she gave birth to a son. The baby was christened Eduardo after his father, but presumably because Scarpetta already had legitimate offspring, it was decided the baby should take his mother's surname. At the age of four, Eduardo De Filippo made his theatrical debut, playing a Japanese child in the operetta *Geisha* at the Teatro Valle in Rome. Two years later, aged only six, the boy was indentured. The apprenticeship was unusual, probably unique. "My father," De Filippo explained, "decided that the way to write for the theater was to learn the mechanics of playwriting and to do that you had to copy other plays. He put me in a room for three or four hours a day just copying out drama. I should add mostly his own plays." At the age of fourteen, De Filippo became a professional actor in the company of his half brother, Vincenzo Scarpetta. Although he was barely adolescent, the three main ingredients for De Filippo's future career were now in place: Naples, writing plays, and acting.

His first big success came in 1931 with his play *Natale in Casa Cupiello (Christmas in Naples)*. He had done two years of military service, returned to Scarpetta's company, and was married to an American, Dorothy Pennington. But both privately and professionally he was deeply unhappy. His marriage was soon ended and he decided that his father's repertoire of plays was too restricting. He set up his own company with his brother Peppino and his sister Tina. They called it La Compagnia Teatro Umoristico di Filippo. But the odd thing was that from then on the leading man was always referred to by colleagues and public alike simply as Eduardo.

They toured the length and breadth of Italy and were immensely successful, so much so that Eduardo's popularity protected him from Mussolini to whom he was bitterly opposed. When the war was over, he and his brother parted company. Eduardo bought and renovated the Teatro San Ferdinando to house his new company, but it was called more easily and accurately Il Teatro di Eduardo. In 1946 he wrote the first of his major plays, *Filumena*. Slowly and emphatically his fame spread beyond Italy. By the end of his life he had written over forty plays.

It is difficult to think of any other major playwright whose heritage and upbringing were so deeply and thoroughly drenched in the blood and sweat of theatrical life. It shows in all his plays — the intricate way his plots are constructed, the truth of his dialogue, the vitality of his characters and, of course, the sheer theatricality of his style. "To know and love Eduardo's plays one must truly love the theatre," wrote Thornton Wilder to an American student preparing a thesis on the playwright. "Not the well-shaped play, not the picture of relatively superficial customs and manners . . . but the show of the people, by the people, for the people — absurd, extravagant, often preposterous, but close to life and the stage."

De Filippo belongs to a select band of dramatists whose work has universal appeal. He explores the "conflict between the individual and society" — his words — the pain and passion of ordinary people, if Neapolitans can be described as ordinary people, and above all the delicious enjoyment of human folly. So, why are his plays not performed more often in English-speaking countries? Why is he not more widely celebrated? Why, when learned critics and scholars write of these things, do they not mention in the same breath with which they cite Moliere, Anton Chekhov, or indeed Berthold Brecht, a greatly inferior playwright — the name of Eduardo De Filippo?

There are, I suspect, at least two reasons inextricably linked. The first is Naples, the second, translation.

Naples is Italy in *excelsis*. It is a great, sprawling city nestling appropriately in the shadow of a volcano. In De Filippo's day, the division between rich and poor was great. The middle classes struggled to keep themselves from slipping into the mud of the slums and so developed pretensions that were triumphantly bourgeois. Neapolitans are skeptics and at the same time deeply religious. They have graceful manners and explosive tempers. The cliché of the gesturing, excitable, loving and passionate Italian is exaggerated in Naples. Neapolitans have developed into caricatures of themselves. I was once foolish enough to drive a car in Naples. It is the only city in the world where I have been verbally abused for stopping at a red light.

At the heart of Neapolitan society is the family, the members bound one to the other by apparently indissoluble bonds. To the outside world, they present a loyal and united front; inside the circle, rivalries, intrigues, loyalties, and betrayers are rife. The one figure exempt from these passions is the mother, an eternal figure of compassion, forgiveness, and love to whom all, husband and children, owe unquestioned allegiance.

Paradoxically, the Neapolitans do not speak Italian. They converse in a popular language that is something more than a dialect and they have a popular theater in which this Neapolitan tongue flourishes. And it was in Neapolitan that Eduardo wrote.

Naples, which inspired Eduardo, can also be described as his prison. To English-speaking sophisticates and cognoscenti, it has been regarded, and to some extent still is, as parochial, too limiting to have universal appeal. Joseph Roth, another great writer, has been similarly neglected because he wrote so compulsively about Vienna, yet his novel *The Radetzky March* is one of the prose masterpieces of the twentieth century. Eduardo's genius, like Roth's, transcends the confines of place. Nevertheless Naples and Neapolitan, I believe, inhibit Eduardo's wider acceptance among the great playwrights of this or any other age. And there is no dodging the fact that Naples and Neapolitan present huge problems to translators, directors, and actors.

"Style," John Gielgud said, "is knowing what play you're in." Much has been made of the influence of *commedia dell'arte* on Eduardo's style, always by theater historians without much knowledge of the theater. I believe this to be irrelevant and misleading, for *commedia dell'arte* is a tradition of exaggeration and slapstick, of mime and gesture, of music and dance. These characteristics are almost entirely absent in Eduardo's work.

In 1973, Franco Zeffirelli directed *Sabato, domenica e lunedi* (*Saturday, Sunday and Monday*) at the National Theatre in London with Laurence Olivier, Joan Plowright, and Frank Finlay. He decided on a style so vulgar that the result was totally baffling and wholly ludicrous. The actors were made to play in phoney Italian accents ("I gotta things-a to do!"), gesticulate wildly and in general behave like refugees from a Rosselini film of the 1940s. The caricature Neapolitans present of themselves was so magnified that the focus was entirely blurred. Of course the production, given the distinguished cast and the director's operatic and cinematic reputation, was highly praised. Audiences flocked to the theater. The play transferred to London's West End and to Broadway. But it did Eduardo no favors, because it transformed his human characters into cardboard stereotypes that would today, I suspect, draw justifiable complaints from the Italian community and very likely the European Court of Justice.

I was a lonely voice in my criticism of the Zeffirelli production, but then I had an advantage: I had seen Eduardo himself act and had some idea of his own style, and he certainly knew what play he was in. He appeared in *Napoli Milionaria* (*Naples Gets Rich*) when it was presented in the World Theatre Season at London's Aldwych Theatre in 1972. I admit to having felt disappointed after he made his first entrance. He seemed to be doing nothing at all. His voice was quiet, his movement restrained. Should he not be more extravagant—more, well, more Neapolitan? But as the evening proceeded I was completely won over, drawn into the world of the play by Eduardo's stillness, his economy of means, and above all by his realism. This was not acting, this was *being*. And I find now an essay by Eric Bentley, written in 1950 for his book *In Search of the Theatre*, in which he writes of Eduardo: ". . . his style is radically different from anything I expected. It is a realistic style. It makes few large departures from life . . . The assumption is that there is more drama in real speech and gesture . . . than in inventing speech and gesture." This is the crux of the Eduardo dilemma. His plays, because they are so particular and precise in their setting, so accurate in their observation, so rich in human emotion, require not embellishment but simplicity and truth.

For the most part, in England at any rate, the adaptations of Eduardo's work have been done by well-known playwrights from literal translations. (This is the fashionable approach and is thought, I suspect, to add commercial spice.) But the heartbeat is inevitably weakened, the color bleached, the brightness dimmed. There have been notions of setting the plays in Liverpool or Glasgow as substitutes for Naples, but these have come to nothing.

Maria Tucci is a distinguished actress, and as her name suggests she has an Italian heritage. It is rare to read translations that, without oneself knowing the original language, utterly convince one both of their theatricality and accuracy. What Ms. Tucci has done is to discover anew Eduardo's essence, to give his plays an English kiss-of-life so that the heart is revived and beats more loudly than ever. She has discovered a style that I believe makes the plays playable with the same realistic technique that Eduardo himself demonstrated. Here is an example of a passionate speech from *Christmas in Naples*:

> CONCETTA: Do you want to see me dead and buried? How could you write that letter? You know what your husband is like, he doesn't waste words. If he finds out about this, he'll kill you. And what about your poor father? This will kill him. Swear to me that you'll never send that letter. Make peace with him and stop this nonsense. Swear it!

The language is direct and uncomplicated, the syntax forthright without for a moment losing the dramatic impulse of character and situation. And she does this throughout the four splendid plays she has translated for this volume. It is to be hoped these texts that so vividly capture Eduardo's spirit will encourage performances of his plays in the United States and elsewhere. Ms. Tucci has precisely caught Eduardo's intentions, which are to transform Naples into the city where we all live and Neapolitan into the language we all speak.

In 1974 Eduardo De Filippo underwent heart surgery but this barely seems to have reduced his energy. Three years later he married Isabella Quarantotti. His last appearance on the stage was in a Pirandello play in 1980. He was made a *Senatore a viata,* a rare honor. His last labor was to translate *The Tempest* into ancient Neapolitan, which he then recorded playing all the parts except Miranda. A nice irony, for *The Tempest* is also the farewell of another great playwright-magician.

Eduardo died in 1984. He lay in state in the Rome Senate. 30,000 people filed past his coffin and paid him homage.

Ronald Harwood
Paris, September 2000

Translator's Note

Few translators start out without the French phrase "Traduire, c'est trahir" running through their minds. Limply translated this is: To translate is to betray. Translating Eduardo De Filippo adds a second betrayal. Eduardo (as he is lovingly and possessively known in Italy) wrote in Neapolitan. This is not simply a dialect, like Cockney, or a particular accent as opposed, say, to Roman or Florentine or Milanese; it is almost another language — almost but not quite. Trying to suggest in English the Neapolitan aspects of Eduardo's Italian is an almost insuperable problem.

I was born in New York City and shipped off to Italy for the summers. Italian was my first language. From my earliest youth, my Tuscan father (the novelist Niccolo' Tucci) thought it important to torment my mother by teaching me the subtle differences between the great bawdy Roman curses and the sharp, stinging Florentine curses. I could spot a Milanese walking down Madison Avenue from three blocks away, and I could do a perfect imitation of a Bolognese train station announcer. In other words I felt equally at home in Italian and English. But Neapolitan, again, is almost a different language — almost, but not quite. Of course every Italian can understand Eduardo's plays, but many of the expressions can float right by them; the delight in catching the Neapolitan way of putting things. After two years of working on Eduardo with help from Neapolitan acquaintances, I was the one who had to translate the rather amorous comments of a museum guard to a Roman friend who was guiding me through Naples. "How can you translate Eduardo?" friends would say. Traitor! Fool! But Eduardo is primarily a storyteller and an actor, and if we can tell his stories simply and clearly, the audiences will laugh and cry at the appropriate places.

I would urge actors not to use Italian accents — much as I like the movie *Moonstruck,* these are not plays about Italian-Americans. We don't do Chekhov with Russian accents or Ibsen with Norwegian accents. The plays are not farces. As with all comedy, the truer it is the funnier it will be.

It's important to remember that there is no word for privacy in Italian. My father used to tell me that in Naples, when people closed their shutters they bowed respectfully to their neighbors, as if apologizing for shutting them out from the view of their lives. Television must have deprived the Neapolitans of so much drama.

The Neapolitans live in one of the most beautiful cities in the world. The Royal Palace, right in the center of town, makes Versailles look small, and nearby are some of the greatest museums and churches in Italy. And then there's the famous Bay. "See Naples and die," goes the saying, but Eduardo tells us, "See Naples and live." Is it the water the makes the spaghetti taste better than anywhere else? The confectionery shops, the courtyards filled with orange trees, the smell of coffee — in almost every play of Eduardo's there's a discussion about the importance of coffee. Fireworks on the bay on New Year's Eve — this is a city that knows how to celebrate. There is joy simply in looking into the confectionery shops or walking down the street of Christmas figurines — open all year, store after store spilling out into the street, tiny replicas of bread stalls and fish mongers and saints in ecstasy, peaches and angels, oranges and cows and shepherds and baby Jesuses. Strolling down this narrow street in August, one can easily understand Luca in *Christmas in Naples*. Whom is he making the crèche for?— for himself. Every time I'm on that street, I come home with the oddest assortment of miniatures. For instance, blue plates of mussels and clams that would have pleased my daughter when she was six . . . or are they for me as a six-year-old? I tuck them away in the rational light of my New York life with the children grown up and my un-religious husband, not quite sure how to explain the seven baroque angels and tiny plates of plaster food.

Eduardo's characters are passionate and practical. As Joe Grifasi, who was so brilliant as *Filumena's* Alfredo, put it: These people are sentimental about their lives but they do not behave sentimentally. They may live in tremendous poverty and thievery in the squalor and grime of the desperate, narrow streets like those on which Filumena grew up, but they are sensible people. Rules are there to be broken, but life must be lived with as much pleasure as possible. None of the plays really have "happy endings." Rather, things get resolved, or accepted. Filumena has her boys safe at last and she is finally able to cry, but is this a romantic ending? In *Christmas in Naples*, Luca sees nothing and does even less, then he becomes ill and dies, happy in his vision of a huge crèche but leaving his family bereft — a strange, surprising ending. In *These Damned Ghosts*, despite the silliness, we once again find the theme of marriages gone sour, of people who no longer talk to each other because of boredom, irritation, or poverty. "On an empty stomach, Mari' . . . Romeo and Juliet would have been at each other's throats." Pasquale Lojacono would rather see ghosts than acknowledge what would be too dreadful for him to accept. In the end there is reconciliation and hope . . . or at least an acceptance. This is clearly one of the themes of *Naples Gets Rich* — the fight between the simple, decent man and the practical, hard-nosed woman who is trying to keep their heads above water. There is no easy resolution.

A note on pronunciation. In *Filumena* all the people in the household call Domenico "Dumi'," which is short for "Don Mimi." This suggests that he was a spoiled little rich boy — in other words, he's Young Master Mimi. In the lovely scene written for the movie version, Sophia Loren invents this name, Dumi', for him when she meets him in the bordello. My fellow actors fell asleep with boredom as I tried to explain these subtleties and they wisely convinced me to give up. "Dumi'" sounded like "dummy," so he became "Don Dome'." Filumena is Filume', as if they were too lazy to finish the whole word. The same goes for Conce' (Concetta) and Rosali' and Alfre' and so on.

For *Filumena,* our splendid designer at Williamstown, Hugh Landwehr, came up with a set that made one instantly feel one was in Naples. High walls of crumbling Neapolitan red with two floors of shuttered windows surrounded the central playing area, as if the house were built around a lavishly furnished courtyard. There were rugs and tables and paintings, and a lush garden was glimpsed upstage right. The kitchen exit was upstage left, the door to Domenico's study downstage left. The second floor gave us the chance to use upstairs windows for a few little scenes. The play began with romantic music and a magnificent scrim painted with baroque cherubs and scrolls, then a sharp change of light and through the scrim we saw two combatants poised for battle. The scrim lifted and the play began.

Films I would recommend seeing are De Sica's *Gold of Naples,* the film version of *Filumena,* especially for the Alfredo and Rosalia; and the Sophia Loren, Marcello Mastroianni *Marriage Italian Style* (the music is a bit soupy, but the chemistry between them and the early scenes of their meeting are wonderful). The film of *Napoli Milionaria,* if only for the opening scenes of street life and Toto's fake death scene, is invaluable. For music I would suggest listening to Roberto Murolo, who has recorded all the great Neapolitan songs simply, with only a guitar, instead of listening to over-produced "big" voices.

I have stayed as close as possible to the printed texts of the play, although I did take some minor liberties with *Christmas in Naples.* We chose to set the play in a house instead of an apartment, rather like the house in *Naples Get Rich,* giving us more sense of the street life — the laundry, the neighbors. And so the charcter of Raffaele, the doorkeeper, had to change, too. I not only took away his profession, I changed his sex and gave his lines in the second act to Carmela (this made the producers happy — one less salary). Then in the beginning of the third act Ninuccia takes over Raffaele's job of serving coffee. I hope I'll be forgiven these very small changes.

I have to give thanks to: Margherita Zanasi, who urged me on, spent hours, days, tossing lines back and forth; without her enthusiasm, I would have never started this project in the first place. She also introduced me to Piero di Porzio and Linda D'Argenio, who came to my rescue over some of the denser Neapolitan lines. To all my superb co-actors, and of course to my directors James Naughton and Dylan Baker. To Michael Ritchie, the producer of the Williamstown Theater Festival, who believed in these plays and gave us the opportunity to put them on. To my publishers, Smith and Kraus, who immediately grasped the importance of translating De Filippo into modern American. To Kay and Elliott Cattarulla — they know why. To my agents, Sarah McNair and Alan Brodie, who dealt valiantly with some thorny permissions issues. To the playwright Keith Bunin, for his hands-on support. To Mimi Gnoli, for everything. I owe special thanks to Ronnie Harwood, for his generous and acute introduction. Finally, my profound gratitude for the support and enthusiasm of Eduardo's widow, the magnificent Isabella De Filippo.

Filumena —
A Marriage Italian Style

(Filumena Marturano)

CHARACTERS

Filumena Marturano
Domenico Soriano, wealthy pastry maker (confectioner)
Alfredo Amoroso, horse trainer
Rosalia Solimene, Filumena's confidant
Diana, young woman
Lucia, the maid
Umberto, student
Riccardo, shopkeeper
Michele, workman
Nocella, lawyer
Teresina, seamstress
First Waiter
Second Waiter

Act One

It is evening, late spring, the last light of day. Filumena, barefoot, in a night-gown, her hair disheveled, stands outside her bedroom door. In the opposite corner, Domenico Soriano is in a dressing gown worn over his pants. He is an elegant man, very well dressed and cared for. He is outraged at the injustice, the treachery that has just occurred. A long dining room table in the center is perfectly set for two, with a beautiful centerpiece of roses. Rosalia (an older woman) is standing next to Filumena, Alfredo (his manservant) is on Domenico's side of the stage.

DOMENICO: *(Slapping his face repeatedly.)* Stupid, stupid, stupid fool! A hundred times a mi — mi — million times!

ALFREDO: W-w-what are you doing?

DOMENICO: I'm an idiot! I should go stand in front of a mirror and spit in my own face. *(Addressing Filumena.)* My whole life wasted . . . on you! Twenty-five years! My health, my strength, my brains, my youth . . . what more do you want? What more can Domenico Soriano give you? Do you want my flesh? Why not, here, take it. You've taken everything else and left me without a shred of dignity! *(Pointing to each of them.)* You, you, you, my neighbors, my own street, all of Naples, the whole world . . . treating me like a fool! I can't think about it. I can't bear to *think* about it! *(He starts to sink into a chair but then bounds up.)* When I think about what you've done . . . ! I should've known! Only a woman like you could sink so low. Twenty-five years and you're still the same. The same! But you won't get away with this! Don't think you've won! For three lire I'd kill you — a woman like you — that's what you're worth: three lire. I'll kill you and all your accomplices, too — the doctor, the priest, and these two pieces of slime I fed every day for years — I'll kill you all! *(Determined.)* My gun . . . get me my gun!

ALFREDO: *(Calmly.)* Your gun? . . . but you said . . .

DOMENICO: Go! *(Alfredo exits.)* "I said!" I've said a lot of things in my life and now I've been tricked into saying more. But that's all over now. I woke up! Understand? You're finished here. Get out! And if you don't walk out on your own two feet, I'll have them carry you out feet first, only this time you'll really be dead. No law on earth can stop me. Alfre'! My gun!

ALFREDO: *(Appears on the upstairs balcony off Domenico's room.)* I took them both to the gun shop to have them cleaned . . . I tried to tell you.

DOMENICO: All right . . . This is fraud! I'll haul you off to jail — all of you! And if you want to dance, Filume', we'll dance, but I'm playing the tune now. When I tell them what you were — the kind of house I took you out of — you won't stand a chance. I'll destroy you, Filume'. Destroy you! *(A pause.)*

FILUMENA: Are you finished? Do you have anything more to say?

DOMENICO: Just don't speak. I don't want to hear your voice. *(He can't trust himself.)*

FILUMENA: You'll have to hear my voice until you've heard everything I've got here inside me, and then . . .

DOMENICO: *(Interrupting.)* Whore! You were a whore and you still are.

FILUMENA: What's the big news? Doesn't everybody know what I was and the house I came from? But you kept turning up there, you and all those others, and I treated you like I treated all the rest of them. Why should I have treated you any different . . . aren't all men the same? If I did something wrong, that's between me and my conscience. But now I am your wife and no one's moving me out of here, not even the army!

DOMENICO: Wife? Whose wife, Filume'? Who do you think you married?

FILUMENA: You.

DOMENICO: You're insane. This is a conspiracy. I have witnesses.

ROSALIA: *(She wants to stay out of it if it's getting serious.)* Who, me? All I know is she got sick, then she was gasping, she was groaning and palpitating, we put her to bed and called the doctor, I was sure she was going to go before my very eyes. She didn't say nothing and I don't know nothing.

DOMENICO: And you, Alfre'? What about you? You don't know anything either?

ALFREDO: *(He's back downstairs.)* Me? Nobody ever tells me anything, I'm always in the dark around here.

ROSALIA: And what about the priest? Wasn't it you who told me to get the priest?

DOMENICO: Because she was calling for him and I wanted her to die . . . happy.

FILUMENA: You were the one who was happy! You couldn't believe your luck. You were jumping out of your pants. I was dying . . . at last I'd be out of the way.

DOMENICO: *(Nastily.)* Good, I'm glad you understand. So, when the priest said: "Marry this poor soul, it's her dying wish," I thought, why not . . .

FILUMENA: "What have I got to lose? Two more hours and she'll be dead." You should have seen your face when the minute the priest left, I sat right up and said, "Dommé, surprise! We're man and wife."

ROSALIA: I was so shocked . . . I jumped . . . my heart landed in my throat . . . I almost fell out of my chair . . . then I started to laugh, I couldn't stop.

(She's still laughing.) I really thought you were dying. You were amazing, you made it all look so real.

ALFREDO: Right up to the final agony . . . the death rattle . . . aaahhhggrrrr . . . *(They are both sharing in the brilliance of her performance.)*

DOMENICO: Quiet! I'll give you both the death rattle! What about the doctor? Didn't he examine her? All those years of medical training, he couldn't tell she was faking?

ALFREDO: Well . . . in my opinion . . . perhaps he made a mistake.

DOMENICO: Shut your mouth, Alfre'. The doctor will pay for this. He'll pay! You bribed him. Isn't that right? You slipped him some money . . .

FILUMENA: Of course that's what you'd think . . . Money! That's all you understand. It bought you everything you ever wanted — even me . . . Because you were Don Domenico Soriano you always had to have the best: the best suits, the best shirts, the fastest horses . . . you made them run! But Filumena Marturano made *you* run, and you've been running without even knowing it and now you'll have to go on running until you learn how to live and behave. I didn't bribe the doctor, he believed me, why not? Any woman after twenty-five years with you *would* be dying in agony. For twenty-five years I was his servant, isn't that true? He'd go off to the races — London, Paris — and if it wasn't for me going every day to check on his factories and the stores, all those trusted workmen of his would've robbed him blind. Then he'd come sailing back saying: "Oh that Filumena, what a woman." I've kept this house for you better than a wife would . . . even when I was a young girl, there I was, washing your feet . . . and never a word of gratitude . . . of appreciation — never once — I was just like a maid he could throw out the door at any moment.

DOMENICO: There it is — that arrogant look. If you had only tried to accept the way things are between us — to understand . . . a man like me with a woman like you . . . and be grateful. I took you out of a whorehouse and you're still dissatisfied. Did you ever ask yourself if you could possibly be in the wrong? If maybe you were hurting me? A woman with no feelings. I've never seen a single tear in your eye — never. In all the years we've been together, I've never seen you cry.

FILUMENA: Why would I cry? For you?

DOMENICO: A woman who doesn't cry, doesn't eat, doesn't sleep! I've never seen you sleep — you're like a creature from hell.

FILUMENA: When could you ever have seen me sleep? The moment you're out on the street you forget you've got a home. Every Christmas, every holiday, I'm here alone like a dog. Do you know when people cry? When they had something good once and it's gone. But Filumena Marturano never had anything good, so why cry? I never had the satisfaction of crying. When he was young, at least he was good looking, but now . . . look at him! . . . he's old . . . fifty-two . . . and he comes home with his handkerchiefs filthy with lipstick . . . You make me sick. *(To Rosalia.)* Where are they?

ROSALIA: I've got them safe.

FILUMENA: He doesn't even try to hide them — from me, what rights do I have — and he's slobbering after that . . .

DOMENICO: That . . . that . . . what? . . . that . . . who?

FILUMENA: That cow. *(Alfredo murmurs "mmmmooo" softly, as if to say "ah yes," then he slaps his own face as if to say that was a mistake.)* Did you think I didn't know? Your problem is you don't know how to lie. Fifty-two years old and you're running around with a girl of twenty-two and you're not even ashamed! Then you try to sneak her into my house saying she's the nurse! Can you believe it! Only an hour ago, I'm dying and they're hugging and kissing at the edge of my bed as if I was so far gone I couldn't see them! You make me sick. What if I'd really been dying, would you have done that? I was dying and you had the table all set for you and that plucked chicken . . .

DOMENICO: Was I supposed to starve? You die and I have to stop eating?

FILUMENA: With roses on the table?

DOMENICO: With roses on the table.

FILUMENA: Red roses?

DOMENICO: Red, green, purple, who cares? I have a right to put roses wherever I want, to eat with whoever I please, and to be happy you were dying.

FILUMENA: But I didn't die . . .

DOMENICO: No, you didn't die.

FILUMENA: No, I didn't die and I won't die.

DOMENICO: No, you won't die.

FILUMENA: No. I won't be dying for a long time, Dommé.

DOMENICO: And so that's our little problem here. *(A pause.)* But there's something I don't understand. If all men are the same, the way you say they are, why do you want to marry me? Why me? And if I've fallen in love with someone else and want to marry her . . . No, I *will* marry her . . . I'm marrying Diana . . . what difference is it to you how old she is?
(He tears off his dressing gown and starts to get ready for his assignation with Diana. Alfredo quietly helps. The dressing continues throughout the scene.)

FILUMENA: Oh, you're so pathetic, you make me laugh. Do you really think I went through all this for you? I don't give a damn about you and I never did. A woman like me, as you say, and as you've been saying for twenty-five years, is only out for herself. Do you expect me to just walk out of here empty-handed?

DOMENICO: *(Triumphant, at last he understands.)* Aha, so it *is* money! Did you really think I would've left you with nothing? Did you believe that Domenico Soriano, the son of Raimondo Soriano, the most famous and distinguished pastry chef in Naples, wouldn't have given you a little house and fixed things up for you?

FILUMENA: Oh stop. It's not your precious money, Dommé. Don't worry — you get to keep it all, and good luck to you. It's something else I want from you, and you're going to give it to me. *(A pause.)* I have three sons.

DOMENICO: Three sons, Filume'? What are you talking about?

FILUMENA: I have three sons, Dommé.

DOMENICO: And . . . whose sons are they?

FILUMENA: Men like you.

DOMENICO: Filume', Filume'! What do you mean, "men like me"?

FILUMENA: Because you're all the same.

DOMENICO: *(To Rosalia.)* Did you know about this?

ROSALIA: Yes sir, I did. This I knew.

DOMENICO: *(To Alfredo.)* And you?

ALFREDO: Me? No, no sir, never, nothing, no no . . . uh unnhh . . .

DOMENICO: *(Still not convinced, as if to himself.)* Three sons? How old are they?

FILUMENA: The oldest is twenty-six.

DOMENICO: Twenty-six?

FILUMENA: Don't look so scared, they're not yours.

DOMENICO: Do they know you? Have you met them? Do they know you're their mother?

FILUMENA: No, but I see them all the time and I even talk to them.

DOMENICO: Where are they? What do they do? How do they live?

FILUMENA: On your money.

DOMENICO: On my money?

FILUMENA: On your money. I've been robbing you, robbing you blind. I've been taking money from your wallet right under your nose!

DOMENICO: Thief!

FILUMENA: Yes, I've been a thief! I sold your suits, I sold your shoes, your hats, your scarves, and you never even noticed. Your ring with the diamond?

ALFREDO: I thought you'd lost it.

DOMENICO: I did!

FILUMENA: I sold it. I took whatever I needed to keep my boys alive.

DOMENICO: I've been harboring a thief in my house! What kind of a woman are you?

FILUMENA: One of them has a store in the next street. He's a plumber.

ROSALIA: *(She is amazed that she can finally talk about it.)* The plumber! He fixes the faucets, unclogs the drains. He plumbs! The other one, what's his name? Riccardo. Oh what a beautiful boy — that boy's got looks! He's got a store on the Via Chiaia, number 74 — not far from one of your own shops — he's a shirtmaker, he makes shirts, and he's got some very fancy customers. Then there's Umberto . . .

FILUMENA: He went to school. He wanted to go to school and now he's a notary, and he sometimes writes for the newspaper.

DOMENICO: So we even have a writer in the family.

ROSALIA: And what a mother she has been to them! Why would I lie? I'm old now and soon, very soon, I'll be standing before God who never listens to stupid people's gossip, so I will tell him that she took care of everything. She found different families to raise them, she couldn't be with them, but the moment they needed anything she found ways to get them medicine, advice . . . even Alfredo helped once *(She looks at Filumena.),* remember?

ALFREDO: What . . . me . . . ?

FILUMENA: You saw me waiting for the bus in the rain and you drove me out to a farmhouse . . .

ROSALIA: She had to get medicine to her baby, she was so upset, and Alfredo passed by in your car and gave her a lift.

ALFREDO: I waited outside with the pigs and the flies . . . I didn't know anything, Don Dommé.

ROSALIA: See, nobody bothered you at all. Your ugly little diamond ring helped the plumber and the shirtmaker open their shops. Two of your suits got Umberto through school, with a little extra for cigarettes. You were left out of it completely.

DOMENICO: I only paid.

ROSALIA: You were just throwing it away.

DOMENICO: It was mine, I could do whatever I wanted with it.

ROSALIA: I know sir, but you never even noticed.

FILUMENA: Rosali', ignore him. Don't even try to talk to him.

DOMENICO: Filumena, what are you trying to do? Destroy me? Now on top of everything else I've got three parasites living off me — laughing behind my back saying: Who needs to work, Don Domenico's loaded . . .

ROSALIA: Oh no, no sir, no! Donna Filumena did everything right, clever, like she had a real head inside that head. The money was delivered by a notary who said it came from a woman who wanted to remain unknown. The boys don't know about her and they don't know about you.

DOMENICO: They only know about my money.

FILUMENA: I should have killed them! That's what I should've done, eh, Dommé? I should have gotten rid of them like so many women do. Then Filumena would have been a good girl. Am I right? Answer me! That's what the girls in the house kept saying: What are you waiting for, get rid of it. Well I thought about it, I really did.

ROSALIA: But then you talked to Our Lady.

FILUMENA: That's right, Our Lady of the Roses.

ROSALIA: Our Lady of the Roses, the little shrine at the end of our old street. She grants a special grace once a day.

FILUMENA: It was three in the morning. I was wandering through the streets wondering what to do. I'd been working in that place six months and here I was *(A gesture to her stomach.)*, who could I ask? What should I do? I kept hearing the girls' voices in my head: "What are you waiting for . . . get it over with . . . we know a good doctor." I kept on walking. I looked up and there I was in front of her shrine, Our Lady of the Roses. So I looked her straight in the eye like this. "You understand everything. You even understand why I've sinned. Tell me what I should do?" *(A pause.)* But she didn't answer! Nothing! "Oh, so you think the less you say, the more we'll believe in you. I'm talking to you, so answer me!" And then I heard it: "A child is a child." I froze. Maybe if I'd turned around I'd have seen that someone was speaking from an open window or from down the street . . . but no . . . It was her. It was Our Lady. I made her listen and she gave me the answer. When the girls kept saying get rid of it, that was her testing me. And I don't know if it was me or her who nodded her head like this . . . but that's when I made her a promise. I swore it. "A child is a child." That's why I've stayed with you and let you treat me the way you've treated me all these years — for my sons. Do you remember that policeman? We'd been together five years, you and I.

ROSALIA: The policeman . . . !

DOMENICO: What policeman? What are you talking about?

FILUMENA: Yes, for once I attracted a decent man — he used to walk me home to the little apartment where you'd set me up after finally taking me out of that "house." You were always traveling . . . and he fell in love with me and wanted to marry me, poor boy, but you got so jealous I can still hear you. "Filume', I've got a wife, I can't marry you, but if you marry this man . . . " and you started to cry — because you're good at crying, not like me, you're really good at crying, isn't he?

ROSALIA: So you said good-bye to the policeman. But two years later your wife died . . .

FILUMENA: You moved me in here — and nothing changed. I kept thinking, he's young, he's not ready to tie himself down again, and I waited . . . Sometimes I'd say, "You know who got married? That girl who lived across the hall from me . . . " And you'd start laughing — just like when you'd be coming up the stairs of that house with your friends, that big fake laugh — and it always sounds the same no matter who's laughing — I could've killed you when you laughed like that. And so I waited . . . I spent twenty-five years waiting for a word from Don Domenico. Now he's old — fifty-two — but he's working so hard to be a young man. He runs after girls, makes a fool of himself, brings handkerchiefs smeared with lipstick here — to this house — to his wife! I'll throw both of you out! We're married. The priest married us. This is my house now.

(Doorbell rings, Alfredo goes to answer.)

DOMENICO: Your house?

FILUMENA: My house.

DOMENICO: Your house?

FILUMENA: My house.

DOMENICO: Now you're really making me laugh.

FILUMENA: Laugh, laugh! I love hearing you laugh now — because soon you won't be laughing anymore. (Alfredo returns looking worried and tries to step between them.)

DOMENICO: What do you want?

ALFREDO: Ahh . . . What do I want? . . . They brought the dinner.

DOMENICO: Why not? Don't I have the right to eat?

ALFREDO: Please, Don Dommé, now? All right. Come on in.

(Two waiters from a nearby restaurant enter with a large food hamper.)

WAITER: Here's the dinner. Signo', we've brought just one chicken because it's certainly big enough for two. Everything you ordered is of the finest quality. (Tells his mate to set down the hamper, and starts to place things on the table.)

DOMENICO: Listen, young man, here's what you've got to do . . . Just get out of here.

WAITER: Yes sir — right away, sir — and we didn't forget the young lady's favorite dessert. Here it is! And here's the wine . . . and . . . did you forget?

DOMENICO: Forget what?

WAITER: Don't you remember? When you ordered the meal this afternoon, I asked if you had any more of those old pants you don't wear anymore and you said, "Tonight. I'm expecting some very good news, and if it all works out, we'll celebrate and I'll give you one of my brand new suits." *(Profound silence.)* Things didn't work out? No good news?

DOMENICO: I said get out.

WAITER: I was just leaving. Come on, Rafe', no good news, only bad news. What rotten luck . . . Have a nice evening. *(Alfredo accompanies them to the door.)*

FILUMENA: Eat. What's the matter? Lost your appetite?

DOMENICO: I'll eat. Later, I'll eat and drink.

FILUMENA: Oh yes, when the cow gets here.

(Alfredo returns, followed by Diana. She is twenty-six, struggling to look twenty-two, and haughty. She speaks to everyone, looking at no one in particular. She's holding some little packets of medicine that she places mechanically on the table.)

DIANA: A mob, an absolute mob in the pharmacy! Domenico, I tried to find all the medicines. Am I too late? Rosali', run me a bath. Oh, red roses! Domenico, you sweetheart! *(Sniffing them.)* Ooh, what a lovely scent . . . Aaaah, I'm ravenous. I found the camphor and the adrenaline but no oxygen. *(She takes a nurse's cap with a big red cross on it out of her bag and starts to put it on.)* Domenico, I was thinking — I don't want to say the word, but — after all — I mean — if she dies tonight, I'll leave early tomorrow. I found a friend with a car. I'd just be in the way here, and I've got a few little things to settle in Bologna and you can tidy things up here. I'll be back in ten days. How is she, still holding on? Did the priest come? *(Diana has not noticed Filumena slowly advancing on her. Filumena speaks with great courtesy.)*

FILUMENA: The priest came. *(Diana turns and shrieks. Filumena keeps talking calmly and advancing on her.)* And seeing I was breathing my last . . . OFF!

DIANA: *(Genuinely perplexed.)* What?

FILUMENA: *(Points to the hat.)* That thing.

ROSALIA: You should take off that white "thing." *(Diana removes it.)*

FILUMENA: Seeing that I was breathing my last . . .

ROSALIA: Now, put it on the chair! *(Diana does as she's told to do.)*

FILUMENA: He encouraged Don Domenico to legitimize our union . . . Down! *(Completely at a loss, Diana has picked up a rose and is sniffing it. Once again she is confused by Filumena's demand.)*

ROSALIA: Put the rose down. (*Diana puts the rose down. Filumena continues to talk, becoming more and more emphatic.*)

FILUMENA: And Don Domenico thought, this is absolutely right. This poor woman has stood by me for twenty-five years, and lots of other little details that are none of your business. So he came right up to my bed, and with two witnesses and the blessings of the Holy Church we were married. Now you know how weddings always make you feel good? Well, I felt so good, I got right up and we *postponed my death!* Naturally when you're not sick anymore you don't need nurses or your filthy carryings-on in front of a dying woman. Because you knew I was dying! So take yourself and all this garbage right out of here to some other house.

DIANA: Oh. (*A giggle.*)

FILUMENA: And I know a perfect one for you — the one where I used to work.

DIANA: (*Still giggling and trying to be charming.*) Oh, yes? Where is that?

FILUMENA: Don Domenico can tell you. He went there a lot — he still does. Get going. (*Filumena has been backing her to the door, Diana keeps smiling as if to say: "I don't know her."*)

DIANA: Thank you.

FILUMENA: Don't mention it.

DIANA: Good night. (*Diana exits. Domenico has been absorbed in his thoughts — either exhausted or paralyzed by the situation, he has sunk into a chair during the previous exchange.*)

DOMENICO: A nice way to treat a young girl!

FILUMENA: It's what she deserves.

DOMENICO: I know you now. I've got to watch and weigh everything you say. You're like a termite, eating me up from the inside. You said there was something else you wanted from me, and it's not money because you know I'd have given it to you. What is it? What's going on in that head of yours? What are you plotting? Answer me!

FILUMENA: Dommé, do you know the song "I'm teaching my sparrow how to sing?"

ROSALIA: (*Eyes heavenward.*) Oh Heavens!

DOMENICO: What does that mean?

FILUMENA: You're the sparrow.

DOMENICO: What are you saying? You're talking in riddles — driving me crazy!

FILUMENA: A child is a child.

DOMENICO: What are you talking about?

FILUMENA: (*Her voice filled with passionate intensity.*) They have to know they've got a mother — who she is and what I've done for them — so they can love me. They mustn't feel ashamed every time they fill out a form — "mother unknown" — every time they're asked who they are. A family — a family, to turn to when they're unhappy . . . for comfort, for advice. They have to have a name.

DOMENICO: A name? What name?

FILUMENA: My name. Soriano. We're married!

DOMENICO: I knew it! But I had to hear it from your mouth — this sacrilege! Now I'm free to kill you! If I cracked your head open, it'd be like squashing the head of a poisonous snake — to protect any poor man who might be unlucky enough to cross your path! Here? Bring them here? To my house! You viper! Give them my name? These sons of a . . .

FILUMENA: Sons of a what . . . ?

DOMENICO: Of *yours*. And who else's? Hmm? who else's? Whose sons are they? You can't tell me — you don't even know yourself. Oh, you thought you'd fix everything up — clear your conscience and save your soul from hell by slipping these three bastards into my house. Over my dead body! They're not setting foot in here! *(Now suddenly very solemn, serious.)* I swear on my father's grave . . .

FILUMENA: *(In a burst of sincerity, she interrupts him.)* Don't swear! Look at me! I swore to Our Lady twenty-five years ago, and to keep that promise I've had to be a beggar in your house ever since. Don't make a vow . . . you won't be able to keep to it. You'll see — one day you'll be begging me.

DOMENICO: What are you plotting now, you witch? I'm not afraid of you.

FILUMENA: No?

DOMENICO: Just keep your mouth shut! *(To Alfredo.)* Bring me my jacket. *(To Filumena.)* Tomorrow you're out of here. I'm getting a lawyer. I'll bring charges against you, and if the law doesn't do the job, I'll kill you, Filume', I'll pick you up and throw you . . .

FILUMENA: Where?

DOMENICO: Back where I found you. *(He tears the jacket out of Alfredo's hand, struggles to put it on, then addressing Alfredo.)* Tomorrow, call the lawyer! Do you hear? And we'll talk, Filume'!

FILUMENA: We'll talk.

DOMENICO: I'll show you what kind of man you're dealing with. Domenico Soriano! *(Domenico is about to storm out. Filumena ignoring him, sits at the table inviting Rosalia to join her.)*

FILUMENA: Rosali', sit down. You must be hungry, too. *(They sit at the table.)*

DOMENICO: Watch your step, Filumena Napoletana!

FILUMENA: I teach my sparrow how to sing.

DOMENICO: *(He laughs as if to destroy her.)* Remember this laugh, Filumena Marturano! *(He laughs again and the curtain comes down.)*

END OF ACT ONE

Act Two

It is the following morning. Lucia is washing the floor, all the chairs are up-turned, some are on the table as the scene goes on. Lucia is putting the room back in order.

ALFREDO: Good morning, Luci'.

LUCIA: Don't you come walking in here with your big feet.

ALFREDO: Oh? Should I walk on my hands?

LUCIA: I've just finished washing the floor, and you're making a mess in here.

ALFREDO: Making a mess? I can't make anything! I'm dead. You know what that means? Dead. Up all night with Don Domenico, not a moment's sleep, standing in the wind, looking out at the bay — getting damp and cold — what a misery working for that man. Why did it have to happen to me? Not that I'm complaining. God knows, I've survived, I've had enough to eat, and we've even had some good times, me and him. Oh, Lord, let him live a thousand years, but quietly! I'm sixty years old now, I'm not a boy, I can't keep up with him. Luci', bring me a little coffee, would you please?

LUCIA: There isn't any.

ALFREDO: There isn't any?

LUCIA: There isn't any. There was some left over from yesterday, but I had a cup and Donna Rosalia didn't want hers so she took it to Donna Filumena, and the last cup I've saved for Don Domenico if he comes home.

ALFREDO: *If* he comes home?

LUCIA: Yes. Donna Rosalia didn't make any more.

ALFREDO: Couldn't you make some?

LUCIA: I don't know how to make coffee.

ALFREDO: You can't even make coffee? Why didn't Rosalia make it?

LUCIA: She went out early this morning. She said she had three urgent letters to deliver.

ALFREDO: Three letters? From Filumena?

LUCIA: Three. One, two, three.

ALFREDO: *(Considering his exhaustion.)* Oh, what'll we do? I have to have coffee. Here's what, Luci', we can take Don Domenico's cup, pour out half for me and fill the rest of his up with water.

LUCIA: What if he finds out?

ALFREDO: I don't think he'll be coming back, he was in such a rage. Anyway, even if he comes, my need is greater than his. Did I ask him to stay up all night in the open air?

LUCIA: I'll warm it up and bring it. *(Rosalia enters, ignoring them. Lucia jumps back to work.)* Donna Rosalia! *(To Alfredo.)* What should I do. Do you still want the coffee?

ALFREDO: Of course. Especially now that Rosalia is back, she can make it. Half a cup — that's all I want. *(Lucia exits. Rosalia continues to ignore him.)* Rosali', what's the matter? Lost your tongue?

ROSALIA: Oh, I didn't see you.

ALFREDO: That's right. I'm so tiny, I'm invisible. I'm just a little flea on this chair.

ROSALIA: A flea with a big mouth.

ALFREDO: You went out early today. Where did you go?

ROSALIA: To mass.

ALFREDO: To mass. And then you delivered three letters for Donna Filumena.

ROSALIA: If you knew, why did you ask?

ALFREDO: *(Feigning indifference.)* I'm in the import-export business here. I like to keep track of what's going in and out of his house. Where did you take them?

ROSALIA: I told you before, you're a flea with a big mouth.

ALFREDO: A big mouth? What's that mean?

ROSALIA: You talk, you talk, you're a sneaky little spy.

ALFREDO: Did I ever spy on you?

ROSALIA: Me? What's to spy on? I've got nothing to hide. My life is as clear as a mountain spring. *(Like a song she knows by heart.)* Born in 1870. You figure out my age. My parents: poor but honest. My mother Sofia Trombetta, washerwoman *(Alfredo mutters "washerwoman.")*, my father Procopio Solimene, blacksmith. *(Alfredo mutters, "Solimene," "blacksmith.")* Rosalia, that's me, and Vincenzo Bagione, umbrella repairman and restorer of wash buckets, were joined in holy matrimony on November 2nd, 1887.

ALFREDO: November second, the Day of the Dead.

ROSALIA: You have something to say about that?

ALFREDO: No, go on with your story.

ROSALIA: From this sacred union came three children in a single birth. When the midwife brought the news to my husband at work she found him with his head in a wash bucket.

ALFREDO: He was rinsing his hair?

ROSALIA: *(She is not amused.)* His head in a wash bucket. A heart attack had cut him off in his prime. So here I was — a widow and an orphan, too, with two parents dead . . .

ALFREDO: One, two . . . Bingo!

ROSALIA: Both of them dead and with four mouths to feed. I went to live right next door to Donna Filumena, who was a child, at 86 vicolo San Liborio, and started selling flyswatters, votive candles, and party hats. I made the flyswatters myself and earned enough to keep my children alive. Filumena and my boys played together, but then they went off to look for work, one to Australia and two to America, and I never heard from them again. I was left alone — me and the flyswatters and the party hats. *I don't want to talk about it!* If it hadn't been for Donna Filumena, who took me with her when she moved in here with Don Domenico, I'd be begging on the steps of the church. That's all. Good night and good-bye. The movie's over.

ALFREDO: If only that were true! We should be so lucky! But if you missed it today, it'll still be playing tomorrow and the next day. And we still haven't heard where those letters went.

ROSALIA: This delicate encumbrance which was entrusted to me cannot be divulged to the public domain.

ALFREDO: You're so mean, your body is all twisted up with meanness and you are ugly. My God, are you ugly!

ROSALIA: I'm not looking for a husband.

ALFREDO: *(Reverts to his usual tone with her.)* Oh look, I lost a button here. Could you sew it on for me?

ROSALIA: *(Moving toward the bedroom rather satisfied.)* Tomorrow, if I have time.

ALFREDO: And I need a string for my underpants.

ROSALIA: Go buy one and I'll sew it on. Now, if you'll please excuse me. *(She exits with great dignity. Lucia enters from the kitchen holding the coffee cup. As she is about to reach Alfredo, Domenico enters from the front door.)*

DOMENICO: Is that coffee?

LUCIA: Yessir.

DOMENICO: Give it to me. *(She turns and gives it to Domenico. He drinks it in one gulp.)* Oh, I really needed that.

ALFREDO: Me too. *(Domenico sits absorbed in his thoughts.)*

DOMENICO: Bring him some coffee. *(Lucia explains with elaborate hand gestures that the coffee she's bringing is already diluted.)*

ALFREDO: So, bring it anyway.

(Lucia exits.)

DOMENICO: What? What was that about?

ALFREDO: *(Smiling forcedly.)* She said the coffee is cold. I told her to bring it anyway.

DOMENICO: She'll warm it up. Have you seen the lawyer?

ALFREDO: Of course.

DOMENICO: When is he coming?

ALFREDO: As soon as he's free. Sometime today.

(Lucia enters with the coffee, gives it to him, then turns at the door to watch him drink it. He grimaces. Lucia exits smiling.)

DOMENICO: What if it's a disaster? What if I find out that there's nothing to do?

ALFREDO: Well then there's nothing to do. I won't drink it. When I leave, I'll go to the café.

DOMENICO: *(Confused.)* What?

ALFREDO: The coffee.

DOMENICO: The coffee? What coffee, Alfre'? I'm saying, what if the lawyer says there's nothing we can do?

ALFREDO: *(He decides to try again and spits it out.)* It's impossible!

DOMENICO: What do you know about these things?

ALFREDO: I know. It's disgusting!

DOMENICO: Yes, you're right, it's disgusting. She thought she could outsmart me. She thought she knew how to do it.

ALFREDO: Don Dommé, she's never known how to do it.

DOMENICO: Well, she'll regret it. I'll destroy her. I'm taking this all the way to the Supreme Court if I have to.

ALFREDO: *(Amazed.)* Good God, Don Dommé, for a cup of coffee? No, I don't think it's worth it.

DOMENICO: What are you talking about? Coffee! I'm worrying about my problems, and you're . . .

ALFREDO: Oh yes, of course, your problems . . . ahh, yes, they're serious, oh yes, Don Dommé.

DOMENICO: Why am I talking to you? What do the two of us have to talk about, the past? I need to talk about the present. The present! Look at you, Alfredo Amoroso, what's happened to you? Your face is sagging, you're losing your hair, you can hardly see, and now you're not making any sense . . .

ALFREDO: And I haven't had a cup of coffee.

DOMENICO: *(Perhaps to make him feel better.)* Ah well, time passes . . . everybody changes . . . remember Mimi' Soriano, remember Don Mimi'?

ALFREDO: *(Not realizing he's referring to himself.)* No sir, Don Dommé . . . is he dead?

DOMENICO: Yes, he's dead. That's right, Don Mimmino is dead.

ALFREDO: Oh . . . *(He gets it.)* You meant you, Don Mimi' . . . oh yes, of course . . . Ahh.

DOMENICO: *(Seeing himself as a young man.)* Black mustache, thin as a reed, up all night. We never slept.

ALFREDO: *(Yawning.)* You're telling me.

DOMENICO: Remember that girl in Capemonte? Gesummina.

ALFREDO: *(Alfredo mimicking the girls passionate cries.)* Mimi', Mimi' . . .

DOMENICO: Oh I can still hear her. And the wife of the veterinarian?

ALFREDO: Oh . . . oooh. Yes . . . the veterinarian's wife, she had the sister-in-law who was a hairdresser. No matter how I tried, she wouldn't look at me.

DOMENICO: But we made our finest conquests on horseback, riding in the park, trotting past the ladies . . .

ALFREDO: You were irresistible!

DOMENICO: Riding hat, crop in hand . . .

ALFREDO: Oooh, what a figure you had!

DOMENICO: My horses! My horses were the finest . . . Remember Silver Eyes?

ALFREDO: Silver Eyes — Holy, Mother of God, Silver Eyes! The little grey mare. That was a horse! She had a fire in her. She had a rump like the moon. When you were face-to-face with her behind, it was like the full moon rising! I fell in love with that horse, that's why I let the hairdresser go. Who could look at a woman after that! When you sold her, it broke my heart.

DOMENICO: Paris, London, the races — always traveling — I was on top of the world — free — no rules, no limits — I had only to say "Don Domenico" and any door would open. Nothing could stop me. And now — look at me: I have no will, no joy, no excitement. *(A pause.)* No . . . *(A decision.)* I'm going to fight. Domenico Soriano doesn't bend. I'll show them I'm still alive! So . . . what's been going on here? What did you find out?

ALFREDO: *(Reticent.)* What did I find out? Well, you know, it's like pulling teeth here . . . it's all secrets here, but I discovered that Rosalia delivered three letters today.

DOMENICO: To who? *(He knows who.)*

(Alfredo starts to answer but sees Filumena entering in a housedress, very busy.)

FILUMENA: Luci'! Here, put that over there, and Rosalia, give me the keys.

ROSALIA: Here you are.

FILUMENA: Luci'! Come here. Hurry up! *(Lucia enters.)* Take these sheets. Make up a bed in the study.

LUCIA: *(Surprised.)* All right. *(Starts to go.)*

FILUMENA: Wait . . . I'll need your room, too. Here are clean sheets, you can sleep on a cot in the kitchen.

LUCIA: *(Visibly upset.)* All right. And my things? Should I move my things?

FILUMENA: I said I need the room.

LUCIA: *(Her voice rises.)* What about my things?

FILUMENA: Use the closet in the hall.

LUCIA: All right. *(She exits. Filumena now decides to notice Domenico.)*

FILUMENA: Oh, you're here?

DOMENICO: Yes, I'm here. *(Cold.)* May I be permitted to ask what's happening in my house?

FILUMENA: Of course. There should be no secrets between husband and wife. I need two more bedrooms.

DOMENICO: For who?

FILUMENA: For my sons. It would have been three, but one is married and has four children, so he'll be staying home.

DOMENICO: So there are even grandchildren. And what's the name of this tribe you're taking under your wing?

FILUMENA: They can have my name for now, and one day they'll have yours.

DOMENICO: Without my consent? I don't think so.

FILUMENA: You'll give it, Dommé, you'll give it. *(Speaking as she exits.)*

ROSALIA: *(To Domenico with great respect as she exits.)* Excuse me.

DOMENICO: *(Shouts through the doorway.)* Over my dead body. Never!

FILUMENA: *(From offstage.)* Shut the door, Rosali'. *(Door slams in his face. Lucia enters.)*

LUCIA: Sir, the young lady is outside, with a man.

DOMENICO: Show her in.

LUCIA: She won't come in, sir, she says you should go out there, she's afraid of Donna Filumena.

DOMENICO: So I've got a mafiosa in my house! Tell her it's all right, I'm here. *(Lucia exits.)*

ALFREDO: If she sees her *(He makes slapping gestures.),* she'll slap her silly.

DOMENICO: Nobody's slapping anybody. This is my house. I'm the master here, *and she's nothing. (Loud voice announcing it to the house.) She just works here, understand?* Let's make that perfectly clear to everybody in this house. This is my house. *(Lucia returns.)*

LUCIA: Sir, she still won't come in . . . She says it's her nerves.

DOMENICO: Who's she with?

LUCIA: A man — she says he's her lawyer — he looks a little nervous, too.

DOMENICO: This is ridiculous! We're three grown men here!

ALFREDO: Leave me out of it. After last night, I'm a wreck. Actually . . . since you have to talk, I'll go in the kitchen and splash a little coff . . . I mean a little water on my face. If you need me, call.

LUCIA: Sir? What should I do?

DOMENICO: I'll go myself. *(Lucia exits to kitchen, Domenico goes off and returns, tugging a resistant Diana.)* Diana, please, don't be silly. This is my house.

DIANA: No, Domenico dear, after last night I absolutely refuse to see that woman.

DOMENICO: Diana, please, there's nothing to be afraid of.

DIANA: I'm not afraid! I just don't want to lose my temper!

DOMENICO: Don't worry. I'm here.

DIANA: You were here last night, too.

DOMENICO: It was all so sudden . . . that will never happen again. Come in, Signor . . . ?

NOCELLA: Nocella.

DOMENICO: Nocella. *(He shakes his hand.)* Come, sit down.

DIANA: Where is she?

DOMENICO: I'm telling you not to worry. Please sit down. *(They sit — Diana's back is to the bedroom door.)* So?

NOCELLA: I live in the same pensione as the young lady, and we met recently . . .

DIANA: He can tell you what kind of life I lead.

NOCELLA: We meet at dinner every night, not that I'm there very often, I'm a busy man . . .

DIANA: *(Unable to hide her fear.)* Excuse me, Domenico, could I change places with you?

DOMENICO: Of course. *(They switch seats so Diana is facing the bedroom door.)*

DIANA: So, last night at dinner I was telling him about you and Filumena.

NOCELLA: Yes . . . we had a few good laughs. *(Domenico glares at her.)*

DIANA: Oh no, no, no, I didn't laugh at all.

DOMENICO: The young lady was here because I had her pretend she was the nurse.

DIANA: I wasn't pretending! I *am* a nurse. I took a course with the Red Cross. I got a great big diploma! I never told you, Domenico?

DOMENICO: *(Surprised.)* No. You didn't.

DIANA: Well, why would I have told you? Anyway, I told him how you were tied to this woman whom you've never cared for. And Signor Nocella explained in great detail . . . *(Doorbell rings.)*

DOMENICO: The bell rang. Excuse me, let's step into my study. It'll be quieter in here.

(Lucia crosses from kitchen to answer the door.)

DIANA: Yes, perhaps we'd better . . .

DOMENICO: Go on in and sit down. *(As Nocella exits, he stops her.)* Any news?

DIANA: *(Intimately stroking his cheek. Domenico is impatient.)* You'll hear. You're a little pale . . .

(They both exit into study. A moment later Lucia enters with Umberto, a serious young man dressed nicely but modestly. His penetrating, observant gaze is a little intimidating.)

LUCIA: Here you are, please come in . . .

UMBERTO: Thank you.

LUCIA: If you'd like to sit down? I don't know where Donna Filumena is.

UMBERTO: Thank you, I'll sit here and wait.

(Lucia starts off for kitchen, then doorbell rings, Lucia exits to open the door. Umberto takes out a little notebook and starts to write as Lucia returns with Riccardo. He is flashily, elegantly dressed.)

LUCIA: Please come in.

RICCARDO: *(Looks at his watch.)* Could you tell me what this is all about? I haven't got much time. I'm a busy man. Hmm. Listen . . . come here. *(She comes over.)* Been working here long?

LUCIA: About a year and a half.

RICCARDO: You know, you're a nice looking girl. You could go far.

LUCIA: Yes, if I don't lose my looks.

RICCARDO: Come see me in my store. I'll see what I can do for you. *(He hands her his card.)*

LUCIA: You've got a store?

RICCARDO: Via Chiaia number seventy-four. I'll make you a shirt.

LUCIA: What? Do you think I'd wear a man's shirt? Go on.

RICCARDO: I serve both men and women. I make shirts for men . . . and for women, I take them off. *(He tries to kiss her.)*

LUCIA: *(Offended, pushing him away.)* No! No. Are you crazy? I'm telling Donna Filumena . . . and there's somebody here. *(Doorbell rings.)*

RICCARDO: *(Notices Umberto and is amused.)* Oh, I didn't see you.

LUCIA: That's right, he doesn't see anything. He can't even see I'm not that kind of girl.

RICCARDO: So. I'll see you at my store?

LUCIA: Number seventy-four? *(She looks admiringly and smiles.)*

RICCARDO: Via Chiaia.

LUCIA: Maybe. *(Exits, tossing him a smile. He walks around the room, then to justify his behavior he speaks.)*

RICCARDO: She's not bad looking.

UMBERTO: So what?

RICCARDO: What are you? A monk?

(Umberto ignores him and keeps writing. Lucia returns with Michele.)

MICHELE: Luci', what's the matter now? That bathtub leaking again? I already put in a new washer. I guess I'll have to change the faucet.

LUCIA: No, the bathtub isn't leaking.

MICHELE: So what's leaking? I have to hurry. I've got to get back to my shop.

LUCIA: Nothing is leaking. Wait. I'll go call Donna Filumena. *(She exits.)*

MICHELE: How do you do? *(Respectfully to Riccardo, who answers with barely a nod.)* Nice morning, eh? I'm the only one in my shop. I had to leave it empty. *(Pulls out a single cigarette.)* Got a light?

RICCARDO: *(Arrogant.)* No.

MICHELE: So, I won't smoke. *(Pause as he looks around.)* Are you a member of the family?

RICCARDO: What are you, the chief of police?

MICHELE: What is that supposed to mean?

RICCARDO: All those questions. You like to talk. I don't.

MICHELE: Well, you don't have to be so rude about it. Who do you think you are? *(Umberto has been writing, he now looks up.)*

UMBERTO: He thinks he's God's gift to women. And he's an animal.

RICCARDO: Who are you calling an animal?

UMBERTO: Excuse me. You walk in here as if you own the place, you can't keep your hands off the maid, and now you're picking on this poor bastard.

MICHELE: Hey, who are you calling a bastard! I'm just minding my own business here. You're lucky we're not out in the street.

RICCARDO: *(To Umberto.)* You know, I've had it with you. I'm going to teach you a little lesson in respect. In fact, I think I'm going to punch you in the face right here.

MICHELE: Oh yeah? Come on, let's see you do it.

RICCARDO: You think I'm scared of you? *(The two men advance slowly on each other. Umberto gets up to protect Michele, but Michele pushes him away.)*

MICHELE: Hey! *(To Umberto.)* You stay out of this.

(Kicks and punches that never land, finally the boys are locked in an elaborate contortion as Filumena enters, followed by Rosalia.)

FILUMENA: Eh! Boys! What's going on? Who started this? What do you think, you're out in the street? *(The boys break apart and assume nonchalant poses.)*

UMBERTO: *(Touching his hurt nose.)* I was trying to stop them.

RICCARDO: Me too.

MICHELE: So was I.

FILUMENA: Who started it?

THE THREE BOYS: He did! *(Each points to the others.)*

FILUMENA: Nonsense, this is disgusting! Aren't you ashamed? Fighting each other! So. Boys. *(Not knowing how to start.)* How's business?

MICHELE: Not bad. Thank God.

FILUMENA: And the babies? One of them was sick last week?

MICHELE: Yes, the little one had a little fever. He ate a couple of pounds of grapes when his mother wasn't looking. I was out. His stomach puffed out to here, like a beach ball. Well, four kids, there's always something. Lucky they all love castor oil. When one of them gets it they all scream for it, so we line them up on four little potties and let 'er rip. You know . . . kids.

UMBERTO: Excuse me, ma'am, when I received your note this morning, your name meant nothing to me. But then I noticed the address. I realized that you must be the lady I run into almost every day on my way to work, and once I walked you home to this address because you hurt your foot. So I remembered the address and figured it was you.

FILUMENA: That's right, I'd hurt my foot.

RICCARDO: What's this all about?

FILUMENA: How's the store in via Chiaia?

RICCARDO: Fine. What could be wrong? Of course, if all my customers were like you, I'd be out of business in a month. You come in three times a week and you've got to look at every piece of fabric — this one yes, this one no — how is this one selling? I know you buy a lot of shirts, but when you leave it's like a tornado hit. It takes three men to get things back in shape.

FILUMENA: *(Maternally.)* Well, in the future I won't be bothering you anymore.

RICCARDO: No, it's fine. The customer is always right. But I sweat through a whole shirt every time you come in.

FILUMENA: All right, boys. Come and sit down so we can talk. *(Almost amused.)* I've called you here on some serious business . . .

(Domenico interrupts entering with Nocella. He is confident, easygoing, and sure of himself again.)

DOMENICO: Filumena, stop. Don't make even more of a mess. Here's the lawyer. He'll explain everything to you. *(To the boys.)* The lady made a mistake. She brought you here for no good reason. We're sorry to have inconvenienced you, you can all go back to work.

FILUMENA: *(Stopping the boys.)* Just a minute! I didn't make a mistake. I asked them here. This is none of your business.

DOMENICO: Do you really want to discuss this in front of them?

FILUMENA: *(Realizing this is serious, she turns to the boys.)* Excuse me, just five minutes. Will you wait out in the garden?

(Umberto and Michele start off a little surprised but obedient.)

FILUMENA: *(To Rosalia.)* Get them some coffee.

ROSALIA: Right away. Go on outside. Sit down and I'll bring you a nice cup of coffee.

RICCARDO: Listen, I can't waste my time here, I've got things to do.

FILUMENA: *(Firmly.)* Go out in the garden and wait with the others. They're waiting, you can wait too. *Go.*

RICCARDO: Yes, ma'am! *(He exits.)*

FILUMENA: So?

DOMENICO: *(Indifferent.)* Here's the lawyer. Talk to him.

FILUMENA: *(Impatient.)* I'm not too friendly with the law. So, what's this all about?

NOCELLA: Actually, Signora, I have nothing to do with this.

FILUMENA: So why are you here?

NOCELLA: No, I have nothing to do with this, because this gentleman is not my client. He didn't call me . . .

FILUMENA: You just walked in off the street?

NOCELLA: No.

FILUMENA: Dropped out of the sky?

NOCELLA: No.

FILUMENA: Then why don't you go home?

DOMENICO: Let him speak!

NOCELLA: The young lady spoke to me about this. Where is she?

DOMENICO: Me, her, it doesn't matter who called you, get to the point.

FILUMENA: Ah, the young lady! She's in there, am I right? She's scared to come out. Go on.

NOCELLA: According to the situation described by her *(Domenico glares.)*, by him anyway, according to Article 101, which I've transcribed here. *(Takes sheets of paper out and reads.)* Article 101: "In the case of imminent peril of death . . . etcetera . . . " explains all the details. However, the imminent peril did not exist, since your life, according to this gentleman, was not in imminent peril and this was, in fact, a fiction.

DOMENICO: I have witnesses. Alfredo, Lucia, Rosalia, her doctor . . .

FILUMENA: His nurse . . .

DOMENICO: My nurse . . . . *(He realizes what he's said.)* everyone. As soon as the priest left, she jumped up out of bed and said, "Dommé, we're man and wife."

NOCELLA: Thus Article 122 is to your advantage: Violence and Error *(Reads.)* "A marriage can be dissolved by those spouses whose consent was extorted with violence or was acquired as a result of error." Extortion did exist. Based on Article 122, the marriage is hence annulled.

FILUMENA: I don't understand.

DOMENICO: I married you because you were supposed to be dying.

NOCELLA: No, the marriage cannot be limited by conditions. In Article —? I don't remember which — it says: If the parties add a condition or special terms, the priest or official of the state cannot proceed with the ceremony of marriage.

DOMENICO: But I thought you said there was no imminent peril of life . . .

FILUMENA: Oh, stop! You don't understand all this garbage yourself. Excuse me, sir, could you talk to me in a language I can understand?

NOCELLA: *(Handing her the papers.)* Here it is, read it yourself.

FILUMENA: *(Defiantly.)* I don't know how to read.

NOCELLA: Signora. Since you were not on the point of death, the marriage is not valid. It's annulled.

FILUMENA: What about the priest?

NOCELLA: He'd tell you the same thing. In fact, it's a sacrilege. It's not valid.

FILUMENA: It's not valid?

NOCELLA: It's not valid.

FILUMENA: I should have died?

NOCELLA: Exactly.

FILUMENA: If I had died . . .

NOCELLA: *(He finished for her.)* It would have been totally valid.

FILUMENA: And he would be free to marry again. Have children?

NOCELLA: Yes, but as a widower. His new wife would be marrying the *widower* of the defunct Signora Soriano.

DOMENICO: Filumena would have become Signora Soriano *Defuncta*.

FILUMENA: So I have been waiting all these years to give my boys a legal name, and now you tell me that it's against the law? That's justice?

NOCELLA: But the law cannot sustain your intentions, however admirable, by becoming accomplice to an act bearing damage to a third party. Domenico Soriano had no intention of marrying you.

DOMENICO: That's right! If you don't believe me, get your own lawyer.

FILUMENA: No, I believe you. Not because you say it, and not because he says it, because *he's* a lawyer. But because I'm looking at you. You think I don't know you? You've got that look again. You're the boss, you're calm, in control.

If you were lying, you couldn't look me in the face. You never knew how to lie, and that's the truth.

DOMENICO: Signor Nocella, proceed.

NOCELLA: Then, with your permission . . .

FILUMENA: No, don't proceed, Mr. Nocella. *(To Domenico.)* I don't want you anymore than you want me. Signor Nocella, it's true. I wasn't dying — it was a trick. I wanted to steal his name. I didn't know it was against the law. The only laws I know are my own — the kind that make you laugh, not the kind that make you cry. *(She calls out to the boys.)* Boys, come here.

DOMENICO: *(Relaxed and superior.)* Filume', aren't you ever going to stop?

FILUMENA: *(Fiercely.)* Be quiet! *(The boys return as Rosalia enters from kitchen with coffee. She stops to listen.)* Boys, listen to me. You are grown men now. And here are two men of the world with all the laws and all the rights on their side, the world that protects itself with pen and ink. Domenico Soriano and this lawyer. And here is Filumena Marturano, who follows her own laws and who doesn't even know how to cry. He's said it over and over again — "If I had only once seen a tear in her eye." So now I say to you — with no tears *(To Domenico)*, see? my eyes are dry as a bone . . . *(Looking straight at them.)* You are my sons!

DOMENICO: Filume' . . .

FILUMENA: Who are you to forbid me to tell my sons that they are mine? Signor Nocella, is this against the law, too? You are my sons and I am Filumena Marturano, and what more is there to say? You are young men. You know your way around, and I'm sure you've heard about me. I don't have to talk about my life today, but until I was seventeen, I lived . . . *(Pause.)* Signor Nocella, do you know those alleys where people live in cellars — caves, really, under the houses — stifling, dark, no windows, no air, no light even in the middle of the day — packed full of people — In the summer you can't breathe from the heat and the sweat, in the winter your body never stops shivering. We lived in one of those holes . . . me and my family. How many of us? I don't know . . . too many. I don't know what happened to them and I don't want to know. I don't want to re-member! Always angry faces, always fighting . . . we'd go to bed without saying good night, we'd get up without a good morning. One thing still makes me shake when I think of it. I was thirteen. My father said, "You're getting big and there's not much food here. Understand?" We'd sit around the table, there was one big pot and I don't know how many forks, and every time I'd put my fork in they'd look at me as if I was stealing. By the time I was seventeen I was watching the girls all dressed up with their beautiful shoes, walking up and down with young men. One night I ran into a friend, I didn't recognize her she was so dressed up. She said to me *(Whispering.)*, "There's this place and there's this and that and the other . . ." I didn't sleep all that night. And the heat . . . the heat. And I met you. *(To Domenico.)* There in that house — it looked like a palace to me! One night I tried to go back home. My heart was pounding. I thought they'd shut the door in my face, but they sat me in a chair and stroked my hair as if I was better than them, someone special. Only my mother, when I said good-bye, her eyes were full of tears. I never went back to my family. *(Almost screaming.)* I made my own family. I didn't kill my sons! *(To the boys.)* For twenty-five years I worked for you — yes, it was me . . . I stole from him to keep you boys alive.

MICHELE: *(Moved.)* It's all right, it's all right, that's enough . . . enough . . . of course you had to do what you did . . . *(He embraces her awkwardly.)*

UMBERTO: There are so many things I'd like to say, but it's hard to talk. I'll write you a letter.

FILUMENA: I can't read.

UMBERTO: I'll read it to you.

(She looks to Riccardo, but he walks out the door.)

FILUMENA: Ah, he's gone . . .

UMBERTO: He's just a difficult person. That's just the way he is, but I'll go talk to him tomorrow in his store. It'll be all right . . .

MICHELE: You can come with me — to my house. It's small, but there's a balcony! The kids are always asking me, "Where's Grandma?" and I say one dumb thing or another. Now, when I walk in the door with you and say, "Here's your Grandma!" you won't believe the shouts, they'll bring the house down.

FILUMENA: *(Decided.)* Yes, I'll go with you.

MICHELE: So let's go!

FILUMENA: One minute — wait outside. *(To Umberto.)* Go out together and wait — ten minutes. I have something to say to Don Domenico.

MICHELE: All right, but hurry. *(To Umberto.)* Are you coming?

UMBERTO: Yes, I'll come down with you.

MICHELE: Good-bye, everybody. *(As they go.)* You know, I was thinking . . .

FILUMENA: Signor Nocella, would you give us a few minutes?

NOCELLA: I was just leaving.

FILUMENA: Just two minutes. I would like you to be here after I've talked to Don Domenico. Please, go inside and sit down *(Nocella exits, Rosalia slips out, Filumena puts her keys down on the table.)* I'm going. Tell the lawyer to do all the legal things. I want nothing, you're free.

DOMENICO: I should think so! You could have had a nice sum of money without going through all this.

FILUMENA: Tomorrow I'll send for my things.

DOMENICO: You're really crazy, you know? Why did you go and upset those boys? Why did you tell them?

FILUMENA: Because one of them is your son.

DOMENICO: *(Looks at her steadily, then tries to respond to his sudden emotion.)* Who's going to believe that?

FILUMENA: One of those three boys is your son.

DOMENICO: *(Not daring to shout.)* That's nonsense.

FILUMENA: I could have told you they all were, and you'd have believed me. I could have told you the truth before, but you'd have ignored the other two, and I wanted them all equal — no one special.

DOMENICO: It's not true.

FILUMENA: It's true, Dommé, it's true. You don't remember. You were going off to London, Paris, the races, other women. Do you remember how you used to give me a 100 lire note every time you left me? Well, one of those nights you came to me and said, "Filume', tonight let's pretend we really love each other." And you turned out the light. And that night I really did love you — but not you, you were just pretending. And when you turned the light back on, you gave me the usual 100 lire note. I took it and I wrote the day, the month, and the year on it — you know how I can write numbers — and then you left. And I waited, and I kept myself as pure as an angel — but you don't remember when that was . . . and I never told you anything. You used to say my life was always the same, that nothing ever happened to me, and when I realized you hadn't noticed a thing, my life went right back to being the same.

DOMENICO: So, which one is it?

FILUMENA: No, I won't tell you. They all have to be treated equally.

DOMENICO: *(After an instant's hesitation, then impulsively.)* It's not true. You'd have told me — to tie me down, to keep me in your clutches. A child was your only weapon — and you, Filumena Marturano, would have used it.

FILUMENA: You would have made me kill it. That's what you were like then, and you still are. I was scared to tell you. You would have made me kill it not once but a hundred times. It's only because of me that your son is alive today.

DOMENICO: So, which one is it?

FILUMENA: No. I want them all treated the same.

DOMENICO: They are the same. They're your sons. I don't want to see them, I don't know them, I won't acknowledge them. Get out!

FILUMENA: Remember yesterday when I said, "Don't swear, because one day you'll be begging me?" This is what I meant. Listen, Dommé, if you say a word about this to my boys, I'll kill you. I mean it, and I'm not like you who's been saying it every day for twenty-five years, but like me, Filumena Marturano: I'll kill you. Understand? Signor Nocella, you can come in now. *(To Diana.)* You too, "nurse," don't be scared. *(Diana enters.)* You've won, I'm leaving. *(She calls for Rosalia.)* Rosali', come here. *(Rosalia enters.)* I'm leaving. *(They embrace.)* Tomorrow Michele will come for my things. Stay well. Good-bye, everybody, you too, Signor Nocella, and forgive me. Listen, Dommé, did you understand what I told you? I'm telling you again in front of everybody — not a word of what I've said, eh? Keep it to yourself. *(Opens the locket worn around her neck and removes a very old, very folded banknote.)* Here's your 100 lire back. *(She tears a corner off and tucks it in her bosom.)* I'll keep these few numbers written on it, a little memento for me. Here *(She holds it out to him until he takes it.)*, you take the money, and I'll keep the child. Good-bye to all of you.

END OF ACT TWO

Act Three

Ten months have passed. The set is the same, but on the side table there are lots of presents and floral arrangements, bottles of wine and cakes, all beautifully displayed. Rosalia enters, she is dressed up, wearing a hat. Domenico is quite changed, all his bluster gone, his hair a little grayer. He seems almost humble, pensive — as if something is gnawing away at him. He sits reading the little notes of congratulations.

DOMENICO: Did you go out?

ROSALIA: I went to run an errand for Donna Filumena.

DOMENICO: What errand?

ROSALIA: Are you jealous? I went to our old neighborhood.

DOMENICO: What for?

ROSALIA: Oooh, he's really jealous.

DOMENICO: I'm not jealous, I'm just curious.

ROSALIA: I'm joking. I'll tell you *(Looks around secretively.)*, but don't tell Donna Filumena, she doesn't want anyone to know.

DOMENICO: Then don't tell me. *(He goes back to reading the notes.)*

ROSALIA: No, no, I think it would be good to tell you, because it shows you what kind of woman she is. She had me take 5,000 lire and fifty candles to Our Lady of the Roses. At six o'clock, at the exact moment you're getting married here, the old lady who takes care of the shrine will light the candles there.

DOMENICO: I understand.

ROSALIA: A saint. You're marrying a saint! And she looks like a girl again — so beautiful! I kept telling her all these months: Don Domenico hasn't forgotten you. He wanted the annulment so he could have a real wedding all proper and now, oooh, it's going to be beautiful. I can see it all when I close my eyes . . .

DOMENICO: Fine. Fine. It's all right. You can go help Filumena now.

ROSALIA: I'm going. *(But she can't stop talking.)* Oh, if it wasn't for her, where would I be? She took me in. She picked me up out of the gutter and set me down here, and here I'll stay until I die.

DOMENICO: Absolutely. Feel free. Make yourself right at home.

ROSALIA: Everything is ready for the day I die. Let's see: a long white gown with a little lace, underwear, white stockings, a little cap. It's all in a chest.

She knows. She'll dress me. She's all I have in the world. If only my sons would come back. Ah, well, I never give up hope. *(As she exits.)* Excuse me. *(Alone, he checks the flowers, the notes, then he says aloud to himself as if he has suddenly made a decision.)*

DOMENICO: All right.

(Riccardo, Michele, and Umberto are heard offstage.)

MICHELE: Six o'clock! The ceremony starts at six!

RICCARDO: We said we'd meet at five.

UMBERTO: I was on time! *(They enter.)*

MICHELE: We said five, I was only a few minutes late.

RICCARDO: A few minutes! It was forty-five minutes. You think that's nothing?

MICHELE: Well, five o'clock always means half an hour later, no? People say five meaning five-thirty or a quarter to six . . .

RICCARDO: Or the next day, or the next month . . .

MICHELE: Look, I've got four kids, they broke all the clocks in the house — I can't afford a new clock.

UMBERTO: *(Noticing Domenico they all speak respectfully.)* Don Domenico, good afternoon.

RICCARDO: Don Domenico.

MICHELE: Don Domenico.

(All three line up in silence.)

DOMENICO: Well, you were talking . . . don't stop because of me!

UMBERTO: Yes . . .

RICCARDO: Well . . . we were talking, and then . . . well . . .

MICHELE: Well . . . we stopped talking.

DOMENICO: The moment you saw me. So, you were late?

MICHELE: Yes sir, Don Dommé.

DOMENICO: And you were on time?

RICCARDO: Yes sir, Don Dommé.

DOMENICO: And you?

UMBERTO: On time, Don Dommé.

DOMENICO: "On time, Don Dommé." *(Pause.)* Sit down. The ceremony is at six. There's time. The priest is coming at six, and we're just the family. Filumena didn't want anyone else. Now listen to me, boys, I wanted to say this, and I've said it before, I think this calling me Don Dommé, well, I don't like it.

UMBERTO: Haahmmm . . .

RICCARDO: Hmmm . . .

MICHELE: Hmmm . . . .

UMBERTO: But you haven't told us what you'd like us to call you.

DOMENICO: I never told you, because I thought you'd have figured it out yourselves. Tonight I marry your mother, I've already talked to the lawyer — tomorrow you will all have my name: Soriano. *(Each boy looks at the others, wondering how to respond — waiting for the others to speak.)*

UMBERTO: Listen, I'll speak for all of us, because I think we all feel the same way. We are not children anymore. We're grown men, and we cannot bring ourselves to call you what you so generously ask us to call you. Some things you just have to feel inside.

DOMENICO: And you don't feel this, ah let us say . . . need, ah, necessity to call one — for instance, *me* — Papa?

UMBERTO: I couldn't lie to you. You just don't deserve that. For the moment, it's not possible.

DOMENICO: And you?

RICCARDO: No, I'm afraid not.

MICHELE: Not me, either.

DOMENICO: Well, in time perhaps you'll get used to it. Meanwhile, I am happy to get to know you, to spend time with you, because you are three fine boys. You all work in your different fields with the same good will and energy. Excellent! Fine. Fine. *(To Umberto.)* You seem serious and passionate about your work. You write articles . . .

UMBERTO: A few short pieces.

DOMENICO: Yes. So you want to become a great writer?

UMBERTO: No, I'm not that ambitious.

DOMENICO: Why not? You're young, I know that to succeed in this field you have to have passion, it's something that's in your blood — that you're born to do.

UMBERTO: Oh no. I don't think this is in my blood. You can't imagine how often I lose heart. I tell myself, "Umberto, you made a mistake. This writing is not for you."

DOMENICO: What would you have wanted to do instead?

UMBERTO: I don't know. You have so many ideas when you're young.

RICCARDO: It's all chance. Why do I have this store in Via Chiaia? Because I was making love to a girl who made shirts.

DOMENICO: *(Catches this one on the fly.)* Do you make love to a lot of girls?

RICCARDO: Yes, quite a lot. But you know, I've never found The One. I see a girl, I like her, I think: "This is it! I'll marry *her!*" Then I see another one, and I like her even better. I don't know what to do. There's always one I like more than the last one.

DOMENICO: *(To Umberto.)* You are different, you're more thoughtful and sensible about women.

UMBERTO: Up to a point. It's hard to be sensible about girls these days . . . You go out in the street, everywhere you look there's a beautiful girl. It's hard to choose. What can you do? . . . Try them all.

DOMENICO: *(Disappointed.)* You. You like women, too?

MICHELE: I like them so much, I got myself stuck right away — I met my wife, got her in trouble, and good-bye — now my feet are nailed to the floor. With my wife you don't fool around. So I just mind my own business, not because I don't like girls but because I'm scared.

DOMENICO: So you like women too. *(Pause, then he tries another approach.)* When I was young, I sang. We'd get together, seven or eight of us. Those were the days of serenading. We'd eat outside, walk up and down the streets, and always end up singing — mandolins, guitars. Which of you can sing?

UMBERTO: Not me.

RICCARDO: I can't.

MICHELE: I sing.

DOMENICO: *(Excited.)* You sing?

MICHELE: I couldn't work if I didn't sing. I sing in my shop, all day.

DOMENICO: *(Happily.)* Let's hear you.

MICHELE: *(Sorry he was showing off.)* Who, me? What should I sing?

DOMENICO: Anything you want.

MICHELE: I'm embarrassed.

DOMENICO: No, please sing for me. You sing in the shop.

MICHELE: That's different. Do you know "Munastero a' Santa Chiara"? What a beautiful song.

> *Munastero a Santa Chiara*
> *tengo 'o core scuro scuro,*
> *ma pecche' pecche' ogni sera*
> *penso a Napule comm'era.*

RICCARDO: *(Interrupts.)* If that's singing, I can sing too. You don't have any voice at all.

MICHELE: This isn't a voice?

UMBERTO: If you call that a voice, I can sing, too.

RICCARDO: What about me?

DOMENICO: With a voice like that, anyone can sing. *(To Riccardo.)* Let's hear you.

RICCARDO: No, I wouldn't dare. I'm not a show-off like him. But I can sing a little.

> Munastero a Santa Chiara,
> tengo 'o core scuro scuro,
> ma pecche' pecche' ogni sera
> penso a Napule comm'era

(The sounds get worse and worse, now Umberto joins in.)

> Penso a Napule comm'era . . .

(Michele adds his voice.)

> No nun e' overo no nun ce crero"

(A horribly dissonant sound.)

DOMENICO: *(Interrupting.)* Stop, stop! Enough. Be quiet! *(They stop.)* It's better if you don't sing. How could this happen? Three Neapolitans who can't sing!

(From offstage we hear Filumena arguing vociferously with the dressmaker. She enters dressed beautifully, earrings, hair swept up. Rosalia and the dressmaker follow her.)

FILUMENA: No, it's not my imagination, there is a problem here.

DRESSMAKER: Donna Filume', there's no problem. When did I ever lie to you?

FILUMENA: You're lying to me right now in my face. I'm not blind!

MICHELE: Good evening, Mamma.

RICCARDO: Good evening and congratulations.

UMBERTO: Good evening, Mamma. Congratulations.

FILUMENA: *(She turns, happily surprised.)* Oh. You're here? *(Back to the dressmaker.)* You know what's wrong? When you cut it, you kept enough to make a dress for your little girl.

DRESSMAKER: Never!

FILUMENA: I saw her in the street — we were wearing the same dress!

ROSALIA: Donna Filumena, you are so beautiful. A perfect bride. *(The dressmaker leaves, muttering, "What the hell did she want that dress to look like? I wouldn't steal . . . ")*

DOMENICO: *(He has been absorbed in his thoughts and he's impatient.)* Filume', I have to talk to you for a minute.

FILUMENA: Madonna, these shoes.

DOMENICO: Take them off.

FILUMENA: What to you want to say?

DOMENICO: *(To the boys.)* Boys, go into the study, have something to drink. Rosali', go with them.

ROSALIA: Come on in.

MICHELE: Come on. Let's go.

RICCARDO: *(To Michele as they're exiting.)* You know, you chose the wrong profession. You should have been a tenor.

MICHELE: Do you mean it? *(Riccardo and Umberto laugh as they exit, Michele follows them off.)*

DOMENICO: *(Looking at her steadily.)* You look beautiful, Filumena — a girl again. If only I were at peace I would tell you that you can still drive a man wild.

FILUMENA: *(Evading.)* I think everything's ready. I've been so distracted today.

DOMENICO: But I am not at peace.

FILUMENA: *(Artfully avoiding.)* Who could be at peace today? The only person you can count on is Lucia — Rosalia and Alfredo are old.

DOMENICO: Don't change the subject. Filumena, you know what I'm talking about. And you're the only one who can give me this peace of mind.

FILUMENA: Me?

DOMENICO: You know I did everything you wanted. After the annulment, I came to see you, many times, but they kept saying you weren't home. Finally I said, Filumena, let's get married.

FILUMENA: And tonight we're getting married.

DOMENICO: And you are happy. At least I think so.

FILUMENA: Of course I am.

DOMENICO: And you've made me happy, too. Sit down. Listen. I've tried so many times to talk to you in these past few months, but I couldn't — I'd always lose courage. I don't want to embarrass you, but we are about to be married, Filume'. We are not like two young people in love. We've lived our life. We have to look at this clearly and honestly. You know why you're marrying me, but I only know I'm doing it because you told me that one of those boys is mine.

FILUMENA: Is that the only reason?

DOMENICO: No. Because I love you. We've been together twenty-five years — that's a lifetime — memories, events — a life shared together. I'd be lost without you, I know that now. And I know I have a son, these are things you can feel and I feel it. But I don't sleep at night. It's been ten months since you told me, and I've had no peace since that night — I don't sleep, I don't eat, I don't walk, I'm not alive. I can't breathe. I do this *(He takes a breath.)* and it gets stuck, here. *(In his throat.)* You can't let me go on like this. You've got a heart, you're a woman who has lived, who understands and maybe even loves me a little. Remember when you told me not to swear, and I didn't swear. So now, Filumena, I'm begging you, on my knees, kissing your hand, your dress. Tell me, Filume', tell me which one is my son, my flesh, my blood. Tell me for your sake — or it will look like you're blackmailing me. I'll marry you anyway, I swear it! *(A long pause. She is looking at her man.)*

FILUMENA: You want to know? So I'll tell you. I'll just tell you which one it is, and then what? You'll take care of him, try to give him a better future, and, of course, you'll find ways to give him more money than the other two?

DOMENICO: So?

FILUMENA: *(Sweetly.)* Well, then help him, he needs it, he has four children.

DOMENICO: *(Anxiously asking.)* The plumber?

FILUMENA: The plumber.

DOMENICO: *(He gets off his knees taking this in.)* A good boy. Solid. Healthy. Why did he marry so young? How can he make a living in such a small shop? It's an art being a plumber. With a little capital he could get a bigger place, hire workmen, he'd be the boss — he could sell modern fixtures. *(Looks at her.)* Ah . . . well, well, of course the plumber — the one with the wife, the one who needs it the most.

FILUMENA: *(She admits she is caught.)* What's a mother to do? She has to help the weakest one. But you're too clever for me. No, it's Riccardo.

DOMENICO: The shirtmaker?

FILUMENA: No, it's Umberto, the writer.

DOMENICO: *(Exasperated, he violently pulls her up out of the chair and throws her back down.)* You just won't help me, will you? You're going to keep me begging right to the end.

FILUMENA: *(Moved by his heartfelt tone, she tries to gather up all her complex feelings, to finally give him a clear and honest explanation.)* Listen carefully, Dommé, and then we'll never talk about this again. I've loved you with all my heart and all my soul from the moment I met you. You were like a god to me . . . and I love you now, maybe more than ever. *(Realizing he still hasn't gotten the point.)* Dommé, why are you making yourself miserable? God gave you everything you needed to be happy: health, good looks, money — and I . . . I can't stand to see you suffer. I never would have said a word — ever. You would have married me and people would've said: "What a generous man to take in three unfortunate boys." *(Pause.)* Dommé, don't ask me again. I can't tell you. You have to be strong and a gentleman and never ask me, because I love you so much that in a moment of weakness, Dommé, I might . . . and that would destroy us. Don't you see? The minute I said he was the plumber, you started to make plans: money, capital, the big store — I know: It's your money, and of course you want to help him — be a father to him. But then the other two — you'd say: "They're not mine, they have no rights." They're three men, they're not three boys, they could end up killing each other over this. Don't think of you, don't think of me — think of them. Dommé, it's too late for us. We've missed the joy of having children. When you hold them all night and you worry because they can't tell you what hurts. Or they come home from school with cold hands and red noses looking for you and jump into your arms saying "Papa." But now that they're men, they're either all our sons or they'll be enemies. Listen, you still have time to change your mind . . . we can leave things as they are and go our separate ways. *(The organ starts tuning up. Rosalia crosses the stage to go open the front door. Domenico and Filumena look at each other, not moving.)*

ROSALIA: He's here, he's here! You should see him! The fancy Monsignor with all the trimmings!

DOMENICO: *(A long look and then a sudden clear decision.)* All right, Filumena, let's go our separate ways . . . Boys! *(They enter from the study.)* I need to talk to you. I am a gentleman and I want to be honest with you.

MICHELE: Yes, Papa?

RICCARDO: Yes, Papa?

UMBERTO: Yes, Papa?

DOMENICO: *(A long look, he is deeply moved, he looks at Filumena, then to the boys.)* Thank you. You've made me very happy. *(Pulls himself together.)* So, when two people marry, the father gives the bride away. But here there is no father . . . there are *sons*. Two will walk with the bride, and one with the groom.

MICHELE: We'll take Mamma. *(Meaning he and Riccardo.)*

DOMENICO: *(To Umberto.)* And you'll go with me.

ALBERTO: *(Enters from above on the balcony.)* It's five minutes to six and these shoes are killing me.

FILUMENA: Rosali' . . . ? *(She goes over to Rosalia, who puts the little wedding veil on her.)*

ROSALIA: It's all arranged. At six o'clock exactly, she's lighting the candles there. *(Filumena walks toward her man, then goes off with a boy on each arm and Domenico and Umberto follow. Alfredo, Rosalia, and Lucia follow into the garden. The lights change to indicate time passing, and the wedding party returns as rice is thrown. Filumena sinks into the sofa.)*

FILUMENA: Madonna! I'm so tired.

MICHELE: You can rest now. We're going. I've got to work tomorrow morning, early.

ROSALIA: *(Carrying a tray of empty glasses.)* What a beautiful ceremony. May you live to be a hundred, my little girl. She really is my little girl.

RICCARDO: It was nice, wasn't it?

FILUMENA: Rosali', a glass of water.

ROSALIA: Right away.

DOMENICO: *(Entering from study with a bottle of wine.)* No guests, no dinner, but at least a special bottle of wine shared with the family. It will help us sleep.

ROSALIA: Here's the water. *(She enters carrying the glass on a little plate.)*

DOMENICO: Who needs water?

ROSALIA: She does.

DOMENICO: Tell my wife that water is bad luck tonight. Call Lucia, and let's not forget Alfredo, trainer of horses.

ROSALIA: Alfre', Alfre', come and have a glass of wine with everyone. Luci', you too.

ALFREDO: Here I am. Ready, sir.

DOMENICO: *(He's handing out glasses.)* Filume', drink! *(To the others.)* Drink.

ALFREDO: Your health.

DOMENICO: Alfre', remember when our horses ran?

ALFREDO: Ah, those horses! Silver Eyes . . . *(He starts to make the shape of her rump with his hands.)*

DOMENICO: And then they stopped. They stopped running long ago. And I didn't want to believe it. I kept thinking we were still going strong. *(Looking at the boys.)* But it's their turn now — these horses. We'd really look stupid trying to run with them, eh, Alfre'?

ALFREDO: With them? Oh, my goodness, never! That would be a terrible idea.

DOMENICO: Drink, Alfre'. *(They all drink.)* A child is a child, and they are a blessing. In any family, a father might have a special feeling for one child — because he's intelligent, or good looking or strong — or foolish, arrogant and ugly — and the others understand, it's almost a father's right. But this won't happen with us, because we found each other too late. Maybe it's better that way. The love I had the right to give one of my sons will be divided between the three of you. *(He drinks.)* To all of us! *(Filumena doesn't answer. She has taken a little bouquet of orange blossoms from her breast and sniffs at them.)* Boys, tomorrow night come for dinner. Come home.

THE THREE BOYS: Thank you.

RICCARDO: We're going now, because it's late and Mamma needs to rest. Take care, and congratulations. We'll see you tomorrow.

UMBERTO: Take care of yourself.

MICHELE: Good night and congratulations.

UMBERTO: Good night, Papa.

MICHELE AND RICCARDO: Papa, good night.

DOMENICO: *(He looks at them gratefully.)* Give me a kiss. See you tomorrow. *(They exit.)*

FILUMENA: *(She comes to sit downstage, looking out at the view. She slips off her shoes.)* Madonna, I'm tired, I'm so tired.

DOMENICO: Running around all day. And the emotion, and all the preparations these last few days, but now it's all done. Rest. What a beautiful night. *(Filumena clears her throat and trembles a moment; sounds that are almost a lament flow out of her, then she fixes her gaze into the night as if waiting for something to happen. Tears start to flow down her face.)* Filume', what's wrong?

FILUMENA: *(Happily.)* Dommé, I'm crying. Oh, it feels so good . . . so good . . .

DOMENICO: *(Holding her close to him, he embraces her tenderly.)* It's all right . . . it's all right. You ran . . . you ran . . . you got frightened . . . you fell . . . you got back up . . . you pulled yourself up . . . you thought and you worried, and thinking is tiring. But now you don't have to run anymore, you don't have to think anymore. Rest. A child is a child — and they're all equal. You were right, Filume'. You were right.

END OF PLAY

Christmas in Naples

(Natale in Casa Cupiello)

CHARACTERS

Luca Cupiello
Concetta, his wife
Tommasino, their son
Ninuccia, their daughter
Pasquale, Luca's brother
Nicolino, Ninuccia's husband
Vittorio Elia, Ninuccia's lover
Carmela, a neighbor
Luigi, her husband
The Doctor
Maria, Armida, Rita, and Alberto, neighbors

Act One

In the Cupiello house, Luca is asleep in the double bed, the other side of the bed is rumpled as if his wife has left it moments before. Tommasino is asleep in a narrow bed hidden by a screen. A towel hangs off the screen and there is an iron washstand with a white enamel bowl and pitcher in front of it. In the left-hand corner, a table where a crèche is being made, with all the equipment necessary for the making of it: paint brushes, paper, cork, and a jar of special glue. On the opposite side is a dresser with saints and a variety of holy pictures, candles, and little unlit votive lights. It is nine in the morning of December 23rd.

Concetta enters. She walks carefully, holding a steaming cup of coffee in one hand and a pitcher of water in the other. Half-asleep, she puts the cup on the dresser and the pitcher on the washstand, goes to the window to open the shutters, then back to the dresser. She picks up the coffee and places it on the bedside table. In a monotone, as if she's done this a thousand times before, she tries to wake her husband.

CONCETTA: Luca, Luca, get up it's nine o'clock.

(*Luca groans, turns around, and goes back to sleep.*)

Luca, Luca, get up, it's nine!

LUCA: (*Wakes up suddenly.*) Ah! (*Yawns.*) Nine o'clock?

CONCETTA: Drink your coffee.

(*Luca reaches for it, but sleep overtakes him. Concetta starts to get his clothes.*)

Luca, Luca, wake up, it's nine o'clock!

(*Luca sits up and starts to remove woolen shawls and scarves that are wrapped around his head.*)

LUCA: Oh, it's nine o'clock? It's already nine. You barely get a chance to get into bed at night and it's nine in the morning. Concetta, is it cold out?

CONCETTA: Yes it is. It's freezing.

LUCA: I noticed. I couldn't get warm all night. Two sweaters, a scarf, shawls, wool socks. Remember these socks you bought? "I got such a bargain," you said, "It's pure wool." Remember, Concetta, remember? Concetta?

(*Concetta brings his clothes to the bed. Luca searches for his glasses.*)

Concetta, where are you? Did you go away?

CONCETTA: I'm right here.

LUCA: Then answer me. Show some sign of life.

CONCETTA: Go on, go on, I'm listening.

LUCA: My feet are frozen. These socks you bought, you said they're pure wool, well you got cheated, they're not wool . . . When you wash wool, Concetta, it shrinks. These, the more you wash them, the more they grow — they stretch — you can hang them out like flags. Where's my coffee, Conce'?

CONCETTA: *(Pointing to the nightstand.)* There.

LUCA: Where?

CONCETTA: Next to your glasses.

LUCA: Where are my glasses?

CONCETTA: Next to the coffee.

LUCA: Oh, now I can see what I'm smelling. Concetta, is it cold out?

CONCETTA: Yes, Luca, it's cold. It's cold. All right?

LUCA: Oh yes, it's cold. This Christmas, God has certainly pulled out all the stops. *(Takes a sip of coffee and spits it out.)* This is disgusting!

CONCETTA: It's just the weather.

LUCA: No, the coffee. Congratulations on the beautiful mess you made.

CONCETTA: So what do you want, cocoa? It may be a little weak, but it's coffee.

LUCA: This cup and coffee have never met.

(Concetta is searching through the drawer for a needle to mend his vest.)

CONCETTA: Woke up with a sense of humor this morning.

LUCA: Concetta, don't get offended, there's a lot of things you know how to do. Your onion frittata, for instance, it's like . . . ahhh. But you don't understand coffee.

CONCETTA: So spare yourself, don't drink it.

LUCA: You don't understand how to make it and you don't understand how to buy it. Because you're cheap. You can't be cheap with coffee. This is garbage. *(Puts cup down.)* It stinks like roach powder. Understand? Good. Is it cold out?

CONCETTA: Yes, Luca, it's cold, it's cold, it's very cold. Are you deaf?

LUCA: What's the matter?

CONCETTA: I've told you three times already — it's cold.

LUCA: Yes, it's cold. Well, this Christmas God has certainly pulled . . .

CONCETTA: Pulled out all the stops. You've said that.

LUCA: And you said *that.* Hmmm.

(Concetta has placed the mended vest back with his other clothes on the bed or near the bed. Luca yawns, looks around as if he's searching for something important but not sure what it is. Suddenly he remembers. In a panic he asks.) The Nativity? Where is it?

CONCETTA: There, it's there. Nobody's touched it.

LUCA: *(Admiring his work.)* Concetta, did you heat up the glue? This year I'm doing something different. I've got designs, plans. Pastorelli, across the way, thinks he's making a great one too. Hah! Wait till he sees mine — his jaw will drop. I'm making a whole hillside with little houses, lights. Concetta, did you warm up the glue?

(Concetta is fixing her hair at the mirror.)

CONCETTA: Luca, would you let me finish getting dressed? I've been cooking for three days, but I have to go buy food for lunch if you want to eat. If you don't want to eat, then I'll sit here and await your orders.

(She sits.)

LUCA: You didn't heat up the glue?

CONCETTA: No.

LUCA: What did I tell you last night? "The minute you're up, even before you make coffee, heat up the glue or else I can't work and the Nativity won't be finished in time."

(She gets up suddenly, grabs the jar of glue, and starts to go off.)

CONCETTA: Fine, I'll heat the glue, so today we can all eat glue for lunch. Christmas is a nightmare. The glue, the paint, the stink, the mess, every little angel, every little shepherd, every little goddam baby Jesus.

LUCA: You're getting old. You've gotten so old!

(She exits and Luca finally decides to get up, goes to the dresser and makes a quick genuflection, raises his eyes in awe toward the saints, crosses himself, then goes to the chair at the foot of the bed, slips on his pants with some difficulty. Back to the night table, his hat is hanging off the headboard and he puts it on. He tries to drink the coffee again, but spits it right out. Still shivering from the cold, he pulls his shirtsleeves down, yawns, goes to the washstand. All through this he has started the same litany Concetta used, to wake his son, Tommasino.) Tommasino, Tommasi', wake up, it's nine o'clock. Eh, I know you're awake, stop pretending.

(He fills the basin with water and soaps up his hands, while occasionally calling out to Tommasino.)

Tommasi', wake up, it's nine. You don't want to stay in bed all day, eh? You great big lunk, sleeping so late. Get up! You know, when I was your age, I'd hop out of bed like a grasshopper at seven o'clock to walk my father to work. I'd walk him right up to the door, I'd kiss his hand — in those days you kissed your parent's hand — then I'd go home and go right back to bed.

(Luca has soaped up his face, and is washing it thoroughly with lots of foam. He can't find the towel, and he is going through all sorts of effort to keep the

water from trickling down his back. Finally, he finds the towel and dries his face. He addresses his son more forcefully.)

I said get up! Understand? All right, I'll just ignore you. We don't want to start the day with a crown of thorns.

TOMMASINO: *(Curled up deep under the covers.)* My milk-bread!

LUCA: That's all you think about, your breakfast, your lunch, your dinner.

TOMMASINO: I want my milk 'n bread!

LUCA: Get up and get your own milk and bread in the kitchen. Your mother is not your servant!

TOMMASINO: I want it here or I won't get up.

LUCA: You get out of bed now or they'll have to carry you out on a stretcher. *(Concetta enters with the steaming pot of glue.)*

CONCETTA: Here's the glue. *(Places it on the table.)* I don't understand, a new Nativity every year, the kids all grown, who needs this? The whole house is a mess, the waste of money, the waste of time. Let's hope at least you know what you're doing.

TOMMASINO: He doesn't.

LUCA: What are you talking about? I've been making Nativities since before you were born. Everyone is the neighborhood comes to me for advice, and you think I don't know what I'm doing.

TOMMASINO: Well, I hate it.

LUCA: That's not true, you don't hate it, you're just showing off, talking tough. Everybody loves the Nativity. It's moving. It makes you feel like Christmas.

TOMMASINO: It makes me feel sick.

LUCA: *(Violently shaking the bed.)* Get up! Get up! Do you hear me? *(Concetta starts to make the bed, put the scarves and socks away.)*

TOMMASINO: I want my milk 'n bread!

CONCETTA: I'm getting it, now get up, sweetheart.

LUCA: *(To Concetta.)* You bring it here, I'll throw it out the window, and you after it. You're raising a criminal.

CONCETTA: *(Conciliatory.)* He's getting up. *(She tries to encourage Tommasino with hidden gestures, but Luca notices first him, then her. Meanwhile, Luca has put on his vest, his jacket, and a woolen scarf, and is starting to work on the crèche with glue, corks, nails, pieces of wood.)*

LUCA: I saw that! I saw that! Smoke signals!

TOMMASINO: *(Shamelessly insistent.)* I want my milk 'n bread!

LUCA: I'll throw it in your face.

CONCETTA: Get up, my angel boy, wash your sweet face and Mamma will bring you a nice bowl of warm milk and bread.

LUCA: No, you won't. *(She ignores him and continues folding clothes and making the bed. After a short pause he asks.)* Is my brother up?

CONCETTA: Yes, he's up. I already brought him his coffee. What a hero, he sneezes twice, he stays in bed for a week.

TOMMASINO: *(Trying to hide his alarm.)* He's up? Do you think he's going out?

CONCETTA: Yes, he says he wants to take a little walk, get some fresh air now that the fever's gone, and then go back to bed.

TOMMASINO: Do you think he's going to get dressed?

CONCETTA: I hope so.

TOMMASINO: No, I mean, do you think he's going to wear his coat?

LUCA: It's December, I guess he'll wear a coat.

CONCETTA: *(Suspicious.)* What's going on?

TOMMASINO: Oh, nothing. I just don't think he should go out. He could get relapsed.

(Pasquale knocks discreetly from offstage.)

PASQUALE: Excuse me please, may I come in?

LUCA: Yes, Pasqua, come on in.

(Pasquale enters all dressed but wearing slippers. Tommasino plunges under the covers.)

PASQUALE: Good morning, Donna Concetta.

CONCETTA: Good morning.

LUCA: How are you feeling?

PASQUALE: Better, better *(He coughs pathetically.),* but still a little weak.

LUCA: *(Taking his pulse.)* I'm so relieved. I was afraid you were going to spend Christmas in bed. Your pulse is normal.

PASQUALE: My tongue, check my tongue.

(Luca examines it carefully.)

LUCA: It's clean, it's clean. Now, listen to me, you're going to have to build yourself up now — red meat, red wine, and a nice walk by the seashore. That'll give us a chance to clean your room, air it out. It's been eight days. Do you hear me, Concetta? A thorough cleaning.

CONCETTA: Yes, yes.

PASQUALE: Actually, I was planning to just go to my office at the lotto parlor for a few minutes, but, Donna Concetta, I couldn't find my shoes.

CONCETTA: Oh? What do you expect me to do about that?

PASQUALE: *(Patiently.)* I don't expect you to do anything, but I've been in bed with a fever for seven days, I was wondering if you'd seen them?

CONCETTA: No, I haven't seen them.

LUCA: Do you remember where you put them before you went to bed?

PASQUALE: Where I always put them, under the bed.

CONCETTA: Well, why don't you look under the bed?

PASQUALE: I looked, Donna Concetta, unfortunately there's nothing there. They seem to have disappeared. Ask Tommasino.

(Tommasino pops right up in bed, on the defensive.)

TOMMASINO: Don't start on me! I'm not the kind of person who'd sell somebody else's shoes!

(Luca recognizes his son's tactics.)

LUCA: He sold your shoes.

PASQUALE: What? He sold my shoes? He sold them? What am I supposed to do?

CONCETTA: That's ridiculous! Why would he sell your shoes?

LUCA: Ask him. He's a thief. You've raised a thief. It sticks out all over him.

TOMMASINO: I didn't sell anything.

CONCETTA: He says he didn't sell anything!

LUCA: Don't lie.

PASQUALE: Confess!

LUCA: Confess!

TOMMASINO: I don't like the Nativity! Jesus, every time something goes wrong in this house, they pick on me.

CONCETTA: From the moment we got up . . .

TOMMASINO: I want my milk 'n bread.

LUCA: *(His hammer in his hand.)* I'll hammer you into the bed! A thief, you've raised a professional thief. I hope you're proud of yourself.

PASQUALE: Now I can't go out. I'm sick in bed for seven days and he sells my shoes.

LUCA: Pasquale, you'd better move out, find a room someplace else.

PASQUALE: Yes, yes. I'm getting out of here.

LUCA: *(To Pasquale.)* The family is breaking up. You'll have to move out. My poor brother, with this gangster in the house, it's not safe, I can't be responsible. *(Pulls his own shoes out from under the bed.)* Here, wear these. After Christmas, I'll buy you a new pair.

(Pasquale takes them and starts to put them on.)

PASQUALE: Well, if you insist, what can I do? But you should lock him up. He's a menace to society. Put him behind bars. Good God, I go to bed with a fever and get up with no shoes. Why did you sell my shoes?

LUCA: What's gotten into you? What right did you have to sell his shoes?

TOMMASINO: I had a right.

PASQUALE: You had a right?

TOMMASINO: Yes. I had a right.

PASQUALE: What do you mean?

TOMMASINO: I thought he didn't need them.

LUCA: Didn't need them?

TOMMASINO: Yeah, wasn't he supposed to die?

PASQUALE: To die? What's he saying?

LUCA: What made you think Uncle Pasquale was going to die?

TOMMASINO: What do you want from me? He lives, he dies. When the doctor came, he said it was serious.

PASQUALE: Serious? What are you hiding from me?

LUCA: Nothing.

TOMMASINO: It's true. He said it was serious, so I sold his coat, too.

PASQUALE: My coat? My camel hair coat?

LUCA: *(To Concetta.)* The camel hair coat.

PASQUALE: The one with the fur collar.

LUCA: *(To Concetta.)* The one with the fur on the collar. *(To Pasquale.)* Your coat.

PASQUALE: With the plaid lining.

LUCA: Yes, your coat.

PASQUALE: The one with the belt.

LUCA: Pasquale, you've only got one coat. *(To Concetta.)* And your son sells Pasquale's coat! The little turd.

(Pasquale throws Luca's shoes on the floor and sits down.)

PASQUALE: Now I can't go out!

LUCA: Pasquale, I told you, go find a furnished room.

PASQUALE: I will, I will, I'm getting out of here. He sells my clothes before I die. Can't you wait till I die before you sell my things?

LUCA: No, who's *he* to decide — when you die, *I* sell your things.

PASQUALE: *(Disgusted.)* Why don't you two fight it out between you and let me know who wins. Vultures! Cannibals. I'm living with a pack of wolves. My own brother, waiting for me to die. Don't hold your breath, I have nothing. People say: "You're so lucky to be living with your brother, they take care of you, they love you." If they only knew. A nest of vipers! If they only knew.

LUCA: Pasquale, I love you like a brother, but I have to tell you you're impossible.

PASQUALE: Me?

LUCA: You. Our sainted father used to say it all the time. "He's impossible!" Your friends are right, you're lucky to have a family. Eh? Let's be honest.

PASQUALE: I am perfectly honest.

LUCA: You pay me five lire a day. My wife brings you coffee in bed, she makes you breakfast, lunch, and dinner. She washes and irons your shirts, darns your socks. Now, just because my boy was having a little fun . . .

PASQUALE: Having a little fun? Having a little fun?!

LUCA: What do you want me to do, shoot him? Here, put the gun in my hand. *(Now he's angry at Pasquale.)* How dare this evil boy touch your precious clothes!

PASQUALE: No, how could I be so selfish as to want to wear my own shoes!

LUCA: *(Gets on his knees, Pasquale imitates him.)* I am on my knees.

PASQUALE: I kiss the floor.

(Luca is fed up.)

LUCA: All right! Fine. Enough. Enough! Take care, Don Pasquale, take care.

PASQUALE: *You* take care. What a family! They call this a family? Some family . . .

(He exits, muttering insults.)

CONCETTA: Listen to him, what a bore.

LUCA: He was right, you know. *(Yanking his son's covers off.)* Get up! Do you hear, get up!

CONCETTA: Luca! He'll catch cold.

LUCA: A cold won't kill him. It would take a bullet.

CONCETTA: Tommasino, come on into the kitchen, I'll warm up the milk.

(She exits, gesturing to Tommasino to get up. Noticing the gestures Luca calls after her.)

LUCA: You're the enemy. My enemy.

(Luca goes back to work. Tommasino has finally gotten up and puts on his pants, starts to wash his face, pours out the dirty water and refills the basin, soaps up his face.)

What are we going to do? You don't listen to anybody. You're a good boy, but you're a savage. You sell your uncle's coat? In December? Have a little common sense, you're not a child anymore. What are we going to do? They kicked you out of every school in Naples. In third grade, you said, "I don't want to study, I want a job." So, get a job. There are signs all over the city, "Clerk wanted."

(Tommasino reacts.)

You have to start somewhere, then you can move up. You know, I'm not going to live forever and we could use the money. I'm going to get you a new suit. The tailor will come after Christmas, he'll make you a nice warm suit, this one is all worn out, and a new shirt. Your mother tells me this one can't be mended anymore. A suit and two shirts.

(Still working on the crèche.)

I'm putting a mountain here, covered with snow and tiny houses — for distance — so they look far away. Then over here, the fish market, the greengrocer and the café, and over here the cave where baby Jesus is born. Do you like it?

TOMMASINO: *(Tying his tie.)* No.

LUCA: Well, of course, it's not finished yet. I'm also getting you a tie, this one's all stretched out, like a rat's tail. And for Christmas I'm giving you ten lire, so when you go out with your friends, you can buy them a drink, make a good impression. I'm putting a stream here, with a fisherman and a waterfall coming down the mountain. Real water.

TOMMASINO: Oh yeah, sure, real water.

LUCA: Real water. I hung the enema bag back here, the tube comes up from behind, and water trickles out. Nice, eh?

TOMMASINO: It's a piece of garbage.

LUCA: How can you say that? This is holy. It's about the birth of Jesus.

TOMMASINO: Jesus — with an enema bag!

LUCA: I'm not talking to you. You'll see when it's finished . . .

TOMMASINO: I won't like it even when it's finished.

LUCA: Then get out of my house.

TOMMASINO: Fine.

LUCA: Go find a job. I don't want to see your face again!

TOMMASINO: Why? Because I don't like your Nativity? Is there a law that says I have to like it?

LUCA: Get out of this house, you lazy bum.

TOMMASINO: Fine, but I still don't like it.

LUCA: So leave. In this house we respect the Nativity.

TOMMASINO: I'm going.

(Concetta enters with a big bowl of hot milk, places it on the nightstand, and starts to make Tommasino's bed.)

First I'll have my milk and bread and then I'll go.

CONCETTA: Luca, so what do you want for lunch today?

LUCA: Here we go again. Every morning she tortures me with "What do you want for lunch?" I say this or that and you go out and get something totally different. Let's just have a nice vegetable broth, you do it so well, and you can toss in 300 grams of elbow macaroni.

TOMMASINO: I don't like elbow macaroni.

LUCA: You don't live here anymore. These macaroni have nothing to do with you.

(Concetta has taken money out of the drawer, she puts some in her handbag and holds five lire in her fist, then she puts on a coat and a mended old hat.)

CONCETTA: And no dessert! Tomorrow is Christmas, we'll be eating so much. Money just disappears at this time of year. So, I'll just take twenty lire for groceries and five for you in case you need a few more shepherds or nails or something.

(She has put five lire next to him on the worktable. Tommasino is finishing his milk.)

TOMMASINO: There. I finished. My last meal at home with the family. This unnatural father throws his only son out in the cold on Christmas Eve. I know what I have to do. I'll get a job, but I won't set foot in this house again.

CONCETTA: What are you saying?

(While he's talking, he sneaks up to the table where Luca is working and deftly pockets the money.)

TOMMASINO: What am I saying? You'll see. Pretend your son never existed. Poof! He vanished, he disappeared!

(Tommasino exits.)

CONCETTA: Tommasino, come back here.

LUCA: *(Notices the money gone.)* He took the money! You're welcome to it, as long as I never have to lay eyes on you again.

CONCETTA: Tommasino, come back. *(To Luca with rage.)* What did you do? What did you do?

LUCA: Don't worry, he'll be back for dinner.

CONCETTA: He said he's leaving home.

LUCA: It's about time. He should get a job. I don't want him in my house anymore.

(Luca works on the crèche. Concetta pulls at his arm.)

CONCETTA: What happened? Tell me what happened? What?

LUCA: Leave me alone! I almost broke it. I can't be distracted. I have work to do!

CONCETTA: Luca, are you building the Basilica of St. Peter's? Just dot it with snow and a couple of shepherds and it'll be fine.

(Ninuccia enters. She is elegantly dressed — hat, gloves, and pocketbook, several heavy gold bracelets. She's obviously in a fury.)

Ninucccia, what are you doing here? So early in the morning!

LUCA: Ninuccia, what are you doing here?

NINUCCIA: Good morning, Papa.

(She takes a chair and puts it in the middle of the room and sits all sullen, sulky, and upset. The parents exchange significant glances. Luca tries to read Concetta's thoughts, but her impassive face reveals nothing. Then Luca addresses his daughter with great patience and sweetness.)

LUCA: What happened? *(No answer.)* Another stupid fight with your husband? I don't understand, he worships you, he gives you everything you want. That apartment! He works hard, when he comes home he needs some peace and quiet. He has hundreds of men working for him. He's got big responsibilities. Why did you fight?

(She's obstinately silent.)

Why did you fight? Why did you fight? *(To Concetta.)* Congratulations, another one of your masterpieces.

(Concetta, ignoring his assessment of her, pulls a chair up close to her daughter. The whispers and mutterings sound more like buzzing than a real conversation. The dialogue should barely be understood, but some of the words could be . . .)

CONCETTA: Ninu', you can't come here every time something goes wrong.

NINUCCIA: But he's driving me crazy.

CONCETTA: What? What, what does he do?

NINUCCIA: He picks at me, he fusses over me, he . . .

CONCETTA: Shhh.

(They stare at Luca who has crept up to overhear. Luca tries hard to catch a phrase here and there that might shed light on the situation, but as his efforts fail he exclaims indignantly.)

LUCA: So, I'm kept in the dark, as usual.

CONCETTA: *(Patronizingly.)* What do you want to know? What do you need to know? Go work on the Nativity.

LUCA: You are the enemy here! I always knew it. My enemy. You want me to go work on the Nativity? Fine, I'll go work on the Nativity. What a family! Jesus, Jesus, I can't believe it! The next time something goes wrong, don't come to me. You can cry your damned eyes out, I'll be working on the Nativity. *(Picks up the jar of glue.)* The glue's cold. What a family! The enemy of your own flesh and blood. *(He starts off, but lingers, hoping to hear.)*

CONCETTA: So then what?

NINUCCIA: I wake up, he's staring at me.

CONCETTA: So?

NINUCCIA: Staring at me!

LUCA: Nothing, nothing, they speak their own dialect. *(He exits into the kitchen.)*

CONCETTA: Then what did he say?

NINUCCIA: I don't know. I turned my back on him and walked out of the house.

CONCETTA: Oh, my God, you know he'll follow you here, and then . . .

NINUCCIA: I don't ever want to see him again!

CONCETTA: What am I supposed to do? Bar the door? Tell him you're not here?

NINUCCIA: I can't take it anymore! He never leaves me in peace, he's so suspicious, he has me followed, he's jealous of everything, it's driving me crazy.

CONCETTA: But, he's right, eh?

NINUCCIA: What do you mean?

CONCETTA: Ninuccia, you think I don't know what's going on? You'd better straighten up and start to behave.

NINUCCIA: Why? What have I done?

CONCETTA: Ninuccia . . .

NINUCCIA: What?

CONCETTA: Eh . . . you think I don't know? I'm your mother.

NINUCCIA: What? What? What do you think I'm doing?

CONCETTA: Ehh . . .

NINUCCIA: What am I doing?

CONCETTA: Hmm.

NINUCCIA: What? Do you want me to do something? Here. *(Pulls out an envelope.)* I'll do something! I'm leaving him. It's official. I'm running away. See. "To Mr. Nicola Percuoco, Urgent" *(Opens the letter.)* "Our marriage was a mistake. I'm in love with Vittorio Elia, and I'm running off with him tonight. Good-bye forever, Ninuccia"

CONCETTA: Are you crazy? You know your husband, he'll kill you. Ninuccia. You don't want to send that letter. Give it to me. *(She tries to grab it.)* Give me that letter!

NINUCCIA: No, Mamma, no!

CONCETTA: Give it to me!

NINUCCIA: No!

CONCETTA: Give it to me! Give it to me!

(Ninuccia throws it on the floor.)

NINUCCIA: Oh all right, take it.

(Ninuccia sits down, furious. Concetta picks up the letter and goes to put it in her handbag, which she lays on the bed. As she goes up to her handbag, she passes the statue of Our Lady.)

CONCETTA: *(To the statue.)* Holy Mother of God, Holy Mother of God, you tell me what to do. *(Turns to Ninuccia.)* All right now. Ninuccia. Listen to me. Listen to me. He's your husband now, I warned you not to marry him, but he's your husband now, and there's nothing you can do.

NINUCCIA: I'm gonna run away.

CONCETTA: And I'm gonna smack you across the face.

NINUCCIA: Go ahead, what are you waiting for? Why don't you plunge a knife into my heart while you're at it? Oh God, what have I done to deserve this? I'm going crazy, I'm going crazy! I can't control myself anymore! I'm gonna smash everything in sight!

CONCETTA: Ninuccia, listen, no no . . .

NINUCCIA: Yes, I'll break everything.

(Ninuccia rushes around the room breaking whatever she finds. Tommasino's bowl of milk, the plate that covered it, the objects on the dresser. Not content, she reaches the crèche and destroys it. Ninuccia's anger has passed. She bursts into tears and sits down, hiding her face in her hands.)

Are you happy now?

(Luca enters, slowly mixing the warmed-up glue in the jar. He stops two steps from the door because his foot bumps into a broken plate. He looks around and asks in a concerned way.)

LUCA: What happened?

CONCETTA: Nothing, nothing.

LUCA: Nothing? It's Pompeii. *(Now he sees the tragic demise of his Nativity scene.)* The Nativity? Who broke the Nativity?

(Ninuccia is crying, Concetta stands there holding blankets and pillows that she has picked up through the struggle.)

LUCA: This is your fault! I always said it, you are my enemy. This is how you raised your children. Now reap what you sow! I'm leaving, I wash my hands of all of you. I'm going to go live alone on a mountaintop.

(Concetta throws the pillow, and finally falls to the floor.)

CONCETTA: Fine. Go. Go. Go. I'm sick of all of you. I can't take it anymore. I can't take it anymore! Help! I can't, I can't take it, I want to die . . .

LUCA: Concetta, Concetta.

NINUCCIA: Mamma, Mamma, what's wrong?

(Ninuccia runs to help her. Luca rushes upstage to call Pasquale. As he passes the dresser, he pulls off his cap and addresses the saints.)

LUCA: Oh, Blessed Mother, help me! Pasquale, Pasquale, my wife is dying! Concetta, say something!

(Pasquale enters holding up his pants, as he will do throughout the scene.)

PASQUALE: What's happened?

LUCA: My wife, she's dying!

PASQUALE: What are you saying?

LUCA: Get the vinegar!

PASQUALE: *(Running off.)* Don't worry, she'll be all right, it's nothing.

LUCA: Where's her rosary?
  (He empties out her handbag in which she has put the letter, the letter falls out unnoticed.)

LUCA: Concetta, talk to me. Say something. Talk! Talk. *(He shakes her.)* Concetta!

NINUCCIA: Shhh, careful, careful.

PASQUALE: *(Returning.)* Here's the vinegar.

LUCA: Go light the candles, Pasqua'. Open your eyes, Concetta!

CONCETTA: *(Reacting to the vinegar.)* Yes . . . Yes . . .

LUCA: Wait, Pasquale', wait, she's talking.

NINUCCIA: Mamma, how are you feeling?

CONCETTA: *(A tiny voice.)* Help me, help me.

PASQUALE: What happened?

CONCETTA: *(Evading.)* Nothing, nothing.

LUCA: No use asking, there are no answers here.

PASQUALE: *(Still holding up his pants.)* By the way, Luca, your son stole my suspenders, too

LUCA: *(Pulls off his own belt.)* Here.

PASQUALE: *(Accepting.)* What are we going to do about that boy?

LUCA: He's a thief, Pasqua', it's his profession. What's there to talk about? Go find a room somewhere else.

PASQUALE: I will, I will. I can't live this way. *(Moves off, still muttering.)* I've got to go, I've got to get out of here. What am I waiting for? One of these days he'll steal me from my own bed. *(He exits.)*

LUCA: How are you feeling now?

CONCETTA: A little better.

LUCA: You really scared me, you know. You should have seen how scared I was. Concetta, there's only you and me now. Forget the children, we already know they're hopeless. *(With genuine bitterness.)* Concetta, we have to think about ourselves now. You worry and sacrifice, you kill yourself, and what's the point? It's as if you've never done a thing. Concetta, if you die, I die too. *(A cry of pain escapes from his throat, he removes his glasses and dries his eyes.)* How are you feeling?

CONCETTA: Better.

LUCA: *(To Ninuccia.)* You can see the color is coming back in her face.

NINUCCIA: Yes, she's better.

(Luca looks at the destroyed crèche; after a brief pause, he speaks almost to himself.)

LUCA: Well, I'll go start the Nativity all over again.

NINUCCIA: Papa, you can think about that now?

LUCA: Stay with her. *(As he passes the dresser, he takes off his cap, and gives a quick nod to the saints.)* Thank you.

(Ninuccia whispers to her mother as if in apology, her mother pulls her aside.)

NINUCCIA: Mamma . . .

CONCETTA: Do you want to see me dead and buried? How could you write that letter? You know what your husband is like, he doesn't waste words. If he finds out about this, he'll kill you. And what about your poor father? This will kill him. Swear to me that you'll never send that letter. Make peace with him and stop this nonsense.

(Nicolino enters, Luca goes up to greet him.)

Swear it!

NINUCCIA: *(Rather unconvinced.)* I swear, Mamma.

(Nicolino is about forty-five, showily dressed. He wears several rings and a gold tiepin. His gestures are slow and large. He is more clever than intelligent. He dressed in a hurry to run after his wife and he's missed some of the details in his usual precise dressing. His vest is incorrectly buttoned, the tie is askew, his shirttails hang out from behind his jacket.)

LUCA: Nicolino, my wife was dying.

NICOLINO: What do you mean?

LUCA: She almost slipped through our fingers.

(Nicolino goes up to the bed with affectionate concern.)

NICOLINO: What happened?

CONCETTA: Nothing. I just felt a little dizzy.

LUCA: She eats nothing, she worries about everything. Ninuccia came here all upset. I suppose you two had a fight, eh? What was it all about?

NICOLINO: Nothing, nothing.

LUCA: *(To the two women.)* Excuse me. *(Takes his son-in-law aside.)* Nicolino, you know, the problem is she never tells me anything — she wants to spare me — but you and I can talk, man to man. Tell me, what did you two fight about?

NICOLINO: Nothing.

LUCA: *(Exasperated.)* This is a conspiracy!

(As Nicolino turns to his wife, his voice rising.)

NICOLINO: Do you want everyone to know about this? Carrying on, making scenes like two buffoons in an opera? I'm a serious man.

(Luca notices Nicolino's shirt sticking out from his fly.)

LUCA: Absolutely, that's what I say.

CONCETTA: *(Almost seductively.)* Nicolino, Nicolino, I know what a busy man you are, you have so many worries, so many responsibilities, all those people dependent on you. You come home, you're tired, you get a little upset, you lose your temper, she understands — It was a little misunderstanding, it was nothing. Go on, apologize to her.

NICOLINO: *(Cordially.)* Well, if it was up to me . . . but she's the one. Who can understand her?

(Concetta moves toward Ninuccia.)

CONCETTA: Oh my little girl.

(Ninuccia turns away from him as Concetta claps her hands together as if she wants to smack her.)

Oh, she's so stubborn.

LUCA: You have to be patient.

(Tommasino enters, sulky and moody. He sits on the bed away from the others.)

Oh, you're back. Off your high horse?

TOMMASINO: I just came to celebrate Christmas and then I'm gone.

LUCA: I knew it! Nicolino, what can I do? I've had no luck with my children. The boy is worse than the girl. It's your fault, Concetta. Don't scream and don't faint, but you spoiled them. The girl, I will admit, is my fault. You know, the first child, a daughter. God knows how much I've suffered, the worry, the disappointments. *(To Concetta.)* Remember when she was sick? Typhoid fever. We made a vow to Our Lady. *(He removes his cap.)* Children are a joy and a misery. She went to school. She read and read. We had books all over the house, not like that one. *(Pointing to Tommasino.)* He's illiterate. When she was little, she'd be reading till two, three in the morning. "Ninu', turn off the light." "Papa, it's just a little light." As if I was worried about the money! It's that children need to sleep. As I said, a joy and a misery. Then one fine day you showed up and asked to marry her, and we were on our knees with gratitude.

NICOLINO: Oh, come now, please . . .

LUCA: Nicolino, we cried day and night up to the day of the wedding.

NICOLINO: Why, did you think she was marrying a hoodlum?

LUCA: Good God, no, we love you. Isn't it true, Concetta? I always talk about Nicolino.

CONCETTA: Absolutely.

LUCA: But you went and bought an apartment. We thought you'd move in with us and make one big family.

NICOLINO: Well, you understand I have certain obligations — salesmen, business partners.

LUCA: I know, of course, you entertain all the time, important people, but imagine a father seeing his daughter ripped out of his arms. She marries and moves away. *(He gets emotional.)* What can you do? What can you do? *(Looking at his son.)* Now, if you'd married *him*, I'd have raised a statue to you — in gold.

(They all laugh.)

TOMMASINO: Oh sure, I'd marry him!

LUCA: No, I mean if you were a woman.

TOMMASINO: I wouldn't marry him.

NICOLINO: *(Joking.)* And I wouldn't marry you.

TOMMASINO: Oh, you're breaking my heart!

LUCA: No, I was saying if you were a girl.

TOMMASINO: I still wouldn't marry him.

LUCA: What a stupid discussion! Forgive me, Nicolino. *(To Tommasino.)* I said, "If you were a woman." Are you a woman?

TOMMASINO: No.

LUCA: If you were a woman, I, as your father, would have a right to say, "Marry him," and you would have to marry him.

TOMMASINO: If I were a woman, I'd say, "I don't like him, and I'd rather rot in hell."

LUCA: Can you believe it? He fights with me even about things that couldn't happen.

NICOLINO: Well, it's typical, eh?

LUCA: Go on, now you and Ninuccia make peace, and let's not hear another word.

(Concetta pushes Ninuccia toward Nicolino and Luca pushes Nicolino.)

TOMMASINO: *(Notices.)* Oh, Nicolino, your fly's open.

(Nicolino looks down and rushes off to the kitchen to tuck the shirt in.)

LUCA: *(To Tommasino.)* I'd noticed it too, but I was waiting for the right moment. You don't just blurt out, "Nicolino, your fly is open."

TOMMASINO: What should I have said?

LUCA: You take him aside and you say, "I believe your shirttails are protruding from your pants."

(Nicolino returns and Luca pushes him toward Ninuccia.)

That poor man, you've made a fool out of him running after you. Go on, you two make peace. People will laugh at you. Tomorrow is Christmas, you'll come here, your mother is preparing a magnificent meal.

NICOLINO: I've ordered four lobsters, I'll have them sent over tonight.

CONCETTA: Oh, I was going to go shopping. I'll be right back.

NICOLINO: Absolutely not. You've just been sick. I'll take care of it. I'll have one of my boys bring over whatever you need.

LUCA: All right, but not too much. We want to eat very simply today, vegetable broth — Ninuccia knows what vegetables to get — and five hundred grams of elbow macaroni.

NICOLINO: Forget the vegetable broth. I'll have one of my boys bring a nice chicken.

LUCA: Yes, well chicken is very good, but we want something light, vegetable broth and five hundred grams of elbow macaroni.

NICOLINO: No, no, it's not enough. I'm sending you a nice chicken.

LUCA: You can send the chicken, but we're eating vegetable broth.

(Concetta and Ninuccia, talking softly, go toward the door and exit.)

NICOLINO: Well, see you tomorrow, Papa.

LUCA: Be patient. I don't know what you were fighting about, but let me tell you, you have to be patient.

NICOLINO: Of course!

LUCA: I know Ninuccia's not easy. I know it's hard to put up with her moods. *(With fervor.)* You have to love her. I'm getting old, Concetta is, too. My Ninuccia, oh God, she's the light of my life. I need to know that when I'm gone, there's a man like you who understands her and cares for her, or I'll never rest in peace.

NICOLINO: Of course, Papa, I love her, I love her so much . . .

(Nicolino doesn't dare add that he would even forgive her if she betrayed him.)

LUCA: Thank you, thank you.

(Luca shakes his hand with great feeling, then brings it to his lips to kiss it. Mortified, Nicolino doesn't have time to pull it away.)

NICOLINO: What are you doing? I'm the one who should kiss your hand.

(He kisses Luca's hand. Luca tries to pull his hand away, but Nicolino thinks Luca wants to kiss it again, so he holds onto Luca's hand and won't let go. Meanwhile Luca is struggling to hold his pants up with his left hand.)

LUCA: Let go, Nicolino, let go.

NICOLINO: No.

LUCA: Nicolino, please, let go! My pants are falling off.

NICOLINO: Excuse me. I'm so sorry, put your belt on. I'm sorry.

(As Luca walks him to the door Concetta enters and looks around the room at the mess.)

CONCETTA: She wrecked half the house.

NICOLINO: Just let me know how much it all comes to. Send me the bill.

CONCETTA: Don't be crazy! It's just old stuff. Don't even think about it.

NICOLINO: See you tomorrow, then.

(As he's picking up the shards, Luca finds the letter, reads the name on the envelope and calls out.)

LUCA: Nicolino! *(Reading.)* "To Mr. Nicola Percuoco."

NICOLINO: *(Turns in the doorway.)* Yes?

LUCA: This must've fallen out of your pocket.

CONCETTA: *(Desperate.)* No, no, no, it's nothing, it's her Christmas letter to you. She wanted to read it to you at dinner tomorrow night.

LUCA: You see, she loves you!

CONCETTA: Here, let me have it, she wouldn't want you to see it yet.

NICOLINO: No. I'll keep it. I'll keep it right here next to my heart until tomorrow night.

(Nicolino exits with his cherished letter.)

LUCA: So now. Back to work. We start all over again. Oh yes, we'll have a nice Christmas Eve, thank God.

END OF ACT ONE

Act Two

A large credenza triumphantly displaying all the splendid Christmas specialties, croccante, struffoli, pasta reale. In the center, the dining room table, set for a grand occasion. In the other corner, in the place of honor, is the finished crèche. Many little silver stars and Christmas decorations hang from the chandelier, and four long streamers made of colored tissue paper are hung from the chandelier to the four corners of the room. It's about nine o'clock. Ninuccia and Nicolino are expected for the gala Christmas Eve dinner and then they'll all go to midnight mass. Concetta has moved the table and the room is now rearranged. As she continues to place cakes and decorations around the room, she's chatting with her neighbor, Carmela, who is carrying in a big bucket of eels.

CARMELA: Donna Concetta, you forgot the eels!

(Concetta enters from the kitchen carrying a pile of plates.)

CONCETTA: Oh, Donna Carmela, the eels!

CARMELA: I thought you were coming over to get them.

CONCETTA: Forgive me, Donna Carmela, I forgot all about them.

CARMELA: I hope you like them. There are two of them, really lively, really fresh.

CONCETTA: They're beautiful. Thank you! Personally I find them disgusting, but Luca loves them. Here, let me take them.

(Concetta puts the plates down to begin setting the table.)

CARMELA: No, no, I'll put them in the kitchen.

CONCETTA: Thank you.

CARMELA: I don't make them anymore.

CONCETTA: I know, I know, but Luca says it isn't Christmas without the eels.

CARMELA: Well, that's that. I put them under the sink.

CONCETTA: Thank you, Donna Carmela. I don't know where my mind has been this Christmas, Donna Carmela. I don't know what to do anymore.

CARMELA: I just saw your husband running down the street, where was he going?

CONCETTA: He said he had to buy a few more shepherds.

CARMELA: Shepherds? Oh, for the Nativity. But it looks fine.

CONCETTA: Can you believe it! A man his age making a Nativity! "What's the point?" I ask him. "Who's going to play with it?" Do you know what he answers? "I'm making it for *me. I'll* play with it." What can you do?

CARMELA: My husband and I say it all the time: You should've been born wearing the pants.

CONCETTA: You never said a truer word. Donna Carmela, this is a man who has never known what it is to work, he and work have never been in the same room together, and my Tommasino has learned from him.

CARMELA: Oh, Tommasino, I saw him the other day, he was . . .

CONCETTA: What?

CARMELA: You don't want to know. What are you going to do about that boy?

CONCETTA: What? He's fine, he's a little wild, but he's young, he'll outgrow it. No, the real tragedy here is my husband.

CARMELA: Well, yes.

CONCETTA: Donna Carmela, I've been cursed with a man who brings disaster wherever he goes, and then who has to fix it?

CARMELA: Well, your daughter must be such a comfort to you. Is she coming tonight?

CONCETTA: Of course, she'll be here soon.

CARMELA: With her husband?

CONCETTA: Yes, of course.

CARMELA: They make such a beautiful couple, so well dressed. Who knew there was so much money in buttons!

CONCETTA: Yes.

CARMELA: Such a happy couple . . . no babies yet?

CONCETTA: No.

CARMELA: Well there's time.

CONCETTA: No. No, her mind is . . . somewhere else, and her father sees nothing, he plays with his toys. What can you do? What can you do?

CARMELA: I know, I know.

CONCETTA: If you only knew.

CARMELA: I know, I know.

CONCETTA: If you only knew.

(*Carmela's husband calls from out his window across the street. "Carmela!"*)

CARMELA: I know, I know. (*She starts to leave.*) Well then, best wishes to you all. And Happy Christmas. If there's anything you need, please call me.

CONCETTA: Thank you, you've been such a help.

(*Vittorio is about twenty-five years old, serious and a bit sad. He is dressed soberly and elegantly in a winter coat with gloves. He slips into the house as Concetta has stepped out into the street to say good-bye to Carmela. He lowers his eyes and mutters a vague greeting. Concetta returns and confronts him.*) Who are you? What are you doing here? Who are you?

VITTORIO: Donna Concetta, forgive me, my name is Vittorio Elia.

CONCETTA: I know who you are.

VITTORIO: Please, Donna Concetta, I have to see your daughter. I have to talk to you.

CONCETTA: To me? What do you want to tell me? I'm telling you, go away. What are you trying to do?

VITTORIO: Donna Concetta, she won't talk to me. I have to see her . . .

CONCETTA: Of course she won't talk to you. She has some sense.

(Pasquale is heard from offstage.)

PASQUALE: Enough! Enough! I can't take it anymore. This has to stop. I can't take it anymore.

CONCETTA: What's happened now?

PASQUALE: *(Entering.)* What do you think happened, Donna Conce'? Who is this?

CONCETTA: Nobody, a friend of Tommasino's.

PASQUALE: A friend of Tommasino's? Then he's a crook! I'm missing five lire again. *(He addresses most of this directly to Vittorio.)* Your friend! Why would he steal from me? I have nothing. I have to work one whole week in that miserable lotto office to earn five lire, and he steals it from me! Disgusting! But this time he's out of luck. I'll get him, the little shit. Last night I marked all my money with a small X. If I find five lire with an X, his days are over.

CONCETTA: Watch what you're saying! You should be ashamed of yourself, talking that way! My son would never take money from this house.

PASQUALE: Donna Concetta, I can't believe you're defending him! He's a danger to society. I'm his uncle, why would I lie about him, but the truth is I've caught him several times with his hand in my pocket.

CONCETTA: He was looking for a pencil.

PASQUALE: A pencil! He just stole my shoes and coat.

CONCETTA: It was an accident.

PASQUALE: An accident?

CONCETTA: He didn't do it on purpose.

PASQUALE: He did it by mistake?

CONCETTA: I don't know what you're talking about.

(Tommasino enters.)

PASQUALE: Ah, speak of the devil.

(Tommasino enters, stops singing noticing that Pasquale is pacing back and forth and shooting him menacing glares, tests the ground.)

TOMMASINO: Uncle Pasqua, good evening, how are you doing? *(Noticing Vittorio.)* Who's this?

CONCETTA: A friend of yours.

(Pasquale continues to circle the room, then he confronts his nephew, poking him in the face with his index finger.)

PASQUALE: You took five lire off my dresser. Don't lie!

TOMMASINO: Me? Never!

PASQUALE: Spit 'em out or you won't live to see Christmas.

TOMMASINO: I didn't take anything. You're out of your mind! How could you embarrass me in front of strangers?

(He starts to sob loudly and not very believably.)

PASQUALE: Stop blubbering and fork over my money.

CONCETTA: Don Pasquale, haven't you done enough? Look at the poor boy, crying his heart out. Have you no shame? Come here, my darling boy.

PASQUALE: Only a mother could be moved by this clown.

TOMMASINO: *(Turns menacingly on him.)* Look out. One of these days, I'll . . .

PASQUALE: Threatening me now! I'm your father's brother, you know. When he gets home, I'll tell him everything. Cough up the money or you'll be coughing up blood!

CONCETTA: *(To get them out of the room.)* Did you look carefully? Maybe it fell on the floor.

PASQUALE: I went over the room with a fine tooth comb, Donna Concetta, but I'll go look again, if you like, and if I don't find my money you can start saying your prayers.

TOMMASINO: All right, but I'm coming with you.

PASQUALE: You don't trust me to tell you if I find it?

TOMMASINO: I don't know, but I've got to be there. If we find the money, I swear on the sacred soul of my mother, I'll . . .

PASQUALE: Good god, it's sacrilege! She's still alive and he's swearing on her soul.

TOMMASINO: Why not? Do you have to be dead to have a soul? I swear on my sacred mother's living soul, I'll get a lawyer.

PASQUALE: And I solemnly swear an oath I have never sworn before, I swear on the head of the director of the Lotto Parlor of Naples, that if I don't find those five lire, you'll spend Christmas in the emergency room.

TOMMASINO: We'll see.

PASQUALE: We'll see.

(They exit.)

VITTORIO: Donna Concetta, forgive me . . .

CONCETTA: All right now, all right, you have to get out of here. Now! My daughter and her husband will be here any minute. I don't want you doing any more damage.

VITTORIO: What do you mean?

CONCETTA: Don't play the fool. It's because of you Ninuccia wrote that stupid letter.

VITTORIO: What letter?

CONCETTA: That letter that her husband is carrying now in his pocket. Thanks to me he thinks it's a Christmas letter from his loving wife. If I can't get it away from him tonight, the family is destroyed.

VITTORIO: *(A brief pause, then.)* Donna Concetta, I love your daughter!

CONCETTA: Oh, good God! He says it to my face! She's married, understand? Married. Do you want to destroy us, coming here? You're lucky I'm a woman alone. If I had a husband, I mean a real husband, or a son — we won't even talk about my son — well he's just a boy — if there was a man in this house . . .

VITTORIO: *(A brief pause.)* We're suffering, your daughter and I! You don't know how much we're suffering. She doesn't love him!

CONCETTA: *(Knowing it's not true.)* She loves him! She loves him. Now go away. Now! Please. Go.

(She goes off quickly to lead him out. Vittorio turns on his heels and slowly starts to leave, but Concetta has seen Luca arriving down the street, she returns, blocking his path, making incomprehensible hand gestures. Luca follows her in, not noticing Vittorio.)

LUCA: Were you going out?

CONCETTA: No.

LUCA: Then why were you opening the door?

CONCETTA: I thought I heard you knocking.

LUCA: No. I didn't knock. Why did you open the door?

CONCETTA: I thought you were coming, and I opened the door.

LUCA: You thought I was coming and you opened the door, and I came.

CONCETTA: Yes.

LUCA: Telepathy.

CONCETTA: *(Not understanding.)* Yes.

LUCA: Do you know what telepathy is?

CONCETTA: No.

LUCA: When I don't knock and you open the door. *(He turns and sees Vittorio.)* Who's this?

CONCETTA: A friend of Tommasino's. He was just leaving. Go on, go on.

LUCA: Just a minute. You are my son's friend? *(Shaking his hand.)* Luca Cupiello, his father.

VITTORIO: Vittorio Elia.

LUCA: Elia, a pleasure, it's nice to see my son has friends who are, well, distinguished, nicely dressed. I always tell my boy to choose his friends wisely. One rotten leaf can hurt the young plant.

VITTORIO: Yes, of course.

CONCETTA: Fine. Go on, Merry Christmas, Happy New Year.

LUCA: Wait a minute, we're talking.

CONCETTA: But he's got things to do.

LUCA: Did you offer him a drink? A little coffee?

CONCETTA: He refused.

LUCA: A pastry? A little cake.

VITTORIO: No, no, I'd better go.

LUCA: Whatever you like. *(Coolly detached.)* Did you see the Nativity?

VITTORIO: No.

CONCETTA: He saw it. He saw it.

LUCA: Did you see it with the lights on?

CONCETTA: Luca.

LUCA: What's the point of making it if people can't enjoy it? Look, here it is. Stand back so you can get the whole effect.
(As Vittorio goes up to it, Luca flips a switch, turning on many little lights, and then says with pride.)
Eh?

VITTORIO: Hmm, nice.

LUCA: I have to admit, I did it all myself.

VITTORIO: *(Cheerfully ironic.)* All by yourself?

LUCA: All by myself. In fact, my family only got in the way. Yes, I had to do it all by myself.

VITTORIO: Good for you.

LUCA: Go on, take your time, feel free to look around. Enjoy it. I couldn't let Christmas pass without making a Nativity. My father used to make one for me and now I make it for my children.

VITTORIO: And the grass, you even put this grass here yourself?

LUCA: Yes.

VITTORIO: Amazing!

LUCA: *(Aside to Concetta.)* I think he's laughing at me.

CONCETTA: Well, what do you expect?

LUCA: What do you mean? I'll smash a plate in his face. *(To Vittorio.)* You don't like it? You don't have to like it. Ah, you're from where?

VITTORIO: Milan.

LUCA: Ah, from Milan. At Christmas, they're made in every house in Naples. But you don't like it?

VITTORIO: No, no, I like it.

LUCA: I bought three new wise men. One had a broken head, so I changed all three, it wouldn't look right — one new and two old! *(He carefully unwraps the little statues.)* There were hundreds, it was so cold, but I chose these.

VITTORIO: Beautiful! You picked these out yourself?

LUCA: Yes, all by myself. Gaspar, Melchior, and Balthazar.

VITTORIO: Bravo!

(Convinced now that he is being mocked, Luca carefully re-wraps the magi and turns off the Nativity lights.)

LUCA: Oh, you're my son's friend, I understand. Is Ninuccia here yet?

CONCETTA: Not yet.

LUCA: My daughter and her husband are coming to spend Christmas here with us. My daughter, she doesn't live here anymore.

VITTORIO: Oh.

LUCA: No, she doesn't. She married the Percuoco Company. Well, she married Nicola Percuoco. You've probably seen the advertisements in the street. "Percuoco." He's got big worries, big responsibilities. He makes buttons, gift items, brooms, boxes, brushes, mirrors. But the big money comes from the buttons. They've got that apartment! Isn't that right, Conce', tell him about the apartment.

CONCETTA: You tell him.

LUCA: When she invites me over, I say: "Ninu', please let me eat in the kitchen," it's all brand new aluminum modern, big and so much light. From the window you can see the sea. I sit there eating my lunch, at a little table, looking out, and I feel better. And the parlor, Concetta, tell him about the parlor.

CONCETTA: Nice, very nice.

LUCA: Paintings, rugs, silverware. And they've got a piano! They hire someone who knows how to play and they give parties, receptions, they sing and dance. Months and months go by and we don't see them. Because I work, too, not now because it's the holidays, but otherwise I hop out of bed like a grasshopper at seven o'clock, and at eight-fifteen I'm at the printing press.

VITTORIO: You're a printer?

LUCA: No, the doorkeeper. I followed in my father's footsteps. This was his job first. I make deliveries, and I have the keys to the printing press. I keep them hidden because it's a responsibility. Concetta, show him the keys.

CONCETTA: What's there to see? It's a big bunch of keys.

LUCA: I lock up at night, I'm the first one there in the morning, or else how could anybody could get in? It's a responsibility. *(A brief pause.)* Where's Tommasino?

CONCETTA: In there. Your brother lost five lire. He accuses our little boy of stealing it. They're looking for it.

LUCA: Well, what can you do? Money really disappears in this house.

(From offstage we hear Pasquale and Tommasino arguing.)

PASQUALE: It's not here.

TOMMASINO: I'm innocent!

(Pasquale entering, sees Luca and is emboldened.)

PASQUALE: Luca, he stole five lire from me.

TOMMASINO: It's not true!

LUCA: Slow down, slow down, let's get the facts.

TOMMASINO: I don't know anything about it.

LUCA: You be quiet! Pasqualino, you've made a mistake.

PASQUALE: A mistake?

LUCA: You can't accuse someone without proof. Let's examine the facts, his mother will be the judge. Now I'm going to shame him in front of his friend. Come here, you, let me check your pockets.

TOMMASINO: Treating me like a thief!

LUCA: I am your father. Let me see. If I find five lire . . .

(Luca pulls out a few objects and finally the five lire note, he takes him aside so no one can hear or see them.)

Here it is.

(Tommasino has no reaction, as if it were his right. He stares back at his father with no shame. Luca asks him under his breath:)

Do you like the Nativity?

(Tommasino realizes that if he says yes he'll get the five lire and be spared, he hesitates briefly, fights with himself, then answers with pride:)

TOMMASINO: No.

(Luca holds up the note for all to see and hands it to Pasquale.)

LUCA: Here it is.

PASQUALE: I knew it!

LUCA: Shame on you! You're a thief.

TOMMASINO: I still don't like it.

PASQUALE: *(Carefully examines it.)* Here's the *X!*

LUCA: Let's see. *(Takes it from Pasquale.)* Here it is! Here's his mark, now you can't deny it.

(Luca notices another mark, the one he made to catch his son, for a moment he's perplexed, then he takes his brother aside and shows him his strange discovery.)

Pasquale, there's also a star here, I made this mark.

PASQUALE: Where? Let me see.

LUCA: Here. I kept losing money, so I put a star on all my money.

PASQUALE: Let me see, at the lotto parlor we have these mistakes all the time . . .

LUCA: So, you steal from me, and he steals from you.

PASQUALE: No, wait a minute . . . maybe your eyes aren't so good . . .

LUCA: Pasquale, keep your hands off my money. Jesus!

PASQUALE: Let me see . . . you made a star and I made . . .

LUCA: Every time I turned around, I'd lose another five lire.

(Pasquale doesn't answer. He's frozen, like someone caught in a trap.)

Now what can I say to my son? He'll say: Even my uncle steals. All right, it's Christmas, let's forget about it.

PASQUALE: *(To his nephew.)* Don't do it again.

LUCA: *(Alluding.)* That's right. Don't do it again.

VITTORIO: I'm sorry. I've got to be going.

LUCA: Why do you have to go?

CONCETTA: Yes, yes, you've got to go.

TOMMASINO: Stay a little longer.

VITTORIO: I'm sorry. I have to go.

LUCA: What are you doing for Christmas?

VITTORIO: My family lives in Milan. I'll go to a restaurant and then to bed.

LUCA: Stay and eat with us.

CONCETTA: No, he can't eat with us, there's no room.

LUCA: Concetta, calm down. There's plenty of food. He's a gentleman, they eat nothing. Stay and eat with us. It makes me too unhappy to think of you alone in a restaurant at Christmas.

(He removes Vittorio's coat, helped by Pasquale and Tommasino. Vittorio protests feebly but then gives in.)

PASQUALE: My brother means it with all his heart.

VITTORIO: I know, but really . . .

LUCA: If you go, I'll get really mad. You are our guest. I cannot allow you to spend Christmas alone.

(Ninuccia and Nicolino enter elegantly dressed, carrying a beautifully wrapped package of sweets.)

NINUCCIA: Merry Christmas!

NICOLINO: Merry Christmas, everybody!

CONCETTA: *(Pulling Vittorio aside.)* You think you're so smart, eh?

VITTORIO: What could I do? I tried to leave.

CONCETTA: You didn't try hard enough.

(Luca helps Nicolino off with his coat and hands it to Pasquale.)

LUCA: Pasquale, please hang this up.

PASQUALE: Yes, yes. I'll take care of it.

(Pasquale, on the move, slips a hand into one pocket, Concetta notices, she goes up to him and pulls the coat out of his hands. Pasquale's thieving hand is still stuck in one of the pockets.)

CONCETTA: Don Pasquale, are we at the border, going through customs?

PASQUALE: I was putting his gloves in the pocket.

CONCETTA: Fine, all right!

(Tommasino has become very helpful, taking his sister's hat and handbag, which he is now going through masterfully. Concetta sees this and pulls the bag away, his hand still stuck inside it. He whimpers as if his hand were hurt. She looks at it in a motherly way, then slaps it. Meanwhile Nicolino attempts a conversation with Pasquale.)

NICOLINO: Pasquale, how's the lotto parlor?

PASQUALE: A lot of work these days. Lots of business at Christmas, the poor are all betting like crazy.

(Nicolino has exhausted his conversation with Pasquale.)

NICOLINO: Is everybody here?

LUCA: Yes! Ah, there's also a friend of Tommasino's whose family is in Milan so I asked him to dinner. I hope you don't mind.

(Ninuccia sees Vittorio for the first time, squeals.)

NICOLINO: Why would I mind?

LUCA: Let me introduce you. Don Vittorio, I want you to meet Nicola Percuoco, button manufacturer. He commands hundreds of men . . . and here's my daughter, Ninuccia.

(Ninuccia and Vittorio shake hands, and she walks away from him.)

NICOLINO: Ninuccia, what's wrong?

NINUCCIA: Nothing.

(Nicolino looks toward Vittorio.)

NICOLINO: What's going on?

(Tommasino claps his arm around his "friend.")

TOMMASINO: Vincenzo.

VITTORIO: *(Under his breath.)* Vittorio.

TOMMASINO: That's right.

LUCA: What's going on?

CONCETTA: Nothing, nothing.

LUCA: What's going on?

(Concetta carries the box of the three kings distractedly down to the table as if it were the centerpiece, or a part of the meal.)

CONCETTA: Nothing, Luca, nothing . . .

LUCA: Concetta, those are the three kings.

CONCETTA: Oh, are they staying for dinner, too?

LUCA: Concetta, you're losing your mind. Did you hear that? "Are they staying for dinner, too?" Nicolino, my wife is losing her mind. She's distracted. *(Pasquale and Tommasino laugh, but Nicolino doesn't.)* He's distracted. Did you and Ninuccia have another fight? I can't turn my back on them. Don Vittorio, see, he and his wife fight all the time. Was it about food again? *(Laughing.)* My daughter tortures him. She doesn't want him to eat pasta, she says he'll get fat, he'll get a big belly. A man who works, what does he care if he gets a belly? That's what you fought about, isn't that right?

(Nicolino casually picks up a knife and plays with it, feigning indifference.)

NICOLINO: No, you're wrong, my wife and I are in complete agreement now.

(Nicolino points the knife toward everyone, one by one, slowly making a semicircle. Luca realizes something is wrong, but he says timidly.)

LUCA: I'm so glad to hear that. You know, Concetta and I, we fight all the time. They can hear us screaming in the street. But you say one word against my Concetta, I'll skin you alive. We love each other. We are a family. And my Tommasino is the same. *(Tommasino has crept up to the crèche and squeezed the enema bag, squirting water.)* What are you doing?

TOMMASINO: St. Joseph looked thirsty.

LUCA: Leave it alone, why are you always hanging around it if you don't like it?

CONCETTA: What a night! Ninuccia, come help me in the kitchen.

(The two women exit.)

LUCA: *(To Vittorio.)* He's a little nervous, but he's a good boy. Do you know how much he loves his Mother? He still writes her a Christmas letter every year. I insist on it. Go on, read us the letter.

TOMMASINO: It's the same every year.

LUCA: Go on, Nicolino wants to hear it. Read it.

PASQUALE: Every year we have to listen to this garbage.

LUCA: If you don't want to hear it, go to your room. Go on, read it. Nicolino, listen to this.

TOMMASINO: Dear Mother, I wish you all the best on this holy Christmas day. Dear mother, from now on I'm going to be good. Dear mother . . .

PASQUALE: Again?!

LUCA: Pasquale, be quiet. You know what he's like. *(To Nicolino.)* He's nervous. Pasquale, I'm warning you, if he throws a plate in your face, I'm not responsible. Look, he's getting nervous, look at his leg.

(In fact, Tommasino is shaking his leg menacingly.)

PASQUALE: I see it. I see it.

LUCA: Go on.

TOMMASINO: Dear Mother, from now on I'm going to be good. Dear mother, I'm going to change, so get me . . .

PASQUALE: My milk-bread, my milk-bread . . .

(Tommasino hurls a plate at him that shatters at his feet.)

Luca! See what he did, he threw a plate at me.

LUCA: I warned you. It's his nerves. He's nervous.

TOMMASINO: Look at my leg, look at my leg!

LUCA: Pasquale, calm down, we have to eat and we don't have a lot of plates.

PASQUALE: I'll calm down, I'll calm down. You are a little shit, you're a turd, a delinquent. *(Turns the chair so his back is to him, muttering.)* Go on read, read, I'm not here.

LUCA: Go on.

TOMMASINO: *(Pleased with his heroism, he continues reading.)* Dear mother, I'm going to change, so get me some nice presents. As I told you last year and I'm telling you this year.

PASQUALE: And as he tells you every year . . .

TOMMASINO: *(Reading again.)* Dear mother, may God let you live a hundred years along with my father, Ninuccia, Nicolino, and me. Dear mother . . .

PASQUALE: What about me?

LUCA: *(To Tommasino.)* Go on.

PASQUALE: Just a minute, I want to know something.

LUCA: I know what you want to know. Go on.

PASQUALE: Just a minute, why didn't you put me on that list?

LUCA: Let it go, Pasquale. Let it go.

PASQUALE: Why should I? I'm his uncle. He should put me on the list.

TOMMASINO: I can't.

PASQUALE: Why not?

TOMMASINO: I can't. There's no room.

PASQUALE: What do you mean there's no room? You got the paper in your hand, you got a pencil. Put me on that list! Put me on that list, boy, or you won't live to see Christmas. Put me on that list or I'll pulverize you. God damn it to hell, I'll slaughter you. Put me on that list or I'll plunge this fork into your skull. I'll make you bleed. God damn it to hell . . .

LUCA: Pasqua', you're not joking? Are you serious?

PASQUALE: I'm not joking!

LUCA: You pick up a fork and threaten the boy? Our father was right, you're a keg of dynamite.

PASQUALE: You're damned right I'm dynamite. I'll blow him off the face of the Earth.

LUCA: If he puts your name on that list, do you really think you'll live a hundred years?

PASQUALE: No.

LUCA: So?

PASQUALE: It's the principle of the thing.

LUCA: All right. I understand. Give him a hundred years too.

TOMMASINO: How can I?

LUCA: Give him a hundred years and then God can make up his own mind what he wants to do.

PASQUALE: (Exasperated.) Pharisees, pharisees! I don't give damn. Go to hell.

(Having rewritten the list, Tommasino reads again.)

TOMMASINO: Dear Mother, I wish you all the best on this holy Christmas day. Dear Mother, may God let you live a hundred years, along with my father, Ninuccia, Nicolino, and me and give Uncle Pasquale a hundred years too, but with a few serious diseases.

PASQUALE: You're a turd.

TOMMASINO: That's it, take it or leave it.

LUCA: (Amused by his son's wit.) Pasquale really got upset. Don Vittorio, we insult each other, but nobody really gets upset. We love each other. Every year, no matter what, I give my wife a present. Two years ago it was fabric for a winter coat, last year I got her earrings out of hock — she was so happy. This year I've pawned the earrings again to buy her something else. Wait, I want to show you.

(Luca exits, Pasquale follows him.)

PASQUALE: I'll go get my present, too.

(Luca returns carrying a woman's umbrella wrapped in paper.)

LUCA: Here it is. She lost her umbrella so I bought her a nicer one. Nicolino, look at this handle, it's real bone.

(Pasquale returns holding a fake leather handbag.)

PASQUALE: And here's my present.

LUCA: When we sit down to eat we'll surprise her — we'll be the three kings bringing presents to the baby Jesus, and we'll sing: Joy to Concetta, we gotcha this umbrella . . .

(This could be to the tune of "Joy to the World.")

TOMMASINO: *(Disappointed.)* What can I do?

LUCA: Nothing, you follow us and go fa la la la . . .

TOMMASINO: I want to carry the handbag.

LUCA: That's Pasquale's present, you can carry your letter on a plate.

(Concetta enters from the kitchen with wine and glasses on a tray. Ninuccia follows her.)

CONCETTA: All right now, everybody, Merry Christmas, let's have a toast, a little glass of wine.

NICOLINO: Ah, now I can read my letter!

CONCETTA: No, no! Not now, not when Ninuccia's in the kitchen.

NINUCCIA: What?

CONCETTA: Get in the kitchen! Go!

(Ninuccia and Concetta go into the kitchen. A loud noise and cries of distress. Concetta cries, "Nicolino! Help" as Ninuccia rushes in.)

LUCA: What happened?

NINUCCIA: We were cutting the eels and one of them got away.

LUCA: I didn't know they were still alive . . .

NINUCCIA: And Mamma tried to catch it and bumped her head on the stove.

LUCA: Is she hurt?

PASQUALE: Let's go see.

(Nicolino removes his jacket and places it on the back of a chair and goes off with the others to help, leaving Vittorio alone onstage. He rushes to the jacket to see if he can find the letter, takes it out and reads it quickly. Concetta and Nicolino come in, followed by Luca, Pasquale, and Ninuccia. Concetta is leaning heavily on Nicolino, she is feeling in the pocket of his vest, while feigning being hurt or overwhelmed. She realizes the letter is not there, notices the jacket on the chair, is aiming for the chair but Luca offers her a different chair where Nicolino deposits her.)

LUCA: Sit here, Concetta.

TOMMASINO: Mamma, are you hurt?

CONCETTA: No.

NINUCCIA: *(Indicating her head.)* Yes.

CONCETTA: *(Concetta understands and quickly puts her hand to her head.)* Yes! *(Ninuccia starts to wrap Concetta's head solicitously with a napkin, under the chin and tied on the top.)*

LUCA: Concetta, does it hurt a lot?

CONCETTA: Ummm.

LUCA: Look at that! A few inches to the left or right and you'd be dead. Where's the eel?

CONCETTA: In the coal, under the stove.

(A huge crashing sound. Tommasino rushes in and right back out.)

TOMMASINO: The credenza fell over.

LUCA: Let's go help.

(As they all go out led by Ninuccia, Concetta gets up to go through Nicolino's pockets, but is interrupted by Tommasino's re-entrance.)

TOMMASINO: Nicolino almost got him, but it got away.

(She starts going through the pockets again, but Vittorio shows her he has the letter, no time to react before the whole group returns from the kitchen, looking disheartened. Luca is hobbling, Pasquale massaging his back, only Tommasino is content: having managed to grab some food, he is furtively eating it.)

LUCA: We almost got him, but he climbed up to the window and slid out into the next house.

CONCETTA: All right, forget the eels.

(Luca and Pasquale seem disappointed.)

Forget the eels. I'll go get the soup.

NICOLINO: *(He's been handling the eels.)* I'd like to wash my hands.

CONCETTA: Come with me. You can wash your hands in the kitchen.

(Concetta and Nicolino exit to kitchen.)

LUCA: Good idea. Let's go wash our hands. Pasquale, do you have a piece of soap?

PASQUALE: Come to my room.

LUCA: *(To Tommasino.)* You come too, you have to wash your hands before dinner. Don Vittorio, we'll be right back. Ninu', entertain him.

(They go off, there is a pause.)

VITTORIO: I didn't want to stay. Your father insisted. I could leave right now.

NINUCCIA: That would be worse. I know what you're doing, you're hoping to make something happen that shouldn't happen.

VITTORIO: *(Bitterly.)* You're right. My poor mother is alone in Milan, crying — she wants to know why her son doesn't come home for Christmas.

NINUCCIA: And why don't you?

VITTORIO: When you talk like that, you make me crazy. *(Showing her the letter.)* So, I mean nothing to you anymore?

NINUCCIA: *(Melting.)* Vittorio, I don't know what to say. I don't even know what I feel anymore.

(He pulls her to him and holds her and kisses her with intense desire. Nicolino

has entered a few moments before, pulls them apart, slapping Vittorio and crying out.)

NICOLINO: You're a worm! We'll finish this out in the street.

VITTORIO: Bastard! She's too good for you!

(Concetta enters with a large casserole.)

CONCETTA: Come on everybody. Let's eat.

(Ninuccia throws herself on Vittorio to stop him.)

NINUCCIA: No, Vittorio, don't!

VITTORIO: She doesn't love you, your wife doesn't love you!

NICOLINO: I'll kill you! Damn you!

(The three other men enter dressed as the three kings, with paper crowns, carrying their objects and wrapped in rugs or a bathrobe and some blankets.)

LUCA, PASQUALE, AND TOMMASINO: Joy to Concetta, we gotcha this umbrella, and this ha-andbag . . . and here's my letter, yes here's my letter . . . and this ha-andbag . . .

NICOLINO: Look at your daughter, defending her lover. You knew it all along.

CONCETTA: Who, me?

NICOLINO: I'll kill you, you coward, hiding behind her skirts, I'll make mincemeat of you. She's mine. *(To Ninuccia.)* I'll deal with you later.

(As Nicolino goes off, Vittorio breaks away from Ninuccia and follows him, crying out.)

VITTORIO: Fine. If you want to fight, fine. I'd die for her any day. You're nothing, you're a button-maker . . .

(Ninuccia tries to get her mother to help, but Concetta has fallen into a chair.)

NINUCCIA: Mamma, they'll kill each other. Mamma, Mamma.

(Concetta tries to show her daughter that she can't move her legs. Meanwhile, Tommasino has been trying to grab the purse from Pasquale. They fight. At the height of the mayhem, Luca collapses.)

END OF ACT TWO

Act Three

Three days later. The table has been pushed back, Luca's bed is restored to the middle of the room. Luca is sitting up in bed almost senseless. Concetta and Carmela sit by the bed. Various neighbors are sitting around being served coffee by a solicitous and sober Ninuccia who comes out of the kitchen carrying a big pot of coffee. She looks as if she has had a deep and sudden sorrow.

CARMELA: Ninuccia, we need more coffee.

NINUCCIA: *(From offstage, entering.)* Yes, yes, I just made more. Donna Carmela, your husband is calling you, he just yelled down from the kitchen window.

CARMELA: What does he want?

NINUCCIA: I was busy with the coffee, I couldn't hear. He said he's on his way over here now. *(Offering her the cup.)* Here. I just made it fresh.

CARMELA: We're keeping going on coffee.

NINUCCIA: Mamma, have a sip.

CONCETTA: I can't, I can't.

CARMELA: Just a sip. You have to, or you can't go on.
(Concetta takes a taste and pushes the cup away. Carmela takes the tray and starts to pour some for the girls and a third one for Alberto.)
Girls, come, have some coffee.

ALBERTO: If I don't have my coffee, I fall asleep on my feet.

NINUCCIA: Wait. This one's for my uncle. *(She takes a cup from the tray and brings it to Pasquale, who is standing away from the group looking out the window.)* Uncle Pasquale, have some coffee.

ALBERTO: Donna Carmela, we need two more cups.

CARMELA: From where? There were four in the kitchen. I brought two of my own, that's all there is.

ARMIDA: Here, take this one. I finished.
(Carmela refills Pasquale's cup.)

MARIA: Wait, you can have mine. *(Drinks it right down.)*
(Luigi, Carmela's husband, enters. A well-dressed, older businessman, in a hurry on his way to his office.)

LUIGI: Donna Concetta, good morning.
(She acknowledges him with a nod.)

CARMELA: What did you want?

LUIGI: I wanted to know if you're staying here or coming back up. I have to run. Here's the key. I didn't even get coffee.

(*Carmela gives her cup to Luigi, leaving Alberto who has been waiting with Maria's empty cup.*)

CARMELA: Here, here. This was my cup.

ALBERTO: (*Requesting what was due him.*) And me?

CARMELA: (*Turns pot upside down to prove it's empty.*) There's none left. Ninuccia will go make a little pot for you.

(*Alberto is resigned. Ninnucia exits to the kitchen.*)

LUIGI: Donna Concetta, how is Don Luca?

CONCETTA: The doctor came last night, I looked him in the face, it was an ugly face.

LUIGI: Did he have a bad night?

CONCETTA: Who could sleep? He kept calling for Nicolino. He wanted Nicolino. It was grand opera!

CARMELA: I think he's going to be all right. He was much worse last night. Now he's resting peacefully.

CONCETTA: No, no, he doesn't look right to me. He can't move his left arm, his tongue is swollen and he talks like this . . . you can't understand him.

LUIGI: Does he recognize you?

CONCETTA: Sometimes yes, sometimes no. Last night I said to him, "Luca, it's me, your Concetta." Guess who he thought I was? He looked at me a bit and then he said; "I know who you are. You're Don Basilio." About three weeks ago we went to *The Barber of Seville.* (*The group laughs.*) They'd given us tickets.

ALBERTO: (*Whispers to the girls.*) She really does look like Don Basilio.

(*The girls laugh some more while the older group silently scolds them to show them that the laughter was inappropriate.*)

CARMELA: Girls, what's going on?

MARIA: (*Trying to cover.*) Nothing, it's just that Alberto didn't get any coffee.

(*Ninuccia enters with a big bowl of soup.*)

NINUCCIA: Mamma, maybe he should have a little soup. I just made it. It's nice and hot.

CONCETTA: I think we should let him be. He just fell asleep. What do you think, Donna Carmela?

CARMELA: It's better to let him sleep. When he's awake, you can heat it up again.

(*Ninuccia puts the bowl aside and covers it with a dish.*)

CONCETTA: When is the doctor coming?

NINUCCIA: He should have been here already.

CONCETTA: And Tommasino?

NINUCCIA: He went to send another telegram to Nicolino. He'll be right back.

LUIGI: *(Looking at his watch.)* I should run, but I want to wait till Don Luca wakes up. I'll stay a bit and then I'll go.

CARMELA: *(To Ninuccia.)* Are you happy now? See what you did?

(Ninuccia lowers her eyes and looks sad.)

CONCETTA: Don't say that! How could she ever have imagined this would happen?

CARMELA: She was stubborn.

CONCETTA: No. I never told Luca anything, I always spared him, so when he found out, it was like he'd been smashed on the head. He got sick, and now here he is, more dead than alive. He keeps calling for Nicolino. He wants to see Nicolino. We've sent Nicolino three telegrams and he still doesn't show up.

CARMELA: Why? Did her husband walk out on her?

CONCETTA: No. He's gone to see some relatives in Rome.

NINUCCIA: He says he never wants to see me again. The family is destroyed.

LUIGI: I have to go.

CARMELA: What are you waiting for? If you have to go, go. You can never make up your mind.

LUIGI: It's just that I think I had something else I had to tell you. *(He suddenly remembers.)* Oh yes, should I come home for lunch?

CARMELA: If you want to come home, come home. I'll make some pasta and butter.

LUIGI: I wish I could stay, Donna Concetta, but I have a client from Milan who needs to see some samples.

(Entering quickly, Tommasino goes right up to his mother.)

TOMMASINO: I sent the telegram. Here's the change. How is he?

CONCETTA: He's resting. Don't let him hear you. Poor boy! I can't tell you what a comfort he's been to me. Look at that face. He hasn't slept in three nights, wouldn't leave his father's bedside. He runs out twenty, thirty times a day, to the pharmacy, to the doctor. And they said you were a heartless son!

(In fact, Tommasino is sitting at the foot of his father's bed.)

LUIGI: All right, I'd better go.

LUCA: *(Suddenly wakes up, babbling.)* Is Nicolino here?

(They all move toward the bed, surrounding him.)

CONCETTA: He woke up. What did he say?

CARMELA: He wants to know if Nicolino is here.

CONCETTA: It's always that damned Nicolino. *(Then sweetly.)* He's coming, he'll be here soon.

NINUCCIA: Papa, have a little soup.

CARMELA: Go heat it up, it's cold.

(Ninuccia goes off with the bowl.)

TOMMASINO: *(Nervously.)* Shouldn't he have his medicine?

CONCETTA: Later. The doctor said every hour.

TOMMASINO: Well, it's been more than an hour.

PASQUALE: No it hasn't.

TOMMASINO: *(Still hostile with him.)* You be quiet.

PASQUALE: I am his brother and I have the right to say whatever I want.

TOMMASINO: *(Menacing.)* Oh yes? We'll see about that.

PASQUALE: *(Answers in the same tone.)* Yes, we'll see.

CARMELA: Hey, this is no time to fight.

RITA: Donna Concetta, the doctor is here.

(Ninuccia returns with coffee and two cups.)

DOCTOR: Good morning everyone, good morning. How is he doing?

CONCETTA: Doctor, we've been waiting for you. Ninuccia, coffee for the doctor. *(Ninuccia has poured coffee and is handing it to Alberto. Concetta takes it out of Alberto's hand and gives it to the doctor.)*

DOCTOR: Thank you. I left my house in a hurry and didn't have time for coffee. *(Ninuccia is giving another to Alberto, but Concetta takes the cup and gives it to Tommasino.)*

CONCETTA: Drink it, Tommasino, drink it. You need it.

ALBERTO: *(To the girls.)* I'll go get one in the cafe.

DOCTOR: Did he sleep well last night?

CONCETTA: He kept us all awake. *(She hands him a piece of paper.)* Here, I kept a chart of the fever.

DOCTOR: *(Takes the paper, glances at it, and speaks to the patient.)* Don Luca, how are we feeling? You look splendid. *(Luca speaks with difficulty, he has a hard time articulating the words, but manages to answer with humor.)*

LUCA: I wish I could say the same for you. *(Seeing Luigi.)* Nicolino . . .

CONCETTA: It's not Nicolino, it's Pastorelli and his wife, Donna Carmela. And here are Signora Armida and Ninuccia's friends Maria and Rita, and Alberto. They all came to see you. *(They all come up to the bed.)*

ALBERTO: Don Luca, you have to hurry up and get well.

LUIGI: We have to go for a long walk.

MARIA: And I want to come too, me too!

RITA: We'll all go.

CARMELA: We'll have a party.

MARIA: A big party when Don Luca is all better.

ARMIDA: Yes, yes, a party!

(*It builds to a crescendo, finally it's so loud the doctor protests, clapping his hands.*)

DOCTOR: Quiet! Quiet! (*To Concetta.*) There are too many people here. I already told you that yesterday.

CARMELA: They just got here, I was the only one here. I came to keep her company through the night.

ARMIDA: We're leaving, we're leaving.

DOCTOR: Yes, you'd better clear out.

(*They all start to go.*)

ALBERTO: I'll go down and get some coffee.

RITA: Wait, give me a cigarette.

MARIA: Me too.

(*Alberto distributes cigarettes and goes out, followed by the girls.*)

LUIGI: (*Moving toward the door.*) I'll wait to hear what the doctor has to say, then I'll go.

(*Ninuccia returns with the broth.*)

NINUCCIA: Mamma?

CONCETTA: Doctor, can I give him some chicken soup?

DOCTOR: Let me examine him first.

(*He pulls up Luca's eyelids, then he feels something unusual. He lifts the covers and pulls out a pair of shoes as if asking for an explanation.*)

CONCETTA: (*Mortified.*) Oh, excuse me, doctor.

PASQUALE: She hid them because she's afraid her son will sell them.

DOCTOR: Really?

TOMMASINO: Oh sure! I'd sell my father's shoes.

PASQUALE: Why not? What's to stop you.

(*After listening to Luca's heart, the Doctor says, not very convincingly.*)

DOCTOR: Good, good, he's getting better.

CONCETTA: Luca, God help us, why don't you say something? The last time you were sick you did nothing but talk. The doctor is here, tell Donna Carmela the one about the pasta and beans.

CARMELA: Yes, please, what about the beans? I want to know.

(*Luca is amused, he realizes this is a good story about the foolishness of doctors.*)

He understands what she's driving at, but soon he loses track of the point of the story.)

LUCA: Yes, that's an important story. Is Nicolino here yet?

CONCETTA: Not yet.

NINUCCIA: Tell us about the beans.

(Luca smiles, but his mouth keeps pulling to the left, making a tragic grimace.)

LUCA: I woke up one morning with a touch of fever and Concetta says, right away: "We have to call the doctor." "Forget it," I said, "It's nothing, the fever will be gone by tomorrow." "No," she says. "We have to call the doctor, what if it gets worse." "All right," I say. That Concetta, once she gets an idea in her head . . . ! The doctor comes, he examines me and says . . . what did he say, Concetta?

CONCETTA: It's intestinal.

LUCA: It's intestinal. He mustn't eat. If he eats, the fever won't go down . . . Where's Nicolino?

CONCETTA: He's coming, he's coming. He'll be here soon.

LUCA: Did you send the telegram?

CONCETTA: Yes, yes, good idea . . . we'll send a telegram. Go on with the story about the beans. That day, what did I make?

LUCA: That day Concetta had made beans and pasta. The smell filled the whole house. I said: "Concetta, why would you make beans today when I'm sick, you know how much I love pasta and beans." She says, "What! I boiled a few vegetables." She knows I hate boiled vegetables. "So why do I smell beans?" "Oh, that's the lady next door." "So ask the lady next door to send some over." "No, you can't eat or the fever won't go away, and the doctor will be offended if we don't follow his advice." "All right," I say. "Fine. We'll see how I feel tomorrow." I'm terrible, aren't I, Concetta?

CONCETTA: That's right. Luca is terrible!

LUCA: Concetta had fallen asleep. I got up and went into the kitchen. I sat myself down at the little table, the spoon was still in the pot, and slurp, slurp, slurp slurp slurp. *(He mimes the spoon going into his mouth.)* I ate them all! Then I slipped myself back into bed. The next day I woke up with no fever. How was I, Concetta?

CONCETTA: Cool as a cucumber.

LUCA: Cool as a cucumber. The genius doctor came and said, "See, if he'd eaten he'd still be sick." What an idiot!

DOCTOR: I'd better be going, I've got some urgent cases to see about.

(The doctor gets up and Concetta, helped by Carmela, goes to rearrange Luca's bed.)

CONCETTA: Forgive me, doctor.

DOCTOR: Of course, of course.

(Ninuccia takes the doctor aside.)

NINUCCIA: Doctor, tell me the truth, how is he?

DOCTOR: You mustn't lose hope. I'll be back in a few days. He certainly had a big shock, but I've seen worse cases who have recovered. We never know.

NINUCCIA: Let's hope.

(She goes back to her mother to tell her what the doctor said. Pasquale has also heard the doctor.)

PASQUALE: Aren't you coming tomorrow?

DOCTOR: What's the point, Don Pasquale? Be brave and give the women some courage.

PASQUALE: What are you saying?

DOCTOR: Only a miracle . . . No, he won't make it. Anyway, let me know if anything happens. Good day, everybody.

(They all say good-bye and walk him out the door).

CONCETTA: Ninu', let's wash up these cups. You'll see, they'll all be back soon.

CARMELA: Let me help.

CONCETTA: I've used up more than two kilos of coffee in three days.

TOMMASINO: That's why they came.

PASQUALE: Well, I'll go tell them to stay away.

CARMELA: Yes, you'd better. They take all the air out of the room. The poor man can't breathe.

(Pasquale is about to go, but he stops as he bumps into Vittorio, who is coming in. Concetta is stunned for a moment. After a brief pause she confronts him.)

CONCETTA: What are you doing here?

VITTORIO: *(Sincerely pained.)* Donna Concetta, please don't send me away. You can't imagine how much I have suffered these three days. I know it's all my fault, believe me, I wanted to die. I've been standing out there walking around for three nights. I just saw the doctor leave, I wanted to kiss Don Luca's hand, please don't deny me this.

(In his delirium Luca mistakes Vittorio for Nicolino. His eyes light up with joy, he cries out and leans out of bed grabbing Vittorio's arm.)

LUCA: Nicolino! Nicolino's here. This is wonderful! They said you weren't coming.

(No one dares to interfere. Vittorio is immobile, his eyes down. Luca pulls him toward him.) He loves me, doesn't he? Where's Ninuccia?

NINUCCIA: *(In tears.)* Here, Papa.

LUCA: Give me your hand. Now you Nicolino, take her hand, go on . . . *(His face clears and he manages to speak with more clarity and strength.)* Swear you will never leave each other again. *(Since they don't speak he insists.)* Go on. Swear.

(Ninuccia looks into Vittorio's eyes, she is crying. From offstage, we hear Nicolino's voice and the neighbors greeting him. "Good morning, Don Nicolino." Concetta is the first to rush to the door, terrified.)

CARMELA: Don Nicolino!

NICOLINO: Where is he?

(Nicolino enters and moves directly to the bed. He sees Vittorio, Ninuccia, and Luca in that pathetic scene. He would like to attack them, but the family pushes him back. Meanwhile the neighbors surround him. With whispers, they beg him to try to understand. He resists, but they manage to pull him away.)

LUCA: They made peace. I made them make peace. Did you see, Concetta? You two were made for each other. You must stay together and love each other. Don't upset Concetta anymore, she's suffered so much.

(Ninuccia and Vittorio let go of each other's hands. Luca is satisfied. He looks around and asks.) Where's Tommasino? Tommasino?

(Tommasino is grief-stricken, he can barely speak.)

TOMMASINO: I'm here.

LUCA: Tommasino, do you like the Nativity?

TOMMASINO: *(There's a knot in his throat, he manages only to say)* Yes.

(Once he has gotten that "yes," Luca's eyes wander off into the distance, as if he were seeing a vision, a Nativity scene as big as the world, with all the comings and goings of many people, but very small people, rushing toward the stable, where a real donkey and real cow, small as they are, are breathing their warm breath on baby Jesus who is very, very big and who fusses and cries like any tiny newborn baby. Lost in that vision he comments on his singular privilege.)

LUCA: What a Nativity! Isn't it beautiful?

END OF PLAY

Those Damned Ghosts

(Questi Fantasmi)

CHARACTERS

Pasquale Lojacono, a lost soul
Maria, his wife, a lost soul
Alfredo Marigliano, an unquiet soul
Armida Marigliano, a sad soul
Silvia, fourteen years old, an innocent soul
Arturo, twelve years old, an innocent soul
Raffaele, doorkeeper, an irritated soul
Carmela, his sister, a damned soul
Gastone Califano, a free soul
Saverio Califan and Maddalena, his wife, useless old souls
Two moving men, suffering souls
Professor Santa, a useful soul, but he never appears

Act One

A large entry hall. All the rooms of the old apartment lead off from here. There are balconies on either side of the stage between the proscenium and the scenic walls. The angle of perspective gives the impression that these balconies continue around the whole apartment. On either side of the set, further upstage, there are two doors to the other rooms. The main entrance to the apartment is upstage right.

The apartment is dark. From offstage we hear:

RAFFAELE: Eh, go on, keep going . . . that's right, you walk ahead and I'll light the way from behind. That's how we did it yesterday, remember? When we brought the other things. You go first, and I'll be here bringing up the rear. Get that through your head.

(A mover enters carrying two chairs, a suitcase, and many men's hats, one inside the other, which he can hardly balance on his head. Raffaele, following close behind, yells:)

Wait! Stop! It's dark! They haven't turned the electricity on yet. All the stuff's in the middle of the room, we'll break our necks. I'll go open the shutters. *(He moves a few steps nervously, then he turns.)* Don't move! *(His voice is strange.)* Are you still out there? Come on in. Are you scared? *(The mover steps in a few paces.)* Good. Now *don't move.* (He has finally opened the shutters on one balcony, daylight pours in.) Oh, thank God, light! *(He goes to the other balcony.)* That's better! *(The mover has put everything in a corner and is leaving.)* Where do you think you're going?

MOVING MAN ONE: I'm going to get the rest of the stuff.

RAFFAELE: Oh no you're not! You're leaving me here alone? What's the hurry? When your pal comes up, he can stay here and then you can go down.

MOVING MAN ONE: And the armoire? You expect me to carry that armoire by myself? It weighs a ton!

RAFFAELE: So we'll wait for the lady. When she comes, you and I will go down. And she can stay here by herself.

(The other mover enters, carrying two suitcases, a broom, dust mop, and a few other things.)

RAFFAELE: Put it here, put it on the floor. What's left downstairs?

MOVING MAN ONE: I told you. The armoire. Come on, Totò. One last trip.

(He's about to go.)

RAFFAELE: Are you deaf? Didn't you hear me? If you go, I go. But I'll have to lock up, because I'm responsible.

MOVING MAN ONE: But it's a waste of time.

RAFFAELE: So what? Is time something you can eat? And if you waste it, will you starve to death? It's your time, so go ahead and waste it. Now, let's wait for a certain personage to show up, and I'll stay here with that personage and you go get the armoire.

MOVING MAN ONE: Why can't you stay here alone?

RAFFAELE: That's none of your business. I suffer from a fear of . . . solicitude. *(Gastone enters. He is about thirty-six years old, charming, cheerful, but he's in a bad mood, so he seems quite arrogant.)*

GASTONE: Is this the top floor?

RAFFAELE: No, sir, there's the terrace.

GASTONE: Isn't there anybody at the front door? There was a woman there, but she couldn't tell me anything.

RAFFAELE: Her hair was all white?

GASTONE: Yes.

RAFFAELE: That's my sister. She's an idiot.

GASTONE: She's an idiot and she's guarding the door?

RAFFAELE: No, no, I'm guarding the door, I just came up for a minute. What can I do for you?

GASTONE: Nothing. I'm going.

MOVING MAN ONE: So we'll go get the armoire.
(They start to go.)

RAFFAELE: *(Yelling.)* Wait! you heard him, he said he's going.
(The two sit down again.)

GASTONE: Is this the new apartment Pasquale Lojacono is renting?

RAFFAELE: That's right.

GASTONE: But he's not here?

RAFFAELE: No sir, he hasn't moved in yet. He rented it almost two months ago, he sent the furniture over — it's all set up, the bedroom, the dining room, the living room, but he hasn't slept here yet. However he has let me know that today he and his wife are finally moving in . . . tonight.

GASTONE: *(Almost to himself.)* His wife. Yes. Is there a lot of furniture? Valuable stuff?

RAFFAELE: Valuable? I don't think so. And there isn't much furniture. As I said, he put some in the bedroom and the dining room, the parlor, the kitchen and this entrance hall, but he's got a long way to go, there are eighteen rooms in this apartment, all of them big . . .

GASTONE: *(Concerned, as if this affected him directly.)* Eighteen rooms?

RAFFAELE: The apartment goes all the way around. It takes up the whole floor of the palazzo. See these two balconies? There are sixty-six more.

GASTONE: Fit for a king!

RAFFAELE: I'll say! This palazzo was built in the sixteenth century by a man who was a helluva lot better than a king. He had his own army and whenever anybody irritated him, he went to war. Rodriguez Los De Rios. His mistress was a young girl, you should've seen her, a beauty. So, since he wanted to make it with her in a different room every night of the year, the palazzo has exactly 366 rooms.

GASTONE: But there are only 365 days in a year!

RAFFAELE: What about leap year? During the French occupation, this was the Court of France. Then the Turks, the Swiss. This palazzo has seen 'em all. And they keep coming, we've gotten used to it by now. On the first floor, for instance, we got a beautiful family of American soldiers.

GASTONE: An historic site.

RAFFAELE: More than historic.

GASTONE: And now Pasquale Lojacono is moving in. It must cost a fortune.

RAFFAELE: I couldn't tell you.

GASTONE: That's right, as long as he pays. I said to that stupid woman, "You'll lose him. You'll lose him. He'll walk out on you." *(To Raffaele, like a warning.)* Husbands shouldn't be irritated! She says, "But the children . . . ?" What children, they're grown, they'll take care of themselves. She's got to think of herself. Eighteen rooms, an historic palazzo! Enough! What's your name?

RAFFAELE: Raffaele, at your service.

GASTONE: Raffaele, here's 500 lire. Listen, I've got to talk to this man's wife when he's not around. So, I'll be back one of these days and if you tell me he's out, I'll come up.

RAFFAELE: *(Pocketing the money.)* Very good, sir

GASTONE: *(Talking to himself as he leaves.)* Good God! Eighteen rooms. I warned her, "You'll lose him! You'll lose him."

(He goes out the front door.)

MOVING MAN ONE: Hey, let's go.

(Rafaelle wanders around the room, he goes through a basket pulling out scarves and ties, examining everything.)

RAFFAELE: I know, I know. Don't rush me. This is good stuff. *(Making sure he's not seen by the movers, he pockets some ties and handkerchiefs, then casually:)* Let's see if anyone's coming? *(Looks out to the balcony.)* Let's see. *(He goes out and waves across to the audience, which is the professor who lives in the palazzo across the way.)* How do you do, Professor. *(Waits for the answer.)* Oh yes, he's moving in today, he'll be out by tomorrow. He won't last! *(Listens.)* Last night? A light? Where? Out on this balcony? On the other one? *(He points to it.)* And on the terrace, too? Of course I believe you, if you say so. And how long has it been since you've seen the elephant head? Twenty days? And the smoke? Last night? With the sparks? And the conquistador hasn't come back again? The conquistador. No. I'll just hand him the keys to the apartment, give him the list of instructions and go.

MOVING MAN ONE: *(Seeing Pasquale arrive.)* Oh, sir — *(To the other mover.)* Get up on your feet!

(The other mover gets up. Pasquale enters from the front door. He is about forty-five, with a tormented face perhaps because he is constantly searching for a way to live without constant worrying and to give his poor wife some relief. He looks like a man who is unhappy but hasn't given up. In other words, misfortune doesn't surprise him. He is very pale, lots of hair sprouts from his head in the most unlikely places. He's dressed simply but well. He's holding a chicken tightly between his upper arm and chest. From the finger of the same hand a large melon dangles from a wire. Under his other arm, various canes and two umbrellas tied together, and hanging from his pinky finger is a cage with a canary. He walks uncertainly, nervously, cautiously, like Raffaele at the opening of the act. He addresses the movers.)

PASQUALE: You're here? You left the armoire downstairs and no one's watching the cart. I was waiting for you to come down. I didn't want to leave it like that.

MOVING MAN ONE: Don Rafe' wouldn't let us go down. He didn't want to be left alone up here.

PASQUALE: That's ridiculous. Where's Raffaele?

MOVING MAN ONE: Out on the balcony.

PASQUALE: *(Calling.)* Raffaele.

RAFFAELE: At your service. *(To the professor.)* Excuse me. *(Re-entering.)* Welcome, sir, here, let me take that.

PASQUALE: *(Puts birdcage on table.)* Here, take this melon.

RAFFAELE: So, you finally decided to move in.

PASQUALE: Where can I put this chicken? I said to my wife, "Let's kill it and eat it." "No, never!" she says, "I love it." As if it was a dog.

RAFFAELE: Here, I'll put her outside on the terrace.

PASQUALE: Yes, but we'll have to clip her wings or she'll get away — she's a friend . . . (*Raffaele takes the hen from Pasquale's arms, but then he notices she's stopped breathing.*)

RAFFAELE: Come here, sweetie, let's go, see the sights. Oh, Don Pasquale, she's dead.

PASQUALE: She's dead? Let me see.

RAFFAELE: She's still warm, feel her. She must've died a couple of minutes ago.

PASQUALE: The minute I walked into this house. A bad sign.

RAFFAELE: It's not a sign. You were holding her tight, with her head under your arm. You smothered her.

PASQUALE: Maybe you're right. She was screeching so loud I couldn't walk. She had a voice that could scratch glass.

RAFFAELE: So, I'll take her away.

PASQUALE: Why?

RAFFAELE: You can't eat a dead chicken.

PASQUALE: Do you eat live ones?

RAFFAELE: No, but you are a gentleman and I know that gentlemen don't eat chickens unless they know how they died.

PASQUALE: Well, we know how it died. This fowl was asphyxiated by accident.

RAFFAELE: Yeah.

PASQUALE: An unfortunate accident, but tomorrow I'll make her into soup.

RAFFAELE: Good luck to you!

PASQUALE: I'll go hang her out on the balcony.

RAFFAELE: I think there's a nail out there.

(*He hangs the chicken and covers it with a cloth.*)

PASQUALE: Yes, here it is. You stay here tonight and in the morning you'll be nice and tender.

RAFFAELE: When is your wife coming?

PASQUALE: Soon. She had to finish fighting with the landlady. That woman accuses us of clogging her drains in that miserable place where we had to use her bathroom and her kitchen. Those drains were clogged before we ever got there, and now she wants us to pay the janitor. . .

RAFFAELE: Well, speaking of paying, let's discuss how much you'll be paying me.

PASQUALE: We'll discuss that later.

RAFFAELE: Well, while we're at it, why not discuss it now? I don't give a damn, but I want the money.

PASQUALE: You don't give a damn, but you want the money?

RAFFAELE: I really don't give a damn, but at the end of the month, if I don't give a damn, what the hell have I got?

PASQUALE: Ah yes, we'll discuss that later.

RAFFAELE: And speaking about discussing it, I've got to discuss certain things with you that the owner wanted me to discuss with you.

PASQUALE: And I've got things to talk about, too.

RAFFAELE: *(To the movers.)* Hey, guys, what's the matter? Are your feet glued to the floor? Go get the armoire.

MOVING MAN ONE: Yes, sir. Actually, sir, since its five-thirty now, and we haven't eaten all day, we'll get a glass of wine across the street, and then we'll bring it up.

PASQUALE: All right, but hurry.

MOVING MAN ONE: Don't worry.

(They go out the front door.)

PASQUALE: So, Raffaele, I've got to talk to you seriously.

RAFFAELE: Tell me.

PASQUALE: Sit down.

(Pasquale sits.)

RAFFAELE: Thank you, your excellency, sir. *(Sits facing him.)*

PASQUALE: *(After a little pause, having fixed him in the eye.)* Raffaele, I'm not crazy!

RAFFAELE: Signore, who said you were?

PASQUALE: Let me speak. I've got my own reasons for coming to live here. If there had been thirty-six or even seventy-two rooms instead of eighteen, I still would've come.

RAFFAELE: Whatever you say.

PASQUALE: I know about this house. I mean, I know what people have believed for hundreds of years: ghosts, spirits, lights, sounds of rattling chains . . .
(Raffaele continues for him, seriously convinced. He doesn't hide the gravity of the facts.)

RAFFAELE: Smoke, the cavalier, the elephant's head.

PASQUALE: Yes, all those stupid stories. Now, I can see you're a clever man. We could make some money, you and me. I've worked hard all my life but I've had no luck. I tried everything, nothing was too low for me, I even worked in the theater, can you imagine, but nothing worked out. My wife, she's got to eat, and me, too. Life is hard. Nobody helps. Or maybe once, they give you a hand just so they can say "I gave him a hand," and then it's "Good-bye," and you never see them again. You can only depend on yourself. The owner is letting me stay here with no rent for five years! He wants me to prove the place is okay. He must've killed himself trying to rent it, but he couldn't.

RAFFAELE: He had it all renovated, spent a pile of money. He moved heaven and earth. Nothing, sir, nothing, nobody wanted it.

PASQUALE: Listen. If I can last here, and I can — I know I can, because I absolutely don't believe one word of what they say — I've got it all figured out. I'll furnish all eighteen rooms and rent them out. A pensione. You can make a fortune these days doing this kind of thing. I haven't told my wife about all this, or she wouldn't come. Now, I assume the owner left specific instructions, which I intend to follow scrupulously.

RAFFAELE: Well. Of course, sir. See, I've been put in personal charge by the owner to personally make sure you carry out these instructions to the letter. And, you'd better not mess up or I'll lose my job. *(Like a proclamation:)* Two times a day, morning and night, you will step out on each balcony to show the neighbors that the house is lived in. There are sixty-eight balconies.

PASQUALE: Sixty-eight. Every day! It'll kill me.

RAFFAELE: Well, that's how it is. *(Picks up the same declamatory tone.)* In the morning you will beat four or five carpets on at least three balconies on all four sides of the palazzo so that people will hear you, see you and stop worrying.

PASQUALE: Unfortunately, I don't have any carpets.

RAFFAELE: Go buy one or borrow one, you can use the same carpet for all twelve balconies.

PASQUALE: It doesn't even have to be a carpet, it could be a coat, who's to know.

RAFFAELE: Certainly. When you're out on the balcony you gotta whistle or sing. I mean, you gotta be cheerful. The people have to see you laughing out there.

PASQUALE: They'll think I'm crazy. All right, maybe I could sing. A man at peace with the world could be singing a little tune out on his balcony and not seem strange. "Oh love, love, hmm . . . hmm . . . my heart." A little bit here, a little bit there. I'll hit all four sides of the palazzo . . .

RAFFAELE: But here's the most important thing: If you run away in terror, you can't tell anybody what you've seen or heard in this house.

PASQUALE: All right. But don't worry, I'm not running away.

RAFFAELE: Don't say that. Nobody's ever lasted here. Every one of them started out as brave as you and after four or five days they ran like rabbits.

PASQUALE: Really? People are pathetic. It doesn't make any sense. What did they see? I know it's nonsense, but you know, I'll admit I'm a little nervous.

RAFFAELE: Sir, you were so scared when you walked in here, you smothered the chicken.

PASQUALE: No. That was a mistake. And what about you? Have you ever seen anything?

RAFFAELE: Of course, I have. A damsel who was loved by a Spanish grandee who was pretending to marry her.

PASQUALE: He was what?

RAFFAELE: Pretending.

PASQUALE: You mean intending

RAFFAELE: Well, anyway she was "making it" with a pale cavalier. And it didn't take long for the Spanish grandee, Rodriguez Los De Rios, to smell a rat.

PASQUALE: A rat?

RAFFAELE: He smelled a rat and found the damsel and her lover. So he had them walled up in the room where they'd been found doing their filthy deeds.

PASQUALE: And that room is here in the palazzo?

RAFFAELE: In this apartment, and we don't know which room it is.

PASQUALE: It could even be this one. *(Raffaele nods.)* But they wouldn't have done their filthy deeds in the front hall with so many other rooms to choose from.

RAFFAELE: Who knows what the custom was in those days?

PASQUALE: This is certainly a fascinating story, but did you, personally, ever see anything?

RAFFAELE: No, because I'm never in here alone, they'd have to kill me first, and after what happened to my poor sister . . . Oh, you should've seen her. Sir, she was a rosebud. Have you seen what happened to her?

PASQUALE: What happened to her?

RAFFAELE: You've never seen her?

PASQUALE: No, I don't know her.

RAFFAELE: Oh, you should see what happened to her! My sister used to go up to the roof to hang out the laundry, since this apartment was never rented. One morning, we heard screams. What can I tell you, she went upstairs all fine and dandy and when she came down, her hair was white and she was an imbecile.

PASQUALE: An imbecile?

RAFFAELE: An imbecile. I mean an idiot, I mean more of an idiot than before.

PASQUALE: So she was an idiot before?

RAFFAELE: Well, she's a woman.

PASQUALE: You mean women are idiots?

RAFFAELE: Well, they're not men. When she talks about it, she starts to babble and you can't understand a word she says.

PASQUALE: But she talks about it?

RAFFAELE: Yes, she tells the whole story, but you can only make out a word or two.

PASQUALE: Send her up to me. Maybe I can figure it out.

RAFFAELE: I'll send her up. Her name is Carmela. Good. So, remember your instructions, and good luck.

PASQUALE: Uhmm. You're going?

RAFFAELE: Yes, sir. You're the one who's got to live here.

PASQUALE: That's right. I'm the one who's got to live here. I was just asking because . . . because I have to put my canary out on the balcony.

RAFFAELE: *(Raffaele takes it out on the left balcony.)* There's a nail out there, I remember. Is it all right here?

PASQUALE: Yes, it's all right.

RAFFAELE: *(Noticing the professor.)* Ah, Professor, your excellency.

PASQUALE: Who's that?

RAFFAELE: Professor Santanna. He gives lessons, in his house. He's a widower, and he married again. He lost his sister in the earthquake in Messina. He has a bit of land in Salierno and a brother in America, who's thirty-two. He's got diabetes. *(Introducing Pasquale.)* The new tenant. *(Pasquale waves.)* Well, let's hope . . .

PASQUALE: Thank you, professor . . .

RAFFAELE: He could tell you. What he's seen from his window — flashes of light on the roof, sparks, the elephant head, the conquistador . . .

PASQUALE: Who is this conquistador?

RAFFAELE: In shining armor with feathers sticking out of his helmet, a white cape, a sword, a trumpet, and he walks up on top there all around the ledge. But nobody's seen him since the war ended.

PASQUALE: Maybe he's on vacation.

RAFFAELE: Don't try to be funny, Mister, there's nothing to laugh about, I'm telling you. You could be inside, and out there there's a wild storm, snow, thunder, lightning, hailstones — you go out on the balcony, the sky is blue, everything's calm. Or, I don't know, one morning you wake up, the house is flooded with sunshine, it's like paradise, you get all dressed up in your white suits, your fancy shoes, you go out, it's raining cats and dogs. These are the kinds of tricks they play. Well, that's enough, I'm going downstairs, sir. *(To the professor.)* See you later.

PASQUALE: *(To the professor.)* Good-bye, so nice to meet you.

(They re-enter the room, Raffaele speaks as he exits.)

RAFFAELE: I'll go send my sister up. *(He turns back.)* Oh, I forgot the most important thing. Everything disappears here. I have to warn you, 'cause we're not responsible. You leave a hat, it's gone. Ties, handkerchiefs, and especially food. If you're missing something valuable, don't come to me about it. *(Suddenly threatening.)* And don't even think of going to the police. These ghosts, they don't fool around, you get kicked, slapped, punched in the head. Halfway down the stairs — they give you a shove and you land with your face in the opposite wall. If you value your life, don't go to the police. Understand? *(Now he's obsequious again.)* So, with your permission, sir, I'll be going downstairs now. Good-bye, Professor, see you later. *(Raffaele exits.)*

(Pasquale, alone, wanders around the room, whistles a little, laughs a little, arranges a few pieces of furniture, but he seems worried, looks over his shoulder, as if someone had called. His worry mounts, he runs around the room as if he were dusting off his jacket, especially on his back, as if there were something invisible tormenting him. He bursts out onto the balcony, violently closing the glass doors. The wooden shutters behind him make a tremendous noise, now he has alarmed the professor who has perhaps asked him what horrible unheard-of event or visions he might have experienced.)

PASQUALE: It's nothing, Professor, nothing. Absolutely nothing. Everything's calm. It's all nonsense. I'm going to beat the rugs now.

(Carmela enters as if she were looking for someone. She is about forty-eight, but looks seventy. Her hair is a mess and all white. After looking around, she stands still near the steps to the roof as if she were holding her pose for a photographer. Pasquale has waved good-bye to the professor, he's cautiously pushing open the glass doors, sees Carmela. Fear stops his cry in his throat and he falls into a chair. Then he gets up and moves swiftly to the other balcony, opens the doors and goes out. Carmela moves away from her spot. Like a figure stepping out of a painting she moves toward the right balcony and she tries to encourage Pasquale to come in with gestures as disconnected and confused as her mind.)

PASQUALE: What do you want? Who are you?

CARMELA: The sister of the janitor, what can I get you? *(She laughs idiotically.)* *(A brief grotesque charade goes on until Pasquale finally realizes she is Carmela and not a ghost.)*

PASQUALE: *(Re-enters the room.)* Oh, you're Carmela, eh? Carmela . . .

CARMELA: Soooo . . . *(She laughs as before.)*

PASQUALE: You are the sister of Raffaele.

CARMELA: *(As if to affirm and deny at the same time.)* Eeeeh!

PASQUALE: Did you understand?

CARMELA: Eeeeh!

PASQUALE: I asked you to come. I want you to tell me about the ghosts on the roof.

CARMELA: *(This is the only thing that interests her. She wants to tell all she saw.)* I was going to hang the clothes on the roof, as usual. I went through this door and up that staircase every week. One Saturday, I didn't feel so good. I hadn't slept all night that day because of the music in my head . . .

PASQUALE: Music?

CARMELA: Yes, music. From far, far away, soft, soft, all violins. I was going up the stairs and the music kept following me, I thought maybe it was coming from the church next door, but it followed me all the way up to the roof. I've never been scared of the dead. When I want to go for a walk I go to the graveyard, I mean Mamma is dead, Papa is dead, I'm not scared of Papa and Mamma. While I was hanging the clothes, I saw a birdie. "What a beautiful birdie you are, what are you doing?"
(With no warning, she lets out a wild cry. Her eyes are fixed and inexpressive and she stops speaking. She starts to whine and cry out, pointing to the front door, then to the roof. Still screaming, she runs away as if she has just relived the past. Pasquale, terrified, tries to gather up hats, umbrellas, suitcases, and starts to rush out, bumping into the movers with the armoire.)

MOVING MAN ONE: Lean it over this way, easy does it, don't let it tip over. Sir, where do you want us to put it?
(Reassured by their presence, he surveys the armoire, front and sides, and decides it goes upstage left.)

PASQUALE: Here, here. I think it looks good here.

MOVING MAN ONE: Good God, four flights, one more step and we'd be dead.
(Raffaele enters with Maria, who has a handbag and packages and a small suitcase. She is a charming twenty-six-year-old. A little sad, perhaps because she's tired. She doesn't feel like talking.)

RAFFAELE: Here she is. The wife. Come in, and welcome to your home.

MARIA: Where's the bedroom?

PASQUALE: Here. *(She starts offstage.)* Do you need something?

MARIA: *(She speaks as she goes offstage.)* The suitcase he brought up.

PASQUALE: *(Taking it from Raffaele.)* Here, give it to me. *(To the movers.)* You can go. Come tomorrow and I'll give you the rest of what I owe you.

MOVING MAN ONE: Fine, we're going. Good-bye and good luck.

RAFFAELE: Sir, can I go now?

PASQUALE: *(Exiting into Maria's room.)* I'll call if I need you.
(Raffaele is alone, he looks around, steps out on the balcony, takes the chicken and exits. The room is empty now. It's sunset. From the balcony, on the left,

a glow of rose-colored light. A single last, cold ray of sun hits the middle of the armoire. Pause, a slow change of lights, then, as if in a fairy tale, the two armoire doors open slowly. A young man of about thirty-six, lit by the sun, cautiously steps out with a big bunch of flowers. He looks around, puts them in a vase, and then places them on the table. He moves like an automaton, takes a package out of the wardrobe, tied in gold thread, unties it carefully, removes a beautiful roast chicken. Puts it on a platter and puts it all in a drawer. He goes back into the wardrobe, always moving slowly, and closes the doors. Pasquale enters from the left, continuing to speak to his wife.)

PASQUALE: I'll go out to buy some candles, or we'll be in the dark tonight. They haven't turned the electricity on yet. *(He starts to go, notices the flowers and is surprised.)* Mari'?

MARIA: What?

PASQUALE: Did you bring flowers?

MARIA: *(From offstage.)* Flowers? No.

PASQUALE: It means they like me. They're welcoming me with flowers. I'll go buy the candles. *(He's about to go, then he looks out to the balcony.)* A beautiful evening, the sky is blue. *(He grabs an umbrella and exits. The wardrobe opens, this time with no hesitation, in fact quickly. The young man places himself to the right of the table where he put the flowers. He is Alfredo Marigliano. His voice might make him seem highly neurotic, but he's merely a passionate free-thinker and a believer in his own personal freedom. Maria enters still talking to her husband.)*

MARIA: What flowers?

ALFREDO: These.

MARIA: *(Surprised but delighted.)* Where's my husband?

ALFREDO: He went out to buy candles.

MARIA: How did you get in?

ALFREDO: I took the elevator. I gave the movers 1,000 lire and they carried me up in the armoire.

MARIA: You're crazy!

ALFREDO: I had to see you. It's been two days.

MARIA: Well, with all the moving . . .

ALFREDO: I had to bring you flowers, to welcome you to your new home.

MARIA: Alfre', do you really love me?

ALFREDO: I won't answer that. You don't deserve an answer. *(Short pause.)* Why am I here? So many risks, so many dangers. Why? Because I left my wife and children a year and a half ago.

MARIA: I've told you so many times go back to her. Go back home.

ALFREDO: You just say that to make your conscience feel better. You've been told it's a sin to follow your heart. Your heart led you to me because you were looking for joy, and you got it, and then to fix things up with God, you said, "Alfre', let's stop. Go back home, to your children." Mari', I respect your ideas, but you know mine. It's not your fault — from the day you were born they told you that joy can only be happy in secret. I know we can't change the structure of the world in a single day, but I can change one world: ours. My children are grown up, they don't need me anymore. Why should I be chained for the rest of my life to a woman who . . . even my wife can't bear to live with me. I'm going mad. Please, Mari', come away with me.

MARIA: What about my husband?

ALFREDO: Your husband! You told me he wanted to start a hotel here, rent out rooms. We'll help him. I'll be his biggest backer. *(Looking around.)* The place is ideal. This could be the reception area. A radio-phonograph here in this corner, with a great selection of records. A reading room, with newspapers, magazines. A telephone right over here. That window is a bit of an eyesore, but that can be fixed. We'll take off the shutters and get a nice planter with some cactus. Yes, it can be fixed up. Guests coming and going, money flowing in. Your husband will be fine. And then, if he still wants to act like a selfish victim, he can put an end to his misery and shoot himself. What are cemeteries for? Funeral directors and grave diggers have to make a living, too.

MARIA: Should I be the one to tell him?

ALFREDO: When the time is right, you'll tell him, or probably he'll tell you, since he'd rather run a hotel than reside in a cemetery. Now, will you do me a favor?

MARIA: What?

ALFREDO: You haven't eaten.

MARIA: I had breakfast this morning.

(He takes out the chicken and puts it on the table.)

ALFREDO: I knew you'd have no time to think about food. It's still warm, eat it. And I brought you dessert, too.

(Pasquale enters with a half-opened package of candles. Alfredo freezes.)

PASQUALE: Here are the candles. I couldn't find any candlesticks. Here.

(Having rummaged in a basket he finds a holder, sticks the candle in, moves toward the table, sees Alfredo and the chicken. He thinks of his chicken, rushes out to the balcony, it's gone! He returns with gestures of awe. A miracle. He wants to speak, notices Alfredo again, tries to light the candle. After three tries

he succeeds. Then he tries to calm down and sits facing Maria.) There were no plain candles, only these. *(Pasquale looks at Alfredo, hoping that he'll be gone the next time he looks.)* Is this a roast chicken?

MARIA: *(Having lost all respect for him, she goes off to her room.)* Yes . . . it's a roast chicken!

(Pasquale looks at the wardrobe again. This time Alfredo moves toward the front door, very slowly. Pasquale follows him. When Alfredo gets to the door, he gives a little smile and a little bow. Pasquale bows back and Alfredo slowly disappears. Pasquale's sense of reality has slipped away, he's completely convinced he's seen a vision. Ashen, trembling with fear, babbling, he sits down very slowly so as not to disturb the air around him. He begins to look like a visionary, a mystic: a man who has seen a ghost.)

END OF ACT ONE

Act Two

The same. But it's renovated, all brand new. It now looks like a lobby of a small pensione, not elegant, but proper. Tables with magazines, a writing desk, a telephone, rugs. A grey velvet curtain with a red border is hung along the corridor — everything as Alfredo described in the first act. Even the window, with the plants. Pasquale is blissfully seated outside on the left balcony. He has put a chair in front of him with a little "Napoletana," the coffee pot used in every Italian house, an espresso cup, and a saucer. He speaks to the professor, while waiting for the coffee to be ready.

PASQUALE: Ah, Professor, we Neapolitans understand we couldn't live without this little comfort out on the balcony in the fresh air. I myself would gladly give everything up except for this little cup of coffee, sipped peacefully out here on the balcony, after a little nap after lunch.

And I make it myself with my own two hands. This is a four-cup machinetta, but you can even stretch it out to six, and if the cups are small, even eight, for friends. Coffee is so expensive. *(He listens.)*

My wife has no respect. She doesn't understand these things. She's much younger than I am, and the younger generation has lost interest in these finer points, which, to me, are the poetry of life. It not only keeps you busy, it calms your spirit. What? No. I follow the rules religiously. On the spout — see the spout? Here, Professor — *(He picks it up to show him.)* here, where are you looking? Here. *(He listens.)*

You like to make jokes. No, go ahead, I don't mind. I put this little paper cap on the spout — it doesn't look like much, but it's important. That's right, it keeps the steam in. That's essential. And you have to boil the water for at least three minutes before pouring it, and, a little secret, put half a teaspoon of fine coffee in here. So that the minute you pour it, you have the full aroma. Me too. Yes, I roast it myself. I told you, my wife doesn't help. The color? Monk's robe, robe of a monk. Yes, well even if my hand slips and some of the coffee gets mixed with the watery part and it's a disgusting mess, I drink it anyway. Professor, it's ready. *(He pours it and drinks.)* Have you had yours? Jesus, this is so good, it's like chocolate! You see how little it takes to make a man happy? A little coffee, sipped peacefully out of doors, in pleasant company . . . I'll save half a cup, and drink it between cigarettes. *(Lights cigarette.)* What? I didn't understand? *(Listens.)* Ahh yes, yes. No, nothing, it's all nonsense. I wouldn't have moved in here if I'd believed that stuff. I've been here six months and you'd think I'd've seen something by now. *(Listens.)* Well, what can I tell you? I'm sure you're right, but here in this house all is calm. You might have seen things on the roof or outside your window, but I'm telling you. I've never seen a thing. All I can say is that since I came here, my life has improved. This house has brought me luck. Now, if only people would start renting rooms, we'd be fine. But ghosts? Ghosts? Not the shadow of a ghost.

(Raffaele enters, he speaks once, then louder the second time.)

RAFFAELE: Sir, the newspaper. Sir, the newspaper.

PASQUALE: Ah, The doorkeeper who is bringing me the paper, excuse me. Let's see.

RAFFAELE: They both have the ad.

PASQUALE: *(Reading.)* "Pensione Lojacono. Ultra clean and comfortable, many bedrooms, running water in the kitchen. Three bathrooms. Modest prices. Proprietor and director, Pasquale Lojacono." I don't get it. Nobody's shown up. Every agency has the listing. Nobody.

RAFFAELE: It's only been three days since you put the ad in the paper, and this house has a reputation. It'll take time. Are you beating the rugs every day?

PASQUALE: Didn't you hear me singing last night? "E Lucevan le stelle." My throat's still sore.

RAFFAELE: Oh, that was you? You got a nice voice. But you've gotta sing early in the morning, we've got offices here, people working. I've got things to do.

PASQUALE: So do I. How long is this going to take?

RAFFAELE: You've got to be patient.

PASQUALE: I'm running out of time. If I don't start seeing results soon, I'll be begging in the streets.

RAFFAELE: I know. You spent a fortune, everybody says so. And speaking of money, here's the bill for what I bought this morning: a bottle of olive oil, meat, vegetables. And what with yesterday's bill that comes to 1,270 lire!

PASQUALE: I can't go on like this! 1,270 lire in a day and a half, and it's all for food.

RAFFAELE: But it's lunch and dinner.

PASQUALE: I know, but it's still too much.

RAFFAELE: Yes, but can I have the money?

(Pasquale lost in thought, walks to the jacket hanging on the door and searches through the pockets, then he takes out some bills.)

PASQUALE: You can have it if I can find it. Oh, I guess I hadn't checked carefully. Here. 3,000 lire and some change. Raffae,' don't tell anybody about this — I have to convince the world that this house is fine. I keep telling the professor I haven't seen a thing, and in a way it's true — no noises, no tricks, no strange sights. They're so generous. I guess they like me.

RAFFAELE: *(Vaguely.)* It's possible.

PASQUALE: Sometimes I feel there's someone behind me when I walk into a room, someone who changes shape and becomes a young man, about thirty-five or thirty-six years old.

RAFFAELE: Yes, I've seen him when he's changed shape too, especially when you're out.

PASQUALE: Really?

RAFFAELE: Yes, I used to ask him where he was going. I still ask. But he gives me a look as if he were saying, "You still don't know where I'm going?" So I'll stop asking, what the hell.

PASQUALE: Don't ask. Let him come and go. So it's true, there's the proof.

RAFFAELE: Of course it is.

PASQUALE: See that pajama top over there?

RAFFAELE: Yes, sir.

PASQUALE: That's not a pajama top — it's a gold mine.

RAFFAELE: Really?

PASQUALE: When I go to bed at night, I slip it on, I put my hands in the pockets, and I find 100, 500, 1,000 lire. So now I leave it right there, only slip it on when I need some cash.

RAFFAELE: That's amazing! I wish I had a pajama top like that.

PASQUALE: Well, the problem is the money kept coming so I kept spending, fixing this place up. I put in three bathrooms. How will I pay for them?

RAFFAELE: Look in the pajamas.

PASQUALE: I've looked, but it's only small change.

RAFFAELE: Well, check your shoes, your hats, under the bed.

PASQUALE: I've looked, I've looked. What can I do? I'll wait. These spirits have to be respected. They must have their reasons. So, how much do I owe you?

RAFFAELE: 1,270.

PASQUALE: Here's 2,000, you can give me the change.

RAFFAELE: Of course. *(Takes money from his pocket.)* Here's 730 in change.

PASQUALE: Exactly.

(Raffaele counts out the money and puts it on the table.)

RAFFAELE: Here you are.

PASQUALE: And here are the 2,000 lire. *(Pasquale puts his money on the table.)*

RAFFAELE: Do you need anything for supper tonight?

PASQUALE: You'd better ask my wife.

RAFFAELE: I'll do that. *(Taking advantage of Pasquale's momentary distraction, he pockets the 730 lire.)* I'll come up and see her later. *(Pasquale has noticed. He's going to beat him at his game. He gets between Raffaele and the 2,000 lire.)*

PASQUALE: Precisely. If I should need you, I'll call. *(Pasquale manages to pocket the money.)*

RAFFAELE: Any time.

PASQUALE: Of course.

RAFFAELE: Permit me. *(He reaches for the money.)* Where's my 2,000 lire?

PASQUALE: Where's my change?

RAFFAELE: Sir, I put the change here.
(Patting the table.)

PASQUALE: I put the 2,000 lire here.

RAFFAELE: What's going on?

PASQUALE: Don't ask me!

RAFFAELE: Sir, I swear I do not have the 2,000 lire in my pocket.

PASQUALE: And I don't have the change. What can you do? It must be the ghosts.

RAFFAELE: *(Bitterly.)* Yes. Sir, maybe the ghost put your change in my pocket and my 2,000 lire in yours. Would you mind looking?

PASQUALE: I think you'd better look for the change first. If you don't find the change, you won't get the 2,000.

RAFFAELE: *(Grinding his teeth.)* Think so? All right. *(Searching his pocket.)* No matter how many tricks they play, they never cease to amaze me, these ghosts. *(Holding up 700 lire.)* See? From the table into my pocket! *(Pasquale takes the money from Raffaele and examines it.)*

PASQUALE: What? Let me see. It's incredible.
(He pockets them.)

RAFFAELE: Sir, now could you see if my 2,000 lire are in your pocket?

PASQUALE: Of course! Obviously, after all this. *(Checks pockets.)* No, Raffe', they're not here.
(Raffaele has no intention of giving into Pasquale's game.)

RAFFAELE: Sir, I'm not crazy, I saw . . .

PASQUALE: What did you see?

RAFFAELE: I saw 2,000 lire on the table.

PASQUALE: And then?

RAFFAELE: *(Beside himself.)* And then it disappeared.

PASQUALE: My change disappeared, too.

RAFFAELE: *(Exasperated, but with a sense of righteousness.)* But then it came back.

PASQUALE: Well, the 2,000 lire didn't come back. What can you do? So many of my things disappear and I don't say a word — handkerchiefs, neckties, bath towels. I lost all my sheets, a spinach frittata. The melon I left on the balcony the day I moved in, I never saw it again.

RAFFAELE: *(Seems irritated, as if he were being reprimanded.)* You're still thinking about that melon. You keep bringing it up.

PASQUALE: And the scissors? And the knife? Not to mention my special hand-made yellow shoes. I haven't worn a hat for months.

RAFFAELE: Just what are you driving at?

PASQUALE: Nothing at all. Let's just consider those 2,000 lire lost. Blame the damn ghosts.

RAFFAELE: *(Resigned and muttering as he exits.)* All right. I'm leaving now. Why would the ghosts pick on me? I'm a poor man. They take my money and don't give it back! What's the world coming to? This ghost is a filthy, cheating, lying son of a . . .

(Maria enters. Picks up a magazine, sees her husband, and is about to go back. Pasquale watches her, then he speaks.)

PASQUALE: Mari', tell me what's wrong. If you're unhappy, if there's something you want to say, tell me. Talk to me.

MARIA: *(Won't even glance at him.)* Are you sure you want me to talk?

PASQUALE: Of course. I don't hide anything from you, Mari'. I tell you everything, except for a few crazy schemes of mine, which I don't tell you about because I don't want to worry you. But I know even that is wrong. If I had the courage to share my fears with you I'd be calmer, freer, more confident . . .

MARIA: So . . . talk.

PASQUALE: You're the one who should talk. I know, it's nobody's fault. Life is hard. At a certain point, especially in marriage, you get an idea in your head, maybe it's all wrong, but you think — "What's *she* thinking?" "What's *he* thinking?" "Why did she do that?" "Why did he . . . ?" All you have to do is ask, everything would become clear. But pride! "Why doesn't she say something?" "It's up to him to say something." And so a wall goes up — coldness, indifference, even hate, Mari'. And . . . I understand, pride, especially for a woman — but you, Mari', you've closed up like a clam. Talk to me, Mari', talk. Help me. Just look at me — not all the time, but once in a while.

MARIA: What do you want from me? I married you five years ago, and you said trust me, I have great plans, you have to have faith, and I had faith and we lived on that faith, God knows how, until today and we're still living on it. I don't talk? You should thank God I don't! I'm here, I do whatever you want, but what kind of a life is this? Where does the money come from? Who furnished this house?

PASQUALE: What difference does it make?

MARIA: What do you mean? People ask.

PASQUALE: It's none of their business. I can't talk about it. I'm not supposed to talk about it to anybody, not even to you. Especially you. This is why you're upset? I knew it! Maria, you want too many explanations. Like all women. You're jealous. Right? Don't be silly, Mari'. Just remember, your husband is no fool. Things are finally looking up. Finally a good soul is lending us a hand, and let's hope he keeps on helping us. You're happy, I'm happy. Tell people to mind their own business.

MARIA: As long as you're full, you don't care who feeds you?

PASQUALE: You think I'm stupid? Why rock the boat?

MARIA: *(Disgusted.)* What kind of a man are you? Who am I living with? You're an animal. A phonograph cabinet with a complete record collection is dropped on the doorstep in this day and age, and you keep it. A fully stocked bar, and you don't say a word. I wake up one morning and a brand new stove appears by magic, one of your little idiotic giggles and it's here to stay. Furniture for five bedrooms? The fairy godmother must've dropped in. A diamond ring? It fell from the sky. You wave a magic wand, and 50,000 lire appear. So now we believe in Santa Claus, the Easter Bunny, and the goose that laid the golden egg. Why don't you hang your stocking on the chimney? Oh that's right, you've got your pajama pockets. I wish I could just accept it, but I can't. I used to think, maybe you really believed or didn't notice, but whatever turns up you accept as if it were perfectly normal. When I ask who pays the bills, you say, "Who cares, I'm happy, you're happy." Well, maybe you can live this way, but I can't. I'm leaving.

(Maria gets up. Pasquale follows her.)

PASQUALE: This is ridiculous, Maria. Excuse me, but this is ridiculous. *(He sees the professor and greets him with a little forced smile.)* Professor. *(He re-enters, with a gesture of irritation.)* That man's always looking out the window. Excuse me, Mari', but if anyone needs an explanation, it's me.

MARIA: Of course!

PASQUALE: And since I don't ask, the subject is closed. Don't worry about me —

there's nothing illegal going on here. Let them talk. They'll say I'm a swine, let them, after a while they'll lose interest. Believe me, I know what's going on here. I know who pays. I know everything, but I can't talk, it's not a good idea. I've heard of people in similar situations and they all say, "Don't talk about it or it will come to an end." Mari', if I told you what I know, you'd run away, you'd leave me and I can't lose you. We couldn't have gone on living the way we were, loving each other like Romeo and Juliet, with me desperate for a suit and you for a pair of stockings. With your heart breaking because once again someone broke his promise about the job he'd been dangling before my eyes. How could we have managed to stifle all that bitterness and find tenderness and passion and complete understanding . . . On an empty stomach, Mari'? On an empty stomach passion is hard to sustain. Romeo and Juliet must've been very rich or after three days they'd have been at each other's throats. Who cares what people say? We finally have a little luck, and Donna Maria is upset. Please! And listen we're not discussing this again, because I want to enjoy life — I want to eat, drink, and dress well, I don't want to have to count every cigarette. I want pastry on Sunday, whatever I need. No, my dear girl. You wait and see. Things will get even better *(Yelling so that he can be heard by the ghosts.)* "Hey, I need 200,000 lire. Now! So give them to me. No excuses, ya hear?" Mari', you deserve to live well, and not have to put up with so little. So, no more of these silly worries. I'm going out for half an hour to the agency to see if there's any news about the pensione, before the weather turns. *(Looks out the balcony.)* Oh yes, it looks bad. *(He goes toward the front door.)* Who pays? Where does it come from? Why ask? Don't mess with a higher force . . . Let's just keep going. *(He exits.)*

MARIA: *(Nauseated, almost crying.)* What a beast. I'm so ashamed.

(Alfredo peeks out of a window in the upstage wall and lights a cigarette.)

ALFREDO: Well, now you know what sort of a man he is. *(He comes down the interior staircase and enters the room.)* You didn't want to believe me. Every time I'd bring it up you'd change the subject, I knew it upset you and I tried to respect your feelings, but the whole thing is, forgive me, so disgusting.

MARIA: Alfredo, please don't humiliate me.

ALFREDO: *(Advances tenderly.)* Humiliate you? Maria, my darling, I just wanted you to see that it's our right, our duty, to get away from him.

MARIA: Alfre'!

ALFREDO: What are we waiting for? I can't leave you in the hands of this parasite. I can't. I heard every word he said, from that window. It made me so furious I wanted to run in and smack him. "And I want 200,000 lire! Now!" When hell freezes over. I want to smack him so hard, I'll turn him into a pizza. Come on, everything's ready, let's go.

MARIA: Alfre', you've got a wife, I've got a husband. We run off together, and then what? Your wife or my husband will call the police, they'll catch up with us and put us in jail.

(Gastone has entered shortly before.)

GASTONE: That's right. The police will come and the romance is over.

(They turn to look at him. Alfredo recognizes him and feels terrible. Maria doesn't know who he is. Gastone meanwhile, comes down the stairs and enters the room. He approaches them silently.)

ALFREDO: Don't say anything mean to her or I'll slap you.

GASTONE: Forget the slaps, Alfre', we have to talk seriously. Oh, my head, I'm exhausted. I was up all night. It's your fault. I've been in the country keeping your wife company. The house is full of animals — crickets, flies, mosquitoes — with my nerves! Last night I raise my sheets, there's a snail in the bed, this big, so I get up, close the windows and the door, I grab a broom, I strike hard. Smash! I'm sure it's dead. I look under the sheets, nothing. I look under the bed, I search the room, everywhere. I don't understand — doors and windows closed—no dead snail. I couldn't sleep a wink. I still think I can feel it crawling on me.

ALFREDO: But how did you get here from that staircase?

GASTONE: See those the stairs to the roof?

ALFREDO: Yes.

GASTONE: From the terrace you scale a little wall and cross a little hallway, then you're in the room on the fifth floor of the apartment next door, which you rented so you could see the lady more easily.

ALFREDO: Who told you that?

GASTONE: Your wife.

ALFREDO: Armida?

GASTONE: Armida.

ALFREDO: How did she find out?

GASTONE: Just because my sister never opens her mouth, never contradicts you, and is always calm and obedient, you think you own her? You told her she had to go to the seashore because the boys had to swim. Swimming has been over for a month. It's October, and she's still there. You think everything is going smoothly? You're wrong. Armida is not happy and she is suffering more than we can imagine. She hired a private detective. She knows every step and breath you take. She has the floor plan of this whole palace and of the apartment you rented next door. It's only because of me you haven't been caught. I convinced her that a scandal would only make things worse, and the poor woman still hopes you'll come back. Poor soul, I hardly recognize her, the children look terrible — they feel their mother's pain. Forced to live in a country house with no plumbing. You have to go to the well in the middle of town to get a bit of water. A few nights ago, she became hysterical, she fainted, wanted to poison herself. She falls on the floor, cracks her head, the children are screaming. You know, I like you. We've been good friends and, well, I've got a wife, too, I've got my own problems. But I don't understand this behavior.

ALFREDO: It's different for you. It's different. Your sister, excuse me for saying so, is an impossible woman. I can't go on, Gastone, I can't. First of all, she's been wildly jealous from the day we married.

GASTONE: What else?

ALFREDO: Everything and nothing, Gasto'. Little things that I'm ashamed to admit drive me crazy. Nothing bad, but there are some things, Gasto', I just can't stand. She dresses terribly. She's convinced she has a beautiful voice. She thinks she has interesting things to say. You see, it all seems like nothing, but these things matter. And she's boring, opinionated, jealous . . .

GASTONE: It's true, it's true, I've told her, not once but a thousand times. "Husbands shouldn't be irritated. Leave him in peace. You'll lose him."

ALFREDO: And she lost me. Gasto', I swear, she lost me, I'm never going back.

GASTONE: Don't say that! What about the children?

ALFREDO: I'll make sure the children have everything they need, whatever the cost, just so long as it's over.

GASTONE: Oh sure, it's easy to get rid of a family, a wife, two kids. Of course, you have so much money you can do whatever you want. But remember, everything has its limits. You're throwing your money away on this woman, she'll ruin you.

MARIA: I have nothing to say in my defense. You're right, I'm guilty, but please change your tone or I'll have to ask you to leave.

GASTONE: Don't worry, I can't wait to get out of here. And as for you, one day you'll find out what kind of a woman she is!

ALFREDO: Gasto', change your tone.

MARIA: You know nothing about me, and you've got no right to judge.

GASTONE: I know everything. I know your husband is a parasite and you are a prostitute.

ALFREDO: Stop! (*To Maria who is crying.*) Mari', please, go in the other room. (*To Gastone.*) And you'd better get out fast, or I'll . . . (*Maria goes off, Al-*

fredo follows her, speaking as he goes.) Nobody's going to tell me what to do. Stay out of my business. Do me a favor and get out of here, you're really bothering us.

GASTONE: Oh, you poor, pathetic fool.

(Gastone is about to leave the way he came, but Pasquale enters from the front hall. Not knowing if it's a ghost or a person, he asks cautiously.)

PASQUALE: Who are you?

GASTONE: Don't ask. I appeared in your house, and I'll disappear right away. But I know you.

(Pasquale is even more convinced that it's a vision and he stares at him with a little half-smile.)

PASQUALE: You know me?

GASTONE: Yes indeed, you're a worm.

PASQUALE: What do you mean?

GASTONE: Could I be any clearer or more accurate? You don't see, you don't hear, you go on pretending that nothing's going on. Aren't you shocked? Aren't you horrified? *(Pasquale looks at him with no expression.)* It's amazing to see a man of flesh and blood surrounded by rotting filth and pretending not to notice. Have you no blood in your veins? Are you a man at all? You slime, you slug! Say something!

(Pasquale loses his temper and screams louder than he.)

PASQUALE: Are *you* a man?

GASTONE: How dare you ask me that?

PASQUALE: You said you appeared out of the blue, and then you'll disappear. Are you a man or a ghost?

GASTONE: Are you crazy?

PASQUALE: *(Totally beside himself.)* Crazy? I'll show you crazy. If you're really a ghost, fine. If you're a man, I'll smash this chair over your head.

GASTONE: Don't act like a clown. Be serious. Well, what would I expect from you! This whole story is so sordid!

PASQUALE: What story?

GASTONE: You don't know? That's right, you know nothing. Well, I'll tell you, you take that money, but that money is cursed.

PASQUALE: Ah so, *you* are a ghost.

GASTONE: Cursed by my sister's husband . . . *(Gastone suddenly stops, transfixed, terrified, staring into the void, then he starts a kind of oriental dance, laughing as if he were being tickled — a wild scream — He beats at his body with both hands as if something were landing on him in different places. Then, with pirouettes and hysterical little cries, he exits crying:)* Out of my way . . .

PASQUALE: What did he see? (He's amused and terrified. A woman enters followed by two children, fourteen and twelve years old, and two old people. She is about forty, her steps are slow, inexorable, and heavy. She is dressed soberly, in dark colors, an unattractive little hat perched precariously on her head, because there is a little square of gauze bandage with a cross of adhesive tape smack in the middle of her forehead. She is pale, her eyes bloodshot from lack of sleep. She walks like a sleepwalker, an impression of great resignation, sadness, and hurt pride. However, she still has her dignity. The girl is dressed in white, even the shoes and stockings are white, she has a green bow at the end of her very tight braids, all dolled-up like a Sicilian corpse. Outside, the storm begins, thunder, sinister lightning, just as Armida starts to move.)

ARMIDA: Sir, this is not a woman standing here before you, this is not a family, these are five ghosts.

PASQUALE: (Reassured by the sweetness of Armida's voice.) Won't you sit down?

ARMIDA: Thank you. (They all sit.) A year and a half ago, we died.

PASQUALE: Oh, recently.

(Thunder in the distance.)

ARMIDA: These two little corpses. Wipe your nose! (She wipes the girl's nose with her handkerchief. The boy has a sudden nervous tic.) And you, stop twitching! You're doing it on purpose. He's always testing me. As I was saying, I died just as my heart, my soul, my senses had reached the pinnacle of total — believe me — total happiness.

PASQUALE: Right at that moment? What a shame!

ARMIDA: I was buried alive in a cold and miserable house.

PASQUALE: You are the young damsel!

ARMIDA: I *was* a damsel! My life was all sunshine, flowers, and music, innocent of all evil. (The two old people lament. A clap of thunder.) No trace of sin on my soul. (To the boy.) Stop it, or I'll smack you. What were we saying?

PASQUALE: (Staring at the boy.) I'm afraid I don't remember.

ARMIDA: God, then you haven't been listening.

PASQUALE: I was looking at the poor little soul. Ah, yes, I remember, your life was all sunshine.

ARMIDA: Yes, yes, be quiet now. (Resuming her melodramatic tone.) I was in the full bloom of youth, but after a year and a half of living death . . .

PASQUALE: (Holding his head in his hands.) Oooh, I've got such a headache! And what happened to the noble cavalier?

ARMIDA: Dead. (Her voice gets louder.) What was he looking for? I gave him everything he could ever want. He loved my homemade pasta with ricotta and parmigiano.

PASQUALE: Ah, you ate things like that even in those days?

ARMIDA: Of course. I made them any time he asked. My wrists would ache. "Armida, the peppers are ripe," Armida would make stuffed peppers. "Armida, it's eggplant time," and I'd make a parmigiana. A spotless jacket, the pants perfectly creased, a handkerchief in his pocket and a second one ready for him, that stinking bastard. He leaves me alone. Sending me to my grave, buried alive with these two little broken spirits. I hope he rots in hell. I hope he suffers the tortures of the damned. He says I drive him crazy. I hope he never gets a moment's peace.

PASQUALE: Maybe you got the wrong impression.

ARMIDA: Why am I so eager to please him, the great big shit? Why do I care about him, the great big turd? What have I gotten out of this? It's hell. Believe me, I'm in hell!

PASQUALE: Of course you are.

ARMIDA: I was never in paradise, believe me.

PASQUALE: Of course not. You use too many bad words.

ARMIDA: When we first met, I adored him. We had to meet secretly, our hearts pounding. I had been forbidden to see him.

PASQUALE: Well, of course. That poor man.

ARMIDA: Who?

PASQUALE: The Spanish grandee.

ARMIDA: The Spanish grandee?

(Pasquale smiles, so as not to offend the ghost.)

PASQUALE: The one who smelled a rat.

ARMIDA: A rat?

(Thunder and lightning.)

PASQUALE: When you were doing your filthy deeds. Well, what do I know? Would you please disappear now, I've got to go to bed.

ARMIDA: I see you find this pitiful scene amusing!

(The boy is twitching away, she goes up and smacks him without changing her tone; he almost loses his balance.)

These pathetic creatures looking for their father's love.

(She changes tone, like a judge delivering a sentence.) Pasquale Lojacono! (Thunder and lightning. Pasquale kneels, rests his elbows on the chair and hides his face in his hands.)

PASQUALE: Don't hurt me.

ARMIDA: You are Pasquale Lojacono, aren't you?

PASQUALE: Why ask, you know everything.

ARMIDA: Yes, I know everything and I know that you know, but I can't believe that you know it, too. That would be monstrous! Open your eyes! Save us!

(They all implore him with their arms outstretched.)

Save us, Pasquale Lojacono! With one simple act you can save these poor souls. You can bring this whole family back to life.

PASQUALE: How can I do it?

OLD MAN: Give us back our lives.

PASQUALE: I could have masses said. I could do good deeds.

ARMIDA: You can. Show your wife the kind of man you are, and if she persists, kill her.

ALL OF THEM: Oh, no, no, no!

ARMIDA: Yes. We'd all be saved.

(Loud thunder, and lightning. As the thunder stops, Alfredo enters as if he were the thunder.)

ALFREDO: Finally! Finally I see what you are. You pretend to be a good Christian soul, full of faith and hope and charity, but you're a vampire, sucking my blood and the blood of my children.

(Thunder and lightning. Pasquale is transfixed. He moves around as if he were watching a magical performance. He climbs on chairs and tables to see better, as if he'd bought a ticket.)

ARMIDA: I knew I'd find you here. Here in this house where you wander undisturbed.

ALFREDO: Yes. Because of you I am cursed to keep on wandering.

THE CHILDREN: Papaaa'!

(They grab hold of him, but the two old people pull them off.)

ARMIDA: You have no heart, you have no soul.

ALFREDO: To hell with you! You poisoned the best years of my life! Go to Hell!

(Gastone speaks from the little terrace window, then he leaves the window. Pasquale gets up onto the sofa in order to see better and gestures to the others that he has disappeared. Then a few moments later Gastone re-enters the room .)

GASTONE: I warned you you'd lose him. You'll lose him!

PASQUALE: He's disappeared!

ALFREDO: *(Hitting himself repeatedly.)* Goddamn it to hell, godamn, damn damn damn it to hell.

ARMIDA: Yes. I've lost him. *(Hysterical and desperate cries.)* I can't take it, I can't take it anymore! I'm destroyed! Madness, madness! *(Pushes the children toward him.)* Here, take the poor souls. I will disappear off the face of the earth. You wanted a corpse, well you'll get one. *(She pulls a bottle from her purse.)* Here. Arsenic.

GASTONE: No! No!

(Gastone throws himself toward her, followed by the old ones and the children. Armida flees, searching for a place to swallow the poison.)

ARMIDA: I'll leave you a corpse. Then you can dance on my grave—

(Gastone and Alfredo and the others all struggle with her, begging, crying, prayers to heaven, with arms upstretched. Sometimes they form groups that resemble allegories of Purgatory. The storm is imminent. The thunder claps and lightning are closer together. Carmela and Raffaele have come upstairs hearing the cries. Pasquale is unable to follow anything anymore, so he's gone out to the balcony and is watching through the glass door, which he has shut behind him. It all looks apocalyptic now. It's about to pour.)

ALFREDO: Armida, Armida. Stop, for God's sake!

RAFFAELE: Sir, for the love of God.

(Gastone manages to pull the poison out of her hands, Maria enters and stops in the doorway.)

GASTONE: Alfredo, I order you to leave this house. Come back to your senses.

THE CHILDREN: Papaaaa . . .

(Maria has withdrawn. Armida has fainted and Alfredo and Gastone are carrying her, followed by the two old people. Pasquale is now drenched in rain, but he doesn't dare come back inside, so he tries to protect himself from the rain as best he can. He peers into the room, then retreats, frightened. He looks out and sees the professor. Naturally he wants to look relaxed and cheerful.)

PASQUALE: Everything's calm, Professor, everything's peaceful.

(He peers in again and pulls back, frightened, since they are hysterical in there, like souls in hell. He laughs foolishly and claps his hands like a child to show the professor that he is not nervous.) Hah, hah, hah, it's not true, not at all. Ghosts don't exist. We made them up. We are the ghosts. Hah hah hah. *(While the storm continues and the people inside are still screaming, Pasquale in an attempt to seem relaxed, sings.)* "Oh, love, love what you do to me . . ."

END OF ACT TWO

Act Three

It is two months later. The room is the same as before, but it's messy, some fur-niture is gone, no radio-phonograph, no bar cabinet, the telephone wires are cut, nails in the wall where pictures once hung. It's evening. Almost eight-thirty. Candles light the room.

GASTONE: *(Continuing a conversation.)* He's been back with his wife and chil-dren for almost two months now. You have been so generous and fine. I cannot thank you enough. My sister, too, says at last she has met a true lady. But he's losing his mind. I'm a man, I understand these things. Poor Alfredo, he's miserable, apathetic, he says yes to everything but with no conviction, no enthusiasm. Last night he told me he wanted to see you. He asked so tenderly I couldn't refuse him.

MARIA: I only did what had to be done.

GASTONE: I told you, you're a saint, a saint, and what about your husband?

MARIA: He frightens me sometimes. He's so agitated, so worried about money. He's already sold some of the furniture. I think the hotel could have worked, we were starting to get some customers, but the plumber is de-manding payment, and do you know what my husband said last night? "Don't worry, I know our benefactor has disappeared, but he'll be back, you'll see."

GASTONE: He's terrible. What kind of a man is he? He's not looking for work?

MARIA: I don't understand him anymore. He always worked. He'd do anything to keep us going.

GASTONE: It's horrible.

MARIA: He says he has to go away tonight. He packed a suitcase, he sent some telegrams.

GASTONE: Where is he going?

MARIA: I don't know. We never talked much, but now we don't even look at each other anymore. He just said he was leaving, he had to go find a friend.

GASTONE: God, could he be going to find Alfredo, to ask him for money?

MARIA: No, no, he wouldn't go that far.

GASTONE: How do you know? I wouldn't put it past him. Oh, I'm sorry.

MARIA: *(Lowering her eyes.)* It's all right.

GASTONE: Well, it's better if he's not here, then there's no risk of meeting him. As I said, Signora, Alfredo wants to see you. He still has the room he rented next door, he paid for the year. He'll be sleeping there tonight. My sister found out, but I told her to pretend she knows nothing. What time is your husband leaving?

MARIA: At nine, at least that's what he said.

GASTONE: Then at nine or at ten-past, Alfredo will come down. I'll come with him so he won't get any ideas. He'll see you and he'll find the strength to go on for a while.

MARIA: And what about me?

GASTONE: Everyone has their cross to bear.

MARIA: You too?

GASTONE: My wife and I get along moderately well. Why? Because I'm patient and always ready to adapt. But the poor thing, what does she get out of life? Nailed to a bed.

MARIA: Why?

GASTONE: Oh, my dear lady, I told you every house has its cross. My wife has been paralyzed for eight years.

MARIA: Is she young?

GASTONE: Thirty-one, thirty-one years old.

MARIA: Poor woman!

GASTONE: I'd give my soul to see her walk again. Her whole personality changed. She doesn't want to see anyone, always in her room in the dark. Once in a while she says something. What can you do, I've gotten used to living alone. I'm thirty-five and I'm dried up like a cork.

MARIA: I never would have thought . . .

GASTONE: Yes, we're not always what we seem. I would have liked a cheerful woman who liked to talk and liked to have fun, travel — a friend who filled our life with life, but instead . . . I'm talking too much . . .

MARIA: Go on, go on, if you need to talk, talk. It will do you good. I'd love to do it myself.

GASTONE: Thank you. Sometime, if you'll let me, I'll come see you, if I'm not disturbing you.

MARIA: Not at all.

GASTONE: And we can talk about our troubles.

MARIA: Exactly

GASTONE: Well, I'm going now. I thank you again, and also for my sister. *(They get up, Maria holds out her hand to shake hands, Gastone holds her hand a bit longer.)*

MARIA: Good-bye.

GASTONE: Your eyes are so sad and tired. Is there anything I can do for you?

MARIA: Thank you. Sometimes a few words are enough. Thank you.

(She exits almost crying.)

GASTONE: Poor woman.

(Gastone follows her with his eyes, then exits by the terrace steps. From off-stage we hear Pasquale, followed by Raffaele.)

PASQUALE: I told you, don't bother me. I'm a nervous wreck. *(They enter.)* Every time I walk in the door you're shoving a summons at me with a blank face, no, with *delight*. If I went out ten times a day, you'd hand me ten summonses. Do you go to the courthouse and search through the garbage bins to find them?

RAFFAELE: So now I've got to swallow this? It's my fault now? They hand them to me and I hand them to you. Why don't I take them, make the sign of the cross over them and they'll turn into 1,000 lire? The man from the bathrooms came again today. You're out of your mind! I don't believe it! I just work here. I sit at the front door.

PASQUALE: You enjoy this. You come up here to destroy me.

RAFFAELE: No, the one who's going to destroy you is the man who installed the bathrooms

PASQUALE: Why don't you tell him to come back tomorrow?

RAFFAELE: And tomorrow we'll tell him something else. You said you were leaving tonight, tomorrow he comes, he doesn't find you here, I have to face him myself. Don Pasca', you're killing me. What are you waiting for? They cut off the phone, the lights, they turned off the water, you haven't found anything in the pajama top. What are you waiting for? Give up!

PASQUALE: This is none of your business. The money stopped the night those dead souls came to visit us.

RAFFAELE: I know. And you haven't seen him again?

PASQUALE: Who?

RAFFAELE: The noble cavalier.

PASQUALE: No. And he hasn't left me a thing.

RAFFAELE: So he was the one . . .

PASQUALE: Now we'll find out *(Calling offstage.)* Mari'.

MARIA: *(Entering.)* What do you want?

PASQUALE: I have to go away, it's urgent, maybe it will solve our problems, it's our last chance. I hope to be back tomorrow, but I'll take a suitcase in case I have to be away a little longer. I'm afraid you'll be alone for a little while. *(He picks up the suitcase that was onstage.)* Good-bye. *(Maria doesn't even look at him.)* Maria, Good-bye.

MARIA: Yes.

PASQUALE: You won't even say good-bye? You won't even give me a kiss?

MARIA: *(Moving away.)* Good-bye

PASQUALE: Good-bye, Mari' *(She sits near the table.)* Look at us, how sad, everything is over — love, enthusiasm — all gone. Months go by and we don't say a word, we don't share a thought. I could go out in the street, I could get run over by a truck, we'd never see each other again, but still we don't talk. How long has it been since I heard your voice? Remember, Mari', when we made love? We'd look at each other, we'd be too shy to speak, but we'd say so many things with our eyes. And I always felt so stupid around you, like I was nothing, and when you feel like nothing, you worry less — it all seems easier, simpler. You joke and laugh, you think everything will be fine, even death . . . you don't think about who is right . . . but maybe by now our hearts are too full of bitterness and sadness and hurt feelings. If we could, just for a second, open up. But no, it's locked up tight, and after a while you lose the key, it's gone, Mari' . . .
(He starts off sadly. Raffaele reminds him of the suitcase and offers to carry it.)

RAFFAELE: The suitcase.

PASQUALE: Thanks, I can manage . . . It's so sad, Mari'.
(He exits.)

RAFFAELE: Madam, I understand. He doesn't mean a key, like a key with a lock, which is a real key. He was making a comparison between the real key and the unreal key, which, after all, is real . . . After a few years of marriage there's a buildup of irritation between husband and wife, so you say: "You . . . know what . . . I really . . . oh, forget it." I suppose it's because I see you today, I see you tomorrow, I see you the next day. I go out and I see you. You go out and you see me. I see you at Christmas, I see you at Easter. You get used to each other so much, you feel like throwing up. Yes, sure, you also get all the good things that are better than what you had before, but a woman doesn't understand this. Just when you're feeling low and you want to be left alone, women start to ask you this and that and then they get sad and you talk but she won't answer, which is the worst. My good sweet wife used to do the same. But I would make her talk. Because I loved her. When I'd see her get sad, one, two days and she'd clam up, I'd give her a good slap and then she'd talk. Eh, poor woman. I remember when I'd hit her, she'd fall into my arms, she'd kiss me, and I'd feel her wet tears and her bloody nose. You, Signora, should beat him up a little, it would do you good. A little blood flowing and you'll love each other more than ever. *(Pasquale crosses over in the back, trying not to be seen by them.)* Well, that's enough. I'll go downstairs now. If you need anything, don't worry about me. Call.

(Maria takes the candle and exits left. It's dark onstage. Pasquale has re-entered in shafts of moonlight from the balconies. He walks on tiptoe. Peeks into Maria's room. He goes out onto the balcony, wraps himself in a blanket, having carefully closed the glass doors, and to make sure he can't be seen by the neighbors, he drapes a blanket over the railing. Alfredo and Gastone enter from the roof-terrace stairs.)

GASTONE: Hurry up, don't make me late. My wife is waiting for me. She's made a date for us to go out with some friends to the theater. She can't stay home even one night, and I always have to go with her. Do you want to join us? *(Alfredo gestures no.)* All right then, hurry up. *(Gastone exits from the roof. As soon as Gastone leaves, Alfredo goes slowly to Maria's bedroom door and mouths softly.)*

ALFREDO: Mari'.

MARIA: *(Enters after a second.)* Alfre'?

ALFREDO: *(Softly but clearly.)* I can't talk. My bother-in-law is watching. Everything's ready, a car, money, everything! Go get your coat and come right back.

MARIA: *(Confused, as if in a dream.)* Alfre' . . . but . . .

ALFREDO: Go on, Mari'.

MARIA: Yes . . .

(She goes off to her room. Alfredo looks at the terrace door, then crosses the stage and almost distactedly goes out on the balcony where he finds Pasquale.)

PASQUALE: Stop. I have to talk to you. *(Pasquale falls to his knees with his face on the ground.)* I'm shaking like a leaf. Oh God, don't kill me. Oh my heart, my heart. I pretended to leave, hoping that I'd finally see you at night. I knew, I knew you wouldn't abandon me. When I came here, they told me there were ghosts, but I didn't believe them. Forgive me. I believe now, because I see you, I can talk to you, and I'm glad. I feel strong, now that I can believe, it gives me hope and courage. They let me stay here for free to prove to the world it wasn't haunted. I never told my wife. I didn't want to scare her. In fact, you only let *me* see you. She never saw you. You helped me fix up the house, gave me money whenever I needed it, and then, all of a sudden, you disappeared and left me with nothing. You've spoiled me . . . I can't go back to the way I used to live. But I can't keep this up by myself. Help me, with a little bit more money I could get this hotel going. It was already starting to work. You are a good spirit and you can understand. I never could give my wife a bracelet, a ring, not even for her birthday. I never could get enough money together to take her to to the seashore. Sometimes I couldn't even let her buy a pair of stockings. If you only knew how sad it is for a man to have to hide his poverty with a little laugh, a little joke. Honest work is hard and miserable. And sometimes you can't even find it. I'm losing her. Every day I lose her a little more and I can't lose her. Maria is my life! I never would have said this to another man, but you're above all those feelings that keep us from opening our hearts to each other. Pride, envy, arrogance, egotism. Talking to you I feel close to God. I feel so small, just a tiny little thing, a nothing, and I'm happy to feel like nothing, to free myself from myself, which is such a heavy weight.

ALFREDO: Thank you, you've released me from my curse. I was cursed to wander in this house until a man spoke to me the way you have spoken to me. The table, look on the table.

(Alfredo exits quickly from the roof terrace exit.)

PASQUALE: He's disappeared. Professor, Professor, you were right. They do exist! There really are spirits. *(He listens and answers.)* Just the way you've told me. Remember when I saw you this morning? I pretended to leave. I came back and hid outside. I was prepared to wait all night, but he appeared right away. I talked to him. He left me some money — look — but he says he's released from his curse and will never appear again. *(Listens.)* What? In other disguises? It's possible. Well, we can hope!

END OF PLAY

Naples Gets Rich

(Napoli Milionaria)

CHARACTERS

Gennaro Jovine, unemployed tram conductor
Amalia, his wife
Maria Rosaria, their daughter
Amedeo, their son
Enrico Settebellezze, unemployed taxi driver
Peppe "the Jack"
Riccardo Spasiano, businessman
Federico, Amedeo's friend, works for the gas company
Pascalino, painter
Part-time priest
Brigadier Ciappa
Adelaide Schiano, a neighbor
Assunta, her niece
Donna Peppenela, a "client" of Amalia's
Teresa and Margherita, friends of Maria Rosaria
The doctor

Act One

The first act takes place during the second year of the war. A big room on the ground floor, smoky, dark with no windows, the front door is the only source of light and air. It is open to the street. On the house across the alley there is a little shrine, a Madonna with votive lights. Neapolitan songs and occasional Fascist speeches blare from the "loudspeaker/radio" outside. Inside, ugly furniture is crammed into spaces, many statues of saints on the dresser. A large brass bed and a table dominate the room. In the stage-left corner there is a tiny area, partitioned off; this is Gennaro's bedroom. Maria Rosaria is washing coffee cups in a tin bowl and lining them up on the big table. A fight is going on out in the street that Maria ignores, it gets louder and louder as the scene progresses. Amedeo enters.

AMEDEO: Is there any coffee?

MARIA ROSARIA: It's not ready.

AMEDEO: It's not ready?

MARIA ROSARIA: I'm boiling the dregs from yesterday.

AMEDEO: The dregs! Jesus, it's always the same, every morning a man has to get up and face the day like an animal. Where's Mamma?

MARIA ROSARIA: She's outside.

AMEDEO: And Papa?

MARIA ROSARIA: He's not up yet.

(From the makeshift room we hear a strange grunting sound, it's Gennaro's voice still heavy with sleep.)

GENNARO: I'm up. I'm up. I've been up since five. Your mother woke me. Do you think anyone in this house could oversleep?

(The argument outside is very loud now. During the following scene it starts to subside.)

Listen to her. Ooh, what a lovely sound.

AMEDEO: That's Mamma? What's she doing out there?

MARIA ROSARIA: Talking to Donna Vincenza.

GENNARO: *(From his room.)* She's not talking to her. She's eating her alive!

AMEDEO: Is it about the coffee?

MARIA ROSARIA: That Vincenza, she's a rotten sneak. She was always hanging around here, and Mamma would give her anything she asked for, a bit of flour, a fresh egg, clothes for that little monkey-faced daughter of hers — you know Mamma, sometimes she sees, sometimes she's blind as a bat —

so she snooped around here, found out who supplies us with coffee, and now she's selling coffee in her place but she charges half a lire less.

GENNARO: So it's a war between the two Grand Cafes of Naples!

MARIA ROSARIA: And she's telling everyone that we stretch our coffee out with chicory.

GENNARO: Not "our" coffee. Your coffee, your mother's coffee, I have nothing to do with this business. What a way to live — always in terror of the police, the inspectors, the Fascists.

MARIA ROSARIA: Oh Papa, if we listened to you we'd all starve to death.

GENNARO: No, you'd live like decent people — anything wrong with that?

MARIA ROSARIA: So it's indecent to sell coffee?

AMEDEO: If we didn't do it, there'd be a hundred others who would. Look at Donna Vincenza.

GENNARO: Last week a man jumped off the bridge just up the street.

AMEDEO: What's that got to do with anything?

GENNARO: Why don't you go jump, too?

AMEDEO: Papa, stay out of this. You don't understand these things, you're living in another time.

MARIA ROSARIA: *(Mutters.)* Just ignore him.

AMEDEO: Well, he's right, you know.

GENNARO: So I'm right, eh? Your sister is telling you "ignore him, he's an idiot. He doesn't know what he's talking about." Oh what a pathetic messed-up generation. Let me tell you something, by dealing in this coffee, your mother's taking it away from the hospitals, the soldiers, the wounded.

AMEDEO: Papa, stop blabbering. You were never too sharp, but you're really getting senile now. What hospitals? What soldiers? This stuff comes straight from the tables of the authorities. What they don't want, they sell to us. Yesterday, the head of the local Fascist group shows up here and tries to sell us five kilos of coffee. But Mamma wouldn't touch it. Listen, they're all a bunch of crooks. Why should they get fat while we starve to death? Listen, if they steal, I'll steal. It's every man for himself.

GENNARO: No. As long as I'm in this house, nobody steals.

AMEDEO: I was just talking.

(Amedeo takes a bowl covered with a plate, a spoon, and a piece of stale bread from the cupboard, Maria looks at him.)

What's wrong? These are my macaroni from last night.

MARIA ROSARIA: I didn't say anything.

(Amedeo sits at the table and uncovers the bowl.)

AMEDEO: What happened to my macaroni?

MARIA ROSARIA: How should I know?

AMEDEO: I didn't eat any last night so that I could eat them this morning. Who ate them? Papa, did you eat my macaroni?

GENNARO: I don't know. Were they yours?

AMEDEO: I've gotta get out of this house. I'm getting out of this house! Didn't you eat yours last night?

GENNARO: What do you want from me? I can't remember. Mine, yours, it's every man for himself.

AMEDEO: I don't believe it! What do you do? Get up in the middle of the night, looking for food?

GENNARO: That's right. I get up in the middle of the night because I've got nothing better to do. Last night after the air-raid siren and two and half hours in the shelter, I came home, I felt a little emptiness in my stomach, I remembered there were some macaroni left over. I didn't know they were yours, they looked exactly like mine.

AMEDEO: And so now I have to go to work on an empty stomach. Keep your hands out of my food! Goddam it to hell! *(Pounding the table.)* I don't mess with other people's things, so don't mess with mine! I swear to God, I'll smash everything in this house.

(Gennaro lifts the curtain of his room. He is in shirtsleeves, his pants half buttoned, with the suspenders hanging down. He is about fifty, thin and wasted, with an open, honest face.)

GENNARO: Smash what? What are you carrying on about? What are you going to smash?

AMEDEO: I'm starving.

GENNARO: It was only a little bit of macaroni. *(Gennaro holds out two fingers to show how little.)*

AMEDEO: It was a plate this full. *(Gennaro picks up a piece of bread, Amedeo tears it out of his hand.)*

This is my bread!

GENNARO: So take it. What a loving son.

AMEDEO: And you're such a loving father you let me go to work on no food. This little piece of bread, look at this, I have to work till noon on this miserable piece of bread. I'm getting out of this house. You'd better watch out. Keep an eye on your things!

(Amedeo goes off to change and Gennaro returns to his room.)

GENNARO: Well, he was right, but I really didn't remember.

(Maria goes to the kitchen. Amalia enters hot and furious, talking to Peppenella. Amalia is about thirty-eight, good-looking, dressed in whatever she

can find, but she wears silk stockings, one of her few little touches of vanity. She's decisive and hard-hearted in business.)

AMALIA: The things I gave her! *(Mocking her past generosity.)* A fresh egg, a piece of meat, a little plate of macaroni. A yard and a half of wool for her little rat-faced daughter. *(Calling off to Maria.)* Has it boiled yet?

MARIA ROSARIA: It just finished boiling.

AMALIA: So, come and get the coffee. *(To Peppenella.)* Donna Peppenella . . . why don't you go on home?

DONNA PEPPENELLA: Please, don't mind me, go on and do whatever you need to do.

(Amalia lifts up the mattress of the big bed, takes out a package tied with string and gives it to Peppenella.)

AMALIA: Here's the flour you asked me for yesterday. That'll be forty lire.

DONNA PEPPENELLA: Eighty lire a kilo? The price went up ten lire?

AMALIA: If you want it, take it, if you don't want it, it's fine with me. I was only trying to help you out. I put myself at risk here, I don't make any money on this. When the "person" comes, I'll give it back to him.

(Gennaro sticks his head out above the curtain.)

GENNARO: If they want flour, let them find their own flour. Why do you get mixed up in all this? *(To Peppenella.)* Can't you find your own flour?

DONNA PEPPENELLA: What can I tell you? *We* can't find it.

GENNARO: Then why come here? Is there a sign over the door that says "Flour mill?" You're right, you're not making any money on this because I won't allow this in my house.

DONNA PEPPENELLA: No! No! Your wife's such an angel, helping me out. She knew I needed a little flour, she's got a heart of gold. *(Glaring at Amalia as if she wants to strike her.)* And here's your forty lire.

AMALIA: *(Stares back coldly.)* Thank you.

DONNA PEPPENELLA: *(Sticky sweet.)* If you happen to run into a couple of beans.

AMALIA: Not a chance, Donna Peppenella. *(Softer now.)* Well, that same "person" who found the flour might be able to find the beans. If he does . . .

DONNA PEPPENELLA: You'll keep me in mind.

AMALIA: If he does, there'll be an increase in price.

DONNA PEPPENELLA: Of course I'll pay the increase. *(Still glaring at Amalia.)* Have a good day.

AMALIA: You too.

DONNA PEPPENELLA: Have a good day, Don Gennaro.

GENNARO: Don't come back.

DONNA PEPPENELLA: Yes, you're right. You're right.

(She exits as Maria enters.)

MARIA ROSARIA: Where's the coffee?

(Amalia lifts the mattress and hands it to her.)

AMALIA: Here. *(Maria starts to go.)* Come back here. *(Maria stops, goes up to her mother, who slaps her.)* I want you home earlier at night. *(Maria puts her hand to her face, but this has happened to her before. She answers hard and irritated.)*

MARIA ROSARIA: I went to the movies, with two of my girlfriends.

(Amalia goes back to her previous business.)

AMALIA: Well, you shouldn't have gone. With the curfew on, you come home at one in the morning! What will people say? Last night it was late, so I didn't make a scene, but if you don't start to behave, I'll kill you. Go make the coffee. The customers are coming.

(Maria exits. Gennaro appears, still disheveled, the shirt hanging out of his pants. During the following scene he starts to lather his face to shave in front of a small mirror that hangs from the wall of the partition.)

GENNARO: You have to watch them like a hawk, these young people.

(Ignoring him, Amalia takes a bunch of beans out from a bag hidden under the mattress, puts them in a colander. Maria enters.)

AMALIA: As soon as the coffee's done, put on the beans.

(Maria takes the beans and exits again.)

GENNARO: So there were beans? No answer!

(Adelaide enters with a bag full of vegetables.)

ADELAIDE: Donna Amalia, I was taking your little Rituccia to school this morning. She's so sweet, and so clever. A five-year-old and she speaks so well. I asked her, "Who do you love?" "Mamma," she answers.

GENNARO: She adores her mother.

ADELAIDE: And what about Papa? "Papa," she says, "is a silly ass." And she pronounced the *s* so perfectly!

GENNARO: I'm supposed to lose sleep over the opinion of a five-year-old? Do you think the words of an infant are going to bother me? But you shouldn't teach the child to talk that way.

AMEDEO: We don't teach her. She picks it up on the street.

GENNARO: *(Re-entering in his gas company uniform.)* She picks it up from you. This is what she learns at home.

AMEDEO: You're an idiot.

GENNARO: Fine. Whatever you say.

(Amedeo mutters something.)

GENNARO: I'm not talking to you.

AMEDEO: So why are you talking to me?

GENNARO: Oh, I fall for it every time!

ADELAIDE: Don Gennaro, don't agitate yourself so much over this. Your little one, she has the soul of an angel.

GENNARO: With the tongue of a devil.

ADELAIDE: She was just having fun. All the way home from school she kept swinging her skirt, singing, "Papa is a silly ass," "Papa is a silly ass."

GENNARO: She doesn't pick this up on the street, she learns it from her mother. *(Amalia shrugs.)* But Papa isn't an ass. He's just a little confused. When I came home from the last war, I couldn't rely on my head the way I used to. I start to do something and I forget what it is. I think of something else and five minutes later, a blank. I see Amedeo's macaroni, I think it's mine and I eat it.

AMEDEO: And I have to work an empty stomach.

(Federico, another gas man, enters, his lunch in a bag under his arm.)

FEDERICO: Amede', let's go.

AMEDEO: Wait a minute. Do you want some coffee?

FEDERICO: I already got some at Vincenza's. Donna Ama', she charges half a lire less.

AMALIA: So go to Donna Vincenza's.

FEDERICO: But your coffee is different. I even told her. *(To change the subject.)* Don Genna', you're shaving?

GENNARO: No, I'm cutting my toenails. Can't you see I'm shaving? What's the point of asking stupid questions? Save your breath and talk when you've got something to say.

FEDERICO: All right. I made a mistake. *(In a light tone.)* Don Genna', what do you say? What about the gas shortages? Are they going to let you tram drivers go back to work? Is it all going to get worse? What do you think?

GENNARO: If I were the minister of I don't know what, it would all be settled already. If they only listened to me.

FEDERICO: *(Amused, giving him rope.)* So come on, Don Genna', what about the shortages?

GENNARO: What shortages? There's no shortage of anything. There's plenty of flour, oil, butter, cheese, shoes, dresses. It's the same old song.

FEDERICO: What do you mean?

GENNARO: *(Still lathering his face.)* Why do you think there are wars?

FEDERICO: Why?

GENNARO: So that we can have shortages!

(They all laugh approvingly. He stops lathering and starts to enjoy it.)

And rationing? Sounds good eh, everything very rational. It was the same in the last war. The minute they start rationing, the business men start to dance, the magic show begins. Poof! Everything disappears. And we poor fools are left with three choices: We can starve to death, we can beg in the streets, or we can go straight to jail. Now, here's my master plan. *(Enrico Settebellezze and Peppe the Jack — two drivers who are out of work; because of the regulations forbidding the use of private vehicles to preserve gas, only military vehicles are allowed. They're both sharp dressers. Enrico is handsome in the popular Neapolitan way, thirty-five, brown-haired, quick eyes, muscular, solid. He smiles easily. He's a charming rascal. Peppe is more vulgar and less clever but stronger. His ample chest, his bull neck, and his special ability to hoist up a car with one shoulder in order to steal the wheels, have given him his name "the Jack." His arms dangle down, he rarely gestures. He seems to be always listening and meditating. He walks and talks slowly.)*

ENRICO: Greetings. Don Genna', I don't want to interrupt, go on, let's hear it, your master plan.

GENNARO: You came for coffee? Drink it and get out.

(Amalia impatiently calls out to Maria Rosaria.)

PEPPE: Why can't we hear it?

AMALIA: Is the coffee ready?

MARIA ROSARIA: Two minutes.

ENRICO: So?

GENNARO: So . . . my master plan . . . it's a complicated business. You can't just explain it in two minutes over coffee, it would take months, years, and all the paper and ink in the world still couldn't begin to cover it.

ENRICO: Oh, just give us a summary.

GENNARO: Don't interrupt.

PEPPE: Don Genna', please don't get mad, but when people talk too much, I'm sorry, my head spins and I gotta go.

GENNARO: So go.

ENRICO: *(To Peppe)* Sit down and listen. Don Genna', go on.

GENNARO: As I was saying, it would take years and years, but I don't want to waste your time. I'm not an educated man, but I'll try to explain to you what I've learned over the years in my hard life. I am an honest citizen who served his country loyally and honorably in the last war, and I can prove it, I have an honorary discharge. Let me show you. *(Enrico, Amedeo, and Federico all make gestures as if to say "we believe you, that won't be necessary, go on.")*

GENNARO: So, as I was saying . . . these professors . . . they make a decree: no streetcars, no cars except for the military.

FEDERICO: Well, they're the professors.

GENNARO: Professors of what? Just because they can read and write they call themselves experts. They say: "Listen, you people are ignorant, you need our help, we'll take care of you, so move over." But we were doing just fine. They tell us we're illiterate, we're lazy, we're stupid, and they talk so much and so loud and make so many speeches that we believe them and give them all the power. And these days the professor are the Fascists. *(Gennaro stops himself, his voice has gotten loud. He lowers his voice.)* Hey, take a look outside.

FEDERICO: *(Goes to look.)* It's all right, there's nobody there.

ENRICO: Don Genna', go on. Don't worry, they're all asleep at this hour.

PEPPE: *(Nervously.)* God, what a way to live. You can't even talk.

GENNARO: So, bit by bit, first with a decree, then a threat, a law, a gun, they take everything away from you. And they keep saying, "It's for your own good." Look at us, we're even afraid to talk.

(They all agree.)

ADELAIDE: Don Genna', sew your lips together tight, tight, for the love of God.

GENNARO: So they make the rules giving everything to themselves, and we? We make our own rules. Now, all of a sudden, they tell us we have to go to war. Why? Who wanted this war? The professors say: "The people wanted it." If the war is lost, we lost it, if it's won, they won it. So now you ask me what's this got to do with the price of coffee? Plenty. If there's no coffee, it keeps us frightened and desperate and that's just what they want.

PEPPE: Don Genna', I didn't understand a thing.

GENNARO: If you'd understood anything, we wouldn't be in this mess.

(Amalia hasn't paid much attention to her husband, she's been busy with practical things and she wants him to change the subject.)

AMALIA: Finish shaving and get dressed.

PEPPE: Don Genna, any ideas for the gas shortages?

GENNARO: Another decree: For every taxi, nine drivers — one at the wheel and eight to push it.

(Riccardo enters dressed in a dark suit, glasses, newspaper tucked under his arm. He is a most dignified, well-off business man. They greet him respectfully. He stops at the entrance.)

RICCARDO: Good morning, everybody.

AMALIA: Good morning, Signor Riccardo. The coffee's just ready. I know you like it nice and fresh.

RICCARDO: Thank you. I didn't sleep all night, I've got a splitting headache. My wife gets so nervous when she hears the sirens. The sirens go off, she starts to shake like a leaf. When we got home after three hours in the shelter, who could sleep?

PEPPE: Did they hit any buildings last night?

RICCARDO: *(Referring to the newspaper.)* Yes, it says here two palazzi and several stores were destroyed.

PEPPE: Near the streetcar depot!

ENRICO: They're getting serious now.

(Maria enters carrying a huge coffeepot to the satisfied murmurs of all. Amalia starts to serve them all. They drink and each one pays.)

AMALIA: *(To Amedeo.)* Close the door and keep an eye on the street.

ENRICO: *(Taking a sip.)* Donna Amalia, it's magnificent, a perfection this morning.

ADELAIDE: Whenever the sirens go off, I drop whatever I'm doing and grab my rosary and run to the shelter.

PEPPE: Oh, they scare the hell out of me.

GENNARO: I get this chill down my back, my stomach turns over, and what can I say, I have to run. I know, I confess, I'm a coward. When I hear the sirens I can't hold it in.

PEPPE: Don Riccardo, what do you say, when is this war going to end?

RICCARDO: Who knows?

PEPPE: But they're saying they'll be dropping more and more bombs, that they're going to wipe out the city.

(Gennaro has finished shaving, dries his face and joins the others, who are asking almost in unison.)

ENRICO: Will the bombing get worse?

FEDERICO: Will they kill us all?

ADELAIDE: They say next it'll be poison gas.

GENNARO: Will they wipe us all out?

PEPPE: This is a war against nature.

RICCARDO: *(Pointing to another piece in the newspaper.)* They say they'll be calling up young boys, and the older men.

ADELAIDE: Oh, my God!

RICCARDO: Well, who knows.

GENNARO: *(Staring at him with disdain.)* Don Riccardo, if you don't know, who does? You're the one who can read the papers. We need to know, we need some reassurance here.

RICCARDO: *(Commiserating, almost tenderly.)* What do you want me to tell you? — there won't be any more bombs, they won't call up any more men, and you'll all get your jobs back? How should I know?

GENNARO: All right, all right, but you wear a suit.

RICCARDO: *(Irritated.)* Do you think people who wear suits know where they're going to drop their bombs and when the war will end?

GENNARO: *(Respectful, to make amends.)* But there, in your office, you spend all day with important people, people who know.

RICCARDO: What people? I don't know anything.

PEPPE: All right, come on, let's go. He doesn't want to talk. *(To Riccardo.)* You're right, it's best to keep your mouth shut these days.

ADELAIDE: That's right, it's none of our business. What can you do?

PEPPE: Let's go, Federico, let's go.

FEDERICO: I'm coming, come on, Amedeo, let's go.

AMEDEO: Let me finish my coffee. *(Swallows it quickly.)* Good-bye, everybody. *(They exit chatting. Enrico stops outside to smoke. Gennaro speaks as he exits to get dressed.)*

GENNARO: You can talk to us, we're people you can trust, you know. We think the same way.

(Riccardo waits for him to leave, then speaks secretively.)

RICCARDO: Donna Ama', did you get the butter?

AMALIA: Not yet, you can try later. The "person" promised he'd bring it, but you know how it is, they find somewhere they can sell it to for more money and they never come back. If he shows up, it's yours. You know we don't use it, first of all because we don't like it, and then because it's so expensive, we can't afford it.

RICCARDO: Of course, and you don't make any money on it.

AMALIA: Ah, Don Riccardo, if that's what you think, I won't be helping you out anymore. I put myself at risk because I know you have little ones. I don't make any money out of this, I swear, *(Gennaro appears dressed in a tie and vest, he gets his jacket off the back of a chair. Amalia has lifted her hand to swear and is looking around for an object to swear on, as an offering to Our Lady, and sees her husband.)* I swear to Our Lady, if I'm not telling the truth . . . may I never see my husband's face again! *(Gennaro stops, freezes for a few seconds, then with saintly patience he murmurs something unintelligible, probably about how dangerous his wife's swearing can be. He takes the jacket and returns to his room. Meanwhile, Amalia has taken a package out from under the mattress and gives it to Riccardo.)*

AMALIA: Here's the sugar you asked for, and the chocolate, and the pastina in this package. Now, that'll be . . . *(Pretends to add and re-add numbers in her head.)* Wait, I'll have to find the piece of paper he left. He'll be here any minute to get his money. *(She fumbles through the mess on her dresser, finds a crumpled piece of paper and pretends to read, putting on a big act so she can get up her courage to announce the huge amount.)* Let's see, two kilos of sugar, one kilo of cocoa, two packages of pastina, then there's what you still owe me from last week . . . *(Almost timidly.)* That'll be exactly 3,500 lire.

RICCARDO: *(Hesitates, then says gently.)* Donna Ama', you see at this moment, the problem is I'm very short of cash what with my wife being ill and, well, you know, the three children, and prices going up every day. I can't even make my salary last till the end of the month, so whatever savings we had, well, you can imagine, they went up in smoke.

AMALIA: *(Smoothly taking the packages back.)* But you own property.

RICCARDO: Property? I have that tiny apartment we live in, and I own two rooms in that slum at Magnocavallo. You call that property? I make three hundred lire a month on them. Are you telling me I should sell them? *(He reluctantly pulls out a little packet and unties a ribbon, displaying it lovingly.)*

RICCARDO: I brought one of my wife's earrings, they tell me it's worth 5,000 lire.

(Amalia fixes her hair, pretending indifference.)

AMALIA: Both of them?

RICCARDO: No, only one. The other one's already at the pawn shop.

AMALIA: Well, I'll show it to that person and maybe he'll accept it.

RICCARDO: I owe you 3,500, so there'll be 1,500 left over . . .

AMALIA: Well, we'll see. *(She tucks it in her bosom.)*

RICCARDO: And could I have my things?

AMALIA: *(Sticky sweet.)* Well, of course, Don Riccardo, they're yours. Actually, tomorrow I should be getting a nice bit of veal. I'll put aside a whole kilo for you.

RICCARDO: Till tomorrow then. *(He puts the packets in his bag, covering them with newspaper.)*

AMALIA: Could you use some fresh eggs?

RICCARDO: If you find any, you know, for the children.

AMALIA: Tomorrow I'll find some for you.

RICCARDO: Thank you and good day.

(He exits. Gennaro comes out of his little room, all dressed. He takes a hat

from a nail in the wall, dusts it off with a handkerchief. He's thinking, and forgets what he's doing and sits down.)

GENNARO: Amalia, I know what's going on here. You can't tell me it's just a few cups of coffee you're selling, always worried about the police, all these people in and out day and night. Butter, rice, beans, Ama' . . .

AMALIA: *(Ready to cut him off.)* I told you, this stuff isn't mine. I'm just helping out a few friends.

GENNARO: Just like that because they've got bright blue eyes?

AMALIA: *(Shouting.)* I'm not making any money.

GENNARO: *(Shouting back.)* So what do we live on? Could you explain this miracle to me? You expect me to believe we're living off the ration tickets? Only an idiot could believe that. If we were living off the rations we'd be dead, buried, and turned to ashes. I don't bring in any money — they're finally going to take all the streetcars off the streets. The number three, gone, the number five, gone, the sixteen gone again. More than half the drivers laid off.

AMALIA: So what can we do?

GENNARO: Don't interrupt! I was saying I figured something out and now I can't remember. *(Stops to think, then suddenly.)* Oh yes, the rations. If you can't live off the rations . . . *(Loses his train of thought again and mutters.)* Oh, I had figured it out. I really had it. I figured out how to live with dignity, without depending on this miserable black market. Without spending every day with your heart in your mouth, terrified of the police . . . *(Totally confused now.)* Ama', please let's be careful.

AMALIA: What are you doing, you're going out?

GENNARO: I'm just going to get a breath of air. Two hours in the shelter last night, I got a chill in my bones. Call me, if you need me.

(Enrico enters, stopping Gennaro as he's going out.)

ENRICO: No. You can't leave now. You see, a few nights ago, I left fifteen kilos of coffee here.

GENNARO: Fifteen kilos?

ENRICO: *(Looking down the street.)* That's right, and Donna Amalia helped me out and . . .

(Enrico gestures to indicate "she hid it.")

GENNARO: I don't like this little game you're playing here. You're going to land me in jail. You don't have a family, you've got nothing to worry about. I know we've all got to help each other out, I don't mind, once, twice, but Don Enrico, I'm scared. These people, they don't fool around, we're talking about being locked up, shipped away for good. I mean, these people, they never look you straight in the eye. *(To Amalia.)* Where did you put it?

AMALIA: In the bed, the second mattress is all coffee.

(Gennaro walks over and pounds the mattress.)

GENNARO: Oh, God help us! And underneath there's all the rest. Pasta, oil, cheese. *(As if he's just remembered.)* Don Enrico, could you get rid of that cheese? Because at night you can't breathe.

ENRICO: Don Genna', please, have a little patience, I've had such a hard time with that cheese.

GENNARO: You might lose a little money, but at least we'll get some sleep. This is bad for our health. You know, the nights are getting colder and when we close the door, the smell, I swear, sometimes when the sirens go off at night I pray to God the bomb lands here and we'll be free.

ENRICO: As I said, you've got to be patient.

GENNARO: *(Indicating the bed.)* Sugar, flour, lard. What is this, the Red Cross? *(He starts to go.)*

ENRICO: That's why you can't go out, because if anything should happen . . . *(Claps his hands to indicate "everyone to their positions.")*

GENNARO: I know. Don't worry. We know what to do. But Don Enrico, please get this stuff out of my house. *(To Amalia.)* I'll stand guard out in the street, but if the sirens go off I'm not hanging around. If the sirens go off, God help us all.

(Gennaro goes outside. Enrico and Amalia are alone.)

AMALIA: So, how much do I owe you?

ENRICO: *(Straightening his elegant tie.)* Don't you worry about it.

AMALIA: *(Smiling.)* What do you mean? It's a present?

ENRICO: Unfortunately, I'm not in a position to give it to you. I'd give you my life if I could, Donna Amalia, I can't accept money from you. When you have placed the goods, we'll subtract the initial expense and the rest is yours.

AMALIA: *(Seductive.)* No, no, you always get half. Always. Look at this, it's an earring.

ENRICO: *(Expertly holds it up to the light.)* It's not bad.

AMALIA: What do you think it's worth?

ENRICO: Let me see the other one.

AMALIA: No. The other one's pawned.

ENRICO: We should see it, to see if the stones match. Do you think you can get the pawn ticket?

AMALIA: Let's see, today is what?

ENRICO: Monday.

AMALIA: *(Sure of herself.)* By Thursday, I'll have it for you.

ENRICO: Good, we'll get it out of hock and see what it's worth.

AMALIA: But what do you think it's worth? About 4,000 or 5,000 lire?

ENRICO: More. Why don't you put it away? Where's the coffee?

AMALIA: *(Lifting up the blanket.)* Here. I sewed it all in here. See? It looks like there's nothing there. Oh, my fingers hurt. This corner here, I had to put two snaps. See? So anytime I need to take out a kilo or two, I slip my hand in . . . *(Meanwhile Enrico has approached her and put his hand on hers, holding tight. She delicately removes his hand and puts it back like an object returned to its proper place.)* And then I take it out.

ENRICO: And I slip it back in again.

(He tries to kiss her. She extricates herself, careful not to offend.)

AMALIA: Eh. Come on, Don Enrico, you've never done this before.

ENRICO: *(Coming to his senses, but still holding on to her.)* Donna Ama', I beg your pardon. Please, forgive me. I won't let you go if you don't forgive me.

AMALIA: Forgive you for what? It could happen to anyone. A momentary . . . phosphorescence.

ENRICO: Thank you, Donna Ama', thank you.

(Kisses both her hands repeatedly. Maria Rosaria enters, watches them, hands on hips as if challenging them. Enrico looks up, suddenly drops Amalia's hand and assumes an air of nonchalance. Amalia turns and sees her daughter. She's upset, then she controls herself and confronts her.)

AMALIA: What do you want?

MARIA ROSARIA: *(Cold and ironic.)* Should I put some garlic in the beans?

AMALIA: Of course, don't you know how to cook beans?

MARIA ROSARIA: There isn't any.

AMALIA: So go get some from Donna Giuvannina.

(She starts off slowly, stops and turns before exiting.)

MARIA ROSARIA: Tonight, I'm going to the movies.

(Maria exits.)

AMALIA: You see? God knows what she's thinking now.

(From offstage we hear Amedeo, then he enters.)

AMEDEO: Mamma, Mamma!

AMALIA: What's going on? Why aren't you at work?

AMEDEO: I just heard from a guy at work that. . . that. . . he was having coffee over at Donna Vincenza's this morning, right after you'd finished screaming at her, she came back furious, kicked everybody out saying no one was going to stop her from selling coffee! She knew people to talk to and she'd destroy you and your coffee. Then she locked the door and went down the street.

AMALIA: *(Calmly.)* All right, calm down.

AMEDEO: She must've gone to the police, that stinky piece of garbage.

AMALIA: So, when the police come, they'll find us here.

AMEDEO: I know, but aren't you glad I warned you?

AMALIA: Yes, yes, you did fine. Now, go find your father, he's out in the street. Whenever you need him, he's not here.

(Amedeo looks down the street and gestures with his hand.)

AMEDEO: Papa! Come here. *(To Amalia.)* I told Peppe to stand guard on the corner. When he lights his pipe . . .

AMALIA: *(To Amedeo)* Stay here, don't move!

(Maria enters holding up a head of garlic.)

MARIA ROSARIA: One head of garlic, two lire.

AMALIA: Hurry up, pull your hair down and put on the black shawl.

(Amalia takes a shawl out of a drawer and puts it on.)

MARIA ROSARIA: When? Now?

AMALIA: No, tomorrow! Do what I tell you.

MARIA ROSARIA: *(Takes a shawl and starts to go.)* I'll be in the kitchen, call me when you need me.

AMEDEO: I'll be right outside. When he lights his pipe. I'll let you know.

GENNARO: *(Entering, knows nothing.)* What's happening? What's wrong?

AMALIA: Go on. Get ready.

GENNARO: Don Enrico, like I was saying, we'll all end up in jail.

(He goes quickly off into his room.)

AMALIA: Call Pascalino the painter and the part-time priest.

AMEDEO: They're on their way.

ENRICO: *(He's in control, heroic.)* Donna Ama', don't you worry. I am not leaving. Your fate is my fate. I'll stand right here like a member of the family.

(Amedeo coming in to report.)

AMEDEO: He lit his pipe! Peppe lit his pipe!

(Gennaro looking out over the partition.)

GENNARO: He lit his pipe?

AMEDEO: That stinking piece of garbage kept her word. Here come Pascalino and the part-time priest!

(They are all hurriedly getting the place ready for something exceptional. Amalia calls to Maria, who enters and joins the others in preparations. Amedeo watches the street.)

AMALIA: Maria, forget the beans and get in here. Gennaro, hurry up!

(Gennaro still in his room, sounds like someone who's hurrying so much he can't get it done.)

GENNARO: I'm coming. I'm trying. Damn it! Call Pascalino!

AMEDEO: He's coming! And the part-time priest!

(Two low characters enter and stand on either side of the bed, facing front, without speaking. They rapidly unfold two black aprons and tie them on their heads. They now look like nuns, they sit. Meanwhile, Amalia, helped by the others, places four lighted candlesticks around the bed.)

AMALIA: Gennaro, come on. Hurry up.

(Gennaro enters wearing a long white nightgown, a large handkerchief wrapped under his chin and tied on top of his head. He is slipping on a pair of white gloves while slowly approaching the bed. Meanwhile the others are hurrying him along with gestures.)

GENNARO: This is what we have to go through just to get a bit of food in our stomachs. Idiots. Total idiots!

AMALIA: Get into the bed.

GENNARO: I'm going to smack your face.

(Then he gives up and Amalia adds the finishing touches. She powders the "dead man's" face with a powder puff and helps him into bed. Maria grabs flowers that are in front of a little statue on the dresser and throws them over the corpse. Each person takes his place as if it had been rehearsed, creating a tragic picture. Amedeo closes the outside wooden door and the inner glass door, he messes up his hair and throws himself at the foot of the bed. Maria kneels next to her mother, clutching a rosary. Enrico pulls a handkerchief out of his pocket, and stands next to the front door. A long pause.)

GENNARO: Are they coming?

AMEDEO: Yes.

(Pause.)

GENNARO: They're not coming.

AMEDEO: They're coming. He lit his pipe.

GENNARO: Oh sure, that idiot, last week I was stuck in this bed seven and a half hours.

(They all make gestures as if to say: "Well, what can you do." Another pause. Then since they have to wait, Adelaide talks.)

ADELAIDE: So, as I was saying . . .

(Suddenly there's knocking on the front door, everyone panics.)

AMEDEO: *(In a whisper.)* They're here!

GENNARO: *(Terrified.)* Good God, that bitch wasn't kidding.

AMALIA: Lie down.

(Gennaro stretches himself out like a corpse, Amalia starts to pray, eyes heav-enward. Pascalino and the part-time priest are mumbling disconnected words that are supposed to sound funereal. The others wail uncontrollably. The knock-ing gets louder, Enrico opens the door, and Ciappa enters, talking to his men offstage, telling them to "Wait outside." Ciappa is fifty years old, tough, sharp-eyed. He understands that, especially in Naples, in certain cases you have to turn a blind eye. Inside, he observes the scene, and without removing his hat he says.)

CIAPPA: What's this? An epidemic? Yesterday we found three people dead right next door to each other and then two more just down the road, and today all five of them are alive and well in Poggioreale. Not Poggioreale the ceme-tery, Poggioreale the jail. So, I don't want to hurt anybody's feelings here *(Pounds the table with both hands!),* but I'm warning you, nobody's going to make a fool out of me. Come on, Lazarus, rise! or I'll clap these hand-cuffs on you and pull you up myself.

AMALIA: *(Beside herself with grief.)* Your excellency, for God's sake, stop! This poor husband of mine, my poorly beloved husband here, passed away last night at two thirty-five A.M.

CIAPPA: Two thirty-five — mustn't forget the five.

AMEDEO: Oh Papa, Papa, Papaaa!

(The two "nuns" are now muttering prayers that sound like curses.)

THE NUNS: Holy Mary full of grace, take this poor man to your holy place.

(Ciappa looks at them sideways. Enrico notices and comes over to the bed.)

ENRICO: This is a great loss.

CIAPPA: It is? All right, that's enough. What do you think, I'm stupid? What a pathetic country this is. Do you think I'm an idiot?

THE NUNS: *(Insistently praying as before.)* Dies Irae dies illa, give a hand to this poor dead fella.

CIAPPA: All right. If he's a corpse, I'm the grave digger. *(Moving toward the bed.)* Come on, I'll pick you up and bury you.

(Amalia grabs his knees, dissolved in tears.)

AMALIA: No, sir. What kind of people do you think we are? My poor husband is dead. Who sent you here? Someone who wants to hurt us. Can't you see how we're suffering? Look at those two fatherless children. *(Outraged.)* Have you no feelings? Come here, come closer, see for yourself, touch him. *(He hesitates.)* Go on, touch him. It's only a sacrilege if he's really dead. Go on, if you're not afraid of being excommunicated. Come on. Touch him.

(Ciappa is impressed by her dramatic tone and by Gennaro's total stillness.)

CIAPPA: No. If he's really dead, I don't want to touch him, I don't know him!

MARIA ROSARIA: *(Crying.)* He's dead, sir, my Papa's dead.

THE NUNS: *(Almost petulantly.)* Dies Irae dies illa, take this poor dear old fella . . .

ENRICO: A prince of a man, and look at him now.

CIAPPA: Holy Mother of God, you're driving me crazy

> *(He doesn't want to be taken for a fool, and decides to catch them by playing along with them.)*

CIAPPA: All right, you say he's dead, I believe you. I believe you so much, I'll sit here and pay my respects. I'll go when the corpse goes!

> *(Ciappa takes a chair and sits center stage.)*

AMALIA: *(With a look of hate toward Ciappa.)* Holy God, please take this fellow . . .

> *(The nuns' blasphemous prayers get louder and clearer. The others keep up the act in a kind of singsong, except for an occasional exchange of looks. Air-raid sirens start in the distance, confusion and voices in the alley, each person in the room looks at the other wondering what to do, hoping the other will make a decision. The nuns pray. The voices outside become more distinct. We hear things like, "Nannina, come on bring the children here." "Eh, don't push." "Stay calm." "Bring some water." "Hurry!" "Open the door to the shelter!" "What's that man doing?" "What should he do?" "I'm here." "Sir, I've told you over and over, you can't bring your dog in here." Meanwhile the sirens have gone on and off until they've completed their cycle. A terrifying silence follows while everyone waits.)*

AMALIA: Officer, we've got a very nice shelter nearby, don't stay on our account, there's no point in risking your life here.

CIAPPA: *(Coolly.)* Go ahead, if you're scared, go on. I hate to leave the poor corpse all by himself. *(He smokes blissfully.)* I'll stay and keep him company.

> *(Sounds of explosions in the distance. The two nuns speaking in falsetto: "We're leaving now. I'm afraid we have to go. Let's go!" As they run out, we see their rear view: rolled up pants, covered in front by the nuns' aprons.)*

CIAPPA: Never seen that before: nuns in pants. *(More explosions.)* Hey, corpse, come on. Listen, let's get up and go to the shelter.

> *(From out in the street the guards call.)*

FIRST GUARD: Come on, forget it, let's go!

CIAPPA: You go, if you're scared.

> *(We hear the sounds of the first bombs falling on the city. Amalia, in terror, is leaning against the wall, clutching the children as if to protect them. Enrico leans up against the opposite wall. Ciappa speaks calmly as the explosions accelerate, the doors rattle.)*

CIAPPA: That bomb was so close you can hear the plane that dropped it. Ah, those are machine guns. *(A more violent explosion.)* Ahh ahh, if a bomb lands here we're finished, these aren't houses, they're cream puffs.
(Ciappa is calmly watching Gennaro who is even calmer and stiller. Slowly it diminishes, finally it's quiet.)
CIAPPA: I guess the bombs don't scare you since you're dead. God, you're a pig-headed corpse. *(Leans on the headboard.)* Get up, listen. *(Shakes the head-board.)* Get up! I'm telling you, you'd better get up.
(He walks around the bed, Gennaro is even more dead. Ciappa lifts the bed-spread with his stick.) Oh look here, so many treasures from heaven.
(After a pause we hear a single prolonged siren that is the all clear. Outside in the alley we hear confused voices, "It's over." "Where's Nenellina?" "Get out of the way, what's this mess?" "Whose is this?" "The fire is down there, they hit a house in the next street!" "The firemen!" We hear the sirens of the fire trucks. Meanwhile, Ciappa is looking at Gennaro with admiration.)
CIAPPA: Listen. Congratulations. You're really good, you are. I know you're not dead. I know it. You've got the whole black market under your bed, but I'm not going to put you in jail. It may be a sin to touch a corpse, but it's worse to touch a man like you. I won't put you in jail. *(Pause.)* But come on. Move. Just give me that little satisfaction. If you move, I swear I won't do a thing, word of honor. *(For Gennaro his word of honor is enough, but he's waiting for another promise and Ciappa instinctively understands.)* I won't even search the place. Word of honor!
GENNARO: So, if you arrest me, you're a filthy son of a bitch.
CIAPPA: I gave you my word. But I'm not an idiot.
GENNARO: Neither am I, Captain.
CIAPPA: *(A large sweeping gesture.)* Good-bye to all of you. It's been a pleasure. *(All follow him toward the door, showing him great respect and reassuring the generous brigadier that he is no fool and that they sincerely admire him.)* Good-bye. Have a good day!
AMALIA: Please, Captain, may I offer you a nice cup of coffee?
CIAPPA: No, thank you, I had one just before I got here.
(Gennaro has risen from his bed and joined the others in their obsequious politeness as they accompany the Captain to the door and out into the street.)

END OF ACT ONE

Act Two

The Americans have landed. There is a mixture of American music blaring from the radio out on the street along with Neapolitan songs. There is an atmosphere of wealth in the house. Everything has changed. The women wear fur coats and jewelry, the men are very well dressed. The house is almost unrecognizable.

ASSUNTA: Donna Amalia, I just got a kilo of meat, but we're all coming here for dinner tonight. Settebellezze invited me too.

AMALIA: Yes, he's invited quite a few people.

ASSUNTA: So I'll cook the meat tomorrow. How's your little Rituccia feeling?

AMALIA: She's not feeling well at all. I'm a little worried.

ASSUNTA: Is my aunt in with her?

AMALIA: Yes. Rituccia always feels better when Donna Adelaide is there.

ASSUNTA: She's so good with kids. I'll just drop this meat off at home, excuse me.
(She exits, then Teresa and Margherita enter, girls of the neighborhood, very made up and dressed very boldly and brightly. Their heels are too high and their skirts are too short.)

TERESA: Good morning, Donna Ama'.

AMALIA: Good morning.

MARGHERITA: Is Maria Rosaria ready?

AMALIA: She's getting dressed. Where are you going at this hour?

TERESA: To take a walk.

AMALIA: A walk? You be careful, girls. Walks! Who is this American sergeant who's chasing after her? Why haven't I met him? Why doesn't he come here and introduce himself?

TERESA: Oh no, Donna Amalia. He's such a nice boy. He's shy, he doesn't know how to speak Italian very well so he's afraid to come here, but we're teaching him.

MARGHERITA: He's a soldier. They work him so hard, and now he's running around trying to get all his papers in order, because in their country, to get married you have to get permission from America itself. He says as soon as it's all done he'll come to meet you and ask for Maria Rosaria's hand.

TERESA: Don't worry about our walks, Donna Ama', there's nothing to worry about. They just like to walk arm in arm with us because we're "frennas."

AMALIA: Yes, but their only "frennas" are girls. I don't see them walking arm in arm with the boys.

TERESA: Oh, they don't do things like that. Your daughter is so lucky, he's so in love with Maria he wants to marry her and take her to America. He thought he was in love with me first, then he met Maria Rosaria and because he's so sincere, he just told me right to my face, "Your frenna is more nice-a," so I say, "Hokei." That night he brings another boyfrenna for me who I really liked more and he fell in love with me so everything was fine. Then I said I got another frenna, Margherita, do you have another frenna for her? And he did. So this way we got six frennas together.

MARGHERITA: Yes, but I don't like my frenna, he's too short.

AMALIA: So tell him, "I want someone more nice-a, get me another frenna who's more nice-a."

(Maria enters in a brightly colored summer dress with little sandals.)

AMALIA: What time will you be home?

MARIA ROSARIA: I don't know. I'll be home when I'm home.

AMALIA: Your sister's not feeling well.

(Amalia goes off to Rituccia's room.)

TERESA: Let's go.

MARIA ROSARIA: Why? I've gone there every day. He hasn't shown up for a week.

TERESA: Maybe he'll be there today.

MARIA ROSARIA: I don't care, Teresi, I really don't care. It's my own fault, I don't blame him, but I'd like to see him, just to tell him he doesn't have to make up all these lies. Why doesn't he just tell me the truth right to my face?

TERESA: But yesterday my boyfrenna told me that he'd bring him today.

MARIA ROSARIA: He's left. Believe me, he's gone. And by tomorrow they'll all be gone.

TERESA: Well, let them go, what do we care? No big loss.

(Maria looks her straight in the eye.)

MARIA ROSARIA: No big loss?

TERESA: Oh, that's right.

(A moment of silent understanding as Teresa remembers that she's in the same boat as Maria.)

MARGHERITA: I don't like mine, he's short.

TERESA: Oh, you don't understand anything. We've got real problems here and she's thinking about too short or too tall.

AMALIA: *(Turns to Adelaide.)* Don't come home too late.

THE THREE GIRLS: All right.

(They go off talking. Adelaide and Amalia come out together.)

ADELAIDE: I think the fever's gone down, I'm glad she's asleep.

AMALIA: They always grow after a fever.

(Part-time Priest enters.)

PART-TIME PRIEST: Donna Amalia, Settebellezze told me to tell you this is very good wine. And here's six loaves of bread made with Allied flour but in our ovens. And these are the cigarettes — American — from Teresina in Furcelle. (He holds up various packs of single cigarettes.) And here's a note from her to you. I'll go put this in the kitchen.

(He exits. Amalia can't read, but doesn't want to admit it. She turns the paper around a lot.)

AMALIA: I can't see too clearly, Donna Adelaide, what does it say?

ADELAIDE: (She has a hard time reading, but she struggles.) Let's see.

PART-TIME PRIEST: (Re-enters) Donna Amalia, Amedeo got two goats for the dinner tonight. I took them to the baker's to roast in the oven and I'll bring them here around seven-thirty along with the parmigiana and the lasagne.

(Part-time Priest leaves.)

AMALIA: Donna Adelaide, if you don't know how to read, don't bother.

ADELAIDE: Ah . . . It says: "Dear Donna Amalia, here are the cigarettes, take 'em. The Engrish sergeant charged me ten lire more a pack. I said to him, but you're Engrish, he said I may be Engrish, but if you won't pay for them I can sell them to someone else."

AMALIA: They've learned how to play the game, too.

ADELAIDE: (Continues reading.) "I paid him what he wanted, but now we have to stick together. No cigarettes for three days and then we can start selling them at 160 lire a pack. Also it's getting cold so we can raise the prices on sweaters, blankets, and tomato paste."

AMALIA: I already made mine.

(Assunta enters.)

ADELAIDE: Well, I'll be going home now. If Rituccia wakes, Assunta will be here. I'll see you later.

ASSUNTA: Donna Ama', I wanted to ask you. (She sniffs the air.) Oh, what a lovely scent. Is it you wearing that delicious perfume? (Goes toward the dresser.) May I take a sniff? I love personal hygiene. I can't bear it! Even the bottle is sensational! Settebellezze gave it to you, didn't he?

AMALIA: Why would he have given it to me? I bought it myself.

ASSUNTA: Oh I just thought, since everyone is saying that you, I mean he, well, ahh . . .

AMALIA: What are they saying? What do they know?

ASSUNTA: Nothing. Don't get mad. I didn't mean any harm. My aunt is always telling me to keep my mouth shut. I'm such an idiot. *(She starts to laugh.)* Sometimes I just start laughing. I don't know why.

AMALIA: Why are you laughing?

ASSUNTA: Don't say anything, it just gets worse.

AMALIA: Stop it!

ASSUNTA: I can't help it. There . . . oops . . . I'll just let a little more out. There, I'm almost done. That is such a beautiful dress you're wearing today, is it new?

AMALIA: I got it from the dressmaker the other day.

ASSUNTA: Oh. It's beautiful.

(Enrico enters wearing a pale grey suit, yellow shoes, a brightly colored tie. A millionaire many times over, he's in another class now. He proudly displays a diamond ring. He has great success with the ladies and he knows it. He notices Assunta. Amalia is eating him up with her eyes.)

ENRICO: Here I am, Donna Amalia, at your service.

AMALIA: Congratulations and best wishes.

ENRICO: Thank you. I am thirty-six years old today. Getting older.

ASSUNTA: Thirty-six! These are best years of your life.

AMALIA: *(A light reproof.)* I was expecting you earlier, actually.

ENRICO: I should have come sooner to thank you for the magnificent bunch of roses you sent me this morning, and to apologize, once again, for all the effort you're going through to celebrate the day of my birth here in your home.

AMALIA: Not at all. You live alone and here you'll find yourself almost as if you were in your own home surrounded by members of your family.

ENRICO: Again, I thank you. However, I must insist you do not lift a finger. Amedeo and I have taken care of everything. *(He sits.)* So, as I was saying, I would have been here earlier, but I had a bit of business to attend to. I had two trucks leaving for Calabria. As you know, if I'm not there to supervise the loading, things disappear. I sent them off, signed the papers, and then I wasted half the day dealing with the Americans getting a permit — all that nonsense and then back down to the docks for half an hour. I went home to change because I looked terrible and now here I am. Is Amedeo back yet?

AMALIA: No. He had some job he had to do tonight.

ENRICO: *(To Assunta.)* Hey, don't you have something to do at home?

AMALIA: She's here in case Rituccia wakes up.

ENRICO: How is the poor little thing?

AMALIA: The fever is still pretty high, but she's asleep now. Assunta, I'll call you if I need you.

ASSUNTA: Oh, yes, I guess I'd better go. *(Starts to smile.)* Yes. *(Tries to stifle a giggle.)* That's right.

AMALIA: Are you starting that again?

ASSUNTA: What can you do? I can't help it. I'm such an idiot. Sometimes I just start laughing and I can't stop. People must think I'm crazy. Excuse me. *(Tries to control her laughter that is now full-blown.)*

ENRICO: What's wrong with her? So . . .

(Peppe and Federico interrupt them as they enter talking.)

PEPPE: That's the best I can do.

FEDERICO: I'll have to give you a check.

PEPPE: I don't want a check.

ENRICO: You can't even finish a sentence in this house.

FEDERICO: Donna Ama', two cups of coffee. Greetings, Settebellezze.

(Amalia prepares the coffee.)

PEPPE: The coffee's on me. But about the tires, there's no way we can work it out.

ENRICO: What's this all about?

PEPPE: I'm talking about five almost new tires from a Mercedes.

FEDERICO: He wants me to pay him 260,000 lire!

PEPPE: They're clean as a whistle. Ask Settebellezze, he's an expert.

FEDERICO: Well, with all due respect, I'm an expert too.

PEPPE: So if you're such an expert you should give me the money, because in four days time they'll cost you 50,000 more.

FEDERICO: But I have to sell them. I've got to make a profit on this, too.

PEPPE: You want to make a profit of 150,000 lire? Well, talk to Amedeo, he's the boss. Maybe he'll give you a break.

(They drink the coffee.)

PEPPE: Tell me, Settebellezze, how's that car I got you?

ENRICO: Fine, but I'm offering 700,000 lire, absolutely no more.

PEPPE: That's what I asked for, seven-hundred-thousand lire.

ENRICO: Oh, yes, I'd forgotten, well that's a very good price. *(Takes a bundle of bills out of his pocket.)* Here you are, 700,000 lire.

PEPPE: It's a pleasure to do business with a man like you. *(Pointing to Federico.)* He's impossible. He thinks I'm trying to cheat him.

FEDERICO: No, no, I trust you. Here. Here's 260,000 lire.

(Amedeo enters, he is also flashily dressed. After greeting them, he starts searching in the dresser and finds a small packet wrapped in newspaper.)

AMEDEO: Good morning, everybody. Ah, here it is. I thought I'd lost it.

(Riccardo enters almost humble, pale, badly dressed and dishevelled.)

RICCARDO: Good morning.

(They barely respond. Amalia, irritated, exchanges a look with Enrico.)

AMALIA: Good morning. Do you want something? *(Riccardo hesitates, making her understand he wants to see her alone.)* All right, yes, wait a minute.

RICCARDO: Yes, I'll wait.

(Riccardo retreats upstage. Peppe takes Amedeo aside.)

PEPPE: Amedeo, I gotta talk to you before tonight.

AMEDEO: We're having a big dinner tonight. Are you coming?

PEPPE: Of course. I was invited.

AMEDEO: So we'll talk then.

PEPPE: We can't talk here. *(He looks around furtively.)* It's about a car with five new tires. Tomorrow night. We've got to talk

AMEDEO: *(Cutting him off.)* All right, step outside.

PEPPE: Donna Ama', here's the money for the coffee.

(Amalia takes it and pockets it.)

FEDERICO: Donna Amalia, are there any cigarettes?

AMALIA: *(Quickly.)* None. They didn't deliver them today.

PEPPE: *(Ironic.)* Ah, yes, no cigarettes today, they disappeared.

FEDERICO: By Papal decree.

PEPPE: Federico, are you coming?

FEDERICO: I'm coming. Good-bye, everybody. Amedeo, are you staying?

ENRICO: Yes, Amedeo's staying here. Amede', I've got to talk to you.

PEPPE: See you tonight at dinner, then. Let's go.

(They all go off together with Federico, talking.)

AMALIA: *(To Riccardo.)* So, what can I do for you?

RICCARDO: *(Timid.)* For that errand I did for you . . .

AMEDEO: *(To Enrico.)* I'll be out in the street. If you want me, give a shout. *(He comes back to get the packet he almost forgot.)* Oh, I almost forgot it again. It's 300,000 lire.

(Realizing he's spoken in front of Riccardo, Amalia tries to repair the damage.)

AMALIA: He's joking. He says he has 300,000 lire.

AMEDEO: It belongs to a friend of mine who's coming to pick it up. Well, I'll be outside.

(Amedeo exits.)

AMALIA: So?

(Riccardo speaks humbly, with no anger. Enrico is happily smoking, Amalia

sits at the opposite end of the table with her back turned on Riccardo, as if she were a little distracted. She finds him almost unbearable.)

RICCARDO: All I can do is appeal to your conscience, Donna Amalia. I have no right to ask you, but the first time I needed money, you said you knew someone who could buy one of my little apartments. I was desperate, so I agreed. Then I was forced to sell the second one. I just found out that you bought them yourself. That's fine — may you enjoy them for the rest of your life. But when the company I worked for closed, I came to you again and borrowed 40,000 lire against the house I live in . . .
(A pause as his words fall on icy silence.) I am twenty days late, I know, but you sent a statement from your lawyer telling me to pay the rent or get out. I have no place to go, but I can't pay the rent this month. Would you really take away my house because I'm late in my rent?

ENRICO: It's not a bad deal. She isn't just taking your house, the contract says she has to give you another 50,000, that's what the lawyer was trying to tell you. Why don't you just take the 50,000 and go live somewhere else?

RICCARDO: Where? With two children?

ENRICO: Well, you don't want this, you don't want that, what do you want?
(Riccardo takes money out of a briefcase.)

RICCARDO: Look, I've got 10,000 lire. I sold two winter jackets and a pair of pants, you can sell anything these days. I'd like to offer you this, for now, and in a few days I should be getting 80,000 lire from my old company. It's just a question of days.

AMALIA: Why didn't you do this six months ago.

RICCARDO: I kept thinking I'd get my job back. Please. Help me. *(They don't respond. Riccardo is almost talking to himself.)* Finding another place to live used to be easy. Even if it was smaller, uglier, it didn't matter so much because you'd go out in the evenings, there'd be people in the streets, you'd nod and smile, you felt protected. You'd look in shop windows, not to buy, just to look. Now, you step outside, it's like being in a foreign country.

ENRICO: *(A bit shaken.)* Well, it's not really up to me. If it's all right with Donna Amalia . . .

RICCARDO: *(With more courage.)* Donna Amalia, here are 10,000 lire. I can't tell you how I hate to beg like this, but my children won't eat today.
(Enrico looks at Amalia who stares back at him, surprised to see a certain weakness in him.)

AMALIA: Oh, don't give me all that! What are you talking about? *(To Enrico, who is still staring at her. She gets up.)* What's he talking about? I didn't steal your apartments, I paid for them. Didn't I? When we couldn't eat, did we come to you? Didn't my children suffer, didn't they go without food? When you had a nice job and went strolling around in the evenings, smiling at people and wasting time looking in shop windows, we were eating stale bread and salt. *(Her rage mounts.)* Don't give me this sob story. No, I'm sorry! Take the 50,000 lire from the lawyer or pay the rent and remember the good old days when you ate while we went to bed hungry. Do me a favor and get out of here. You're wasting my time, I've got things to do. Get going, Go.

(Riccardo speaks almost politely as if not to upset her.)

RICCARDO: Fine, I'm going. Don't get upset. We'll find . . . we'll leave . . . I'll go to the lawyer first thing tomorrow.

(He's confused and tries to leave from the wrong door.)

AMALIA: I think he got the point, eh? Did you go to the docks?

ENRICO: I gave the guys 400,000 lire and I got these, they're worth about three million. *(Unwrapping two diamonds.)*

AMALIA: They're beautiful.

ENRICO: No defects, pure.

(Amalia looks outside, picks up a tile under the bed, and takes money out of a little cloth bag. Puts the diamonds in the bag and replaces the tile.)

AMALIA: I'm always nervous. So, this is my share?

(Enrico has gotten up and stopped at the door, looking distractedly out at the street.)

ENRICO: Yes, it's your share, since you still find it so hard to link your name with mine.

AMALIA: *(Getting serious.)* Listen, Settebellezze, you know how much I admire you and care for you. Sometimes when I feel you looking at me, I could almost slap myself for the thoughts that go through my head. Sometimes I wish . . . *(Enrico lowers his eyes, she gets stronger.)* We set up this business, me buying and selling and you with trucks. We've done well, we should thank God. Now don't ask me to commit a sin. I have a grown daughter, and what about my husband?

ENRICO: You haven't heard from him in over a year. I don't mean to be cruel, but don't you think you would have heard from him if he was alive? If the Germans got him, where would they have taken him? They were hanging people in the streets or shooting them. Maybe a bomb got him. If you ask me, he's dead.

AMALIA: *(Amalia takes a letter out.)* This came three days ago, it's addressed to Gennarino. It's from a man who was with him all this time, he just sends greetings and news of himself. Gennaro must've given him this address.

I don't know where he is, or what happened to him, but I know he's alive. One of these days I'll see him standing here in front of me.

ENRICO: *(Insinuating.)* Well, that will certainly make you happy.

AMALIA: Happy and unhappy. You know, he'll start asking questions. What's this, what's that, how do we make our money? In other words, my hands will be tied.

ENRICO: *(Getting closer and closer.)* Yes.

AMALIA: *(She moves away.)* It'll be hard. I'll miss the business.

ENRICO: And what else?

AMALIA: All . . . those things.

ENRICO: And me? What about me?

(Amalia hasn't the strength to resist anymore, she looks him straight in the eye and folding her arms slowly and sensuously she murmurs.)

AMALIA: And you, too.

(He slowly moves his face toward her — a long kiss. Peppe enters, searching through his pockets, he notices the scene. Stunned, he stays to watch, then turns to leave. They break apart and separate, Amalia goes off to the kitchen.)

ENRICO: What do you want?

PEPPE: I left my matches in the kitchen.

ENRICO: So go get them.

PEPPE: *(Suppressing a smile.)* I don't need them anymore. *(Enrico glares at him.)* Oh well, I guess I'd better get them. *(He goes off, looking at Enrico slantways. Amedeo enters.)*

AMEDEO: You wanted to see me?

ENRICO: *(Plunges right in.)* Yes. Listen to me. You've got to stop. I know what I'm talking about, I grew up in the streets. Let me tell you, you've got to stop.

AMEDEO: Stop what?

ENRICO: Listen to me. I know. I see. I understand. You're making some bad choices.

AMEDEO: What are you talking about?

ENRICO: Your friend, Peppe the Jack. Stay away from him, you're too young to get mixed up in that business. You don't want to end up behind bars. You know why he's called the jack, don't you?

AMEDEO: *(Pretending not to know.)* Why?

ENRICO: *(Ironically.)* You don't know, huh? He wanders the streets at night with a friend, and when they spot the right car he gets under it, jacks it up with his shoulder, and then *you* take the wheels off.

AMEDEO: Me?

ENRICO: You don't get it? I'll explain a little more clearly. *(Amalia enters, so he takes Amedeo's arm and starts to drag him outside.)* We're going out for a little walk.

AMEDEO: Don Enrico, there's some mistake.

ENRICO: Come on. *Walk!*

(*As they exit, Maria Rosaria enters, looks at her mother, folds her arms, and stays still, an accusatory silence.*)

AMALIA: Oh, back so soon? What did the bridegroom say?

MARIA ROSARIA: The bridegroom's gone, he's left. He's not coming back.

AMALIA: *(Almost amused.)* Well, what do you care? You'll find another one.

MARIA ROSARIA: *(Coldly.)* I'll find whoever I want and whoever I like, understand? You just worry about your own business.

AMALIA: *(Joking.)* Oh, poor thing. You really had your heart set on going to America.

MARIA ROSARIA: I had my heart set, but not on America — *on him.* You could've noticed. You should've paid attention, now it's too late.

AMALIA: What do you mean it's too late? What did you do?

MARIA ROSARIA: You should've paid attention. What did you care where I was going, it left you free to do whatever you wanted. Instead of worrying about business, you should've been worrying about me.

AMALIA: I worried about you. I've practically killed myself to keep this family alive.

MARIA ROSARIA: You? You didn't have time to worry about me. What about Settebellezze, who was worrying about him? Me?

AMALIA: *(Barely restraining her anger.)* Listen, I'm telling you one more time, Settebellezze and I are in business. Buying and selling, that's all. But you. What? Tell me. When? Where?

MARIA ROSARIA: Here. We met here. When you'd go out at night for your little dinners with Settebellezze.

AMALIA: Here? In my house? You should be ashamed! I'll slap you so hard, I'll . . .

MARIA ROSARIA: Go ahead. Call Settebellezze, let him slap me too, why not. You've given him the right to do whatever he wants.

(*Amalia barely controls her voice so that they don't hear her on the street.*)

AMALIA: Whore, you are a whore.

MARIA ROSARIA: And so are you.

AMALIA: I'll kill you, understand?

(*She goes after her and Maria runs into the next room followed by Amalia. We hear the fight. Meanwhile, out in the street there is a murmur of voices. Something extraordinary has happened. We hear words like: "Holy Mother of God!" "It's a miracle!" "I can't believe it!" "He's back!" "Don Gennaro!"*)

*It builds to a chorus. "Don Gennaro, we all thought you were dead." Finally
we hear Gennaro's voice.)*

GENNARO: Instead, I'm alive, and I've come home.

(Adelaide enters.)

ADELAIDE: Donna Amalia, Donna Amalia!

AMALIA: *(Coming back in.)* What's happened?

ADELAIDE: Your husband.

GENNARO: Thank you, thank you all. Later, I'll tell you everything.

*(He's miserably dressed — an Italian soldier's hat, American pants, a Ger-
man windbreaker all greasy and torn. He seems very thin, exhausted. He looks
around, stunned at the changes in the house. He doesn't recognize Amalia and
is about to excuse himself and go away, as if he'd come to the wrong house.)* Excuse me, Signora.

ADELAIDE: Come back, Don Genna, this is your house. See, there's your wife.

*(Gennaro hardly dares to stay. He looks at Amalia with admiration and fear.
Amalia has turned to stone, she can't speak. She sees how her husband has
suffered. Finally she speaks with a thread of a voice.)*

AMALIA: Gennarino.

*(Gennaro advances toward her timidly, as if to excuse himself for not having
recognized her. He'd like to cry or speak, but all he manages to do is repeat
her name.)*

GENNARO: Amalia, forgive me. Amalia! *(They embrace, holding tightly and tenderly. Amalia starts to cry.)* Such a long time, so long. *(He bursts into tears.
A pause, Amalia is the first to recover, and to give him strength, she says.)*

AMALIA: All right, all right, now come sit, rest. Tell me, where have you been?

GENNARO: I can't, not now, I can't begin to tell you. There's not enough time
to ever tell you what I've seen, what I went through. It would take moun-
tains of paper to write the story of these past thirteen, fourteen months.
It's all here — in my eyes, in my head. I don't know where to begin. I
feel like I've forgotten everything, my house, you, my street, my friends.
Slow down. Slow down. Tell me about you, the house, Amedeo, Rituccia, Maria Rosaria.

AMALIA: Rituccia's not well.

GENNARO: What's wrong?

AMALIA: Nothing, a little fever.

GENNARO: Is she in there?

ADELAIDE: Poor Don Gennaro, you really look terrible. *(He exits to Rituccia's
room.)* Good God, good God, he's so old. I'll leave you now, Donna
Amalia. I'll see you later.

(Exiting, she speaks directly to the statue of the Madonna across the street, "Oh Dear lady, Holy Mother of God. Help him. You've got to help him.")

AMALIA: Come out here, come! Your father's home!

(Maria appears, drying her eyes and fixing her hair.)

MARIA ROSARIA: Papa has come back?

AMALIA: Don't let him see you like that, don't tell him anything, it would kill him.

AMEDEO: *(Entering from the street.)* What? Papa has come back?

(Gennaro re-enters talking.)

GENNARO: Ama', she's got a high fever. I don't like the way she's breathing.

AMEDEO: Papa.

(Gennaro turns, the words are caught in his throat. They embrace.)

GENNARO: Amedeo, it's a miracle.

AMEDEO: Eh, Papa, bravo!

(Gennaro sees Maria half-hidden in a corner. At first he waits for her to come to him, then he speaks.)

GENNARO: Mari', Papa is here.

(She runs to him, embraces him. He is now in total joy, caught tightly between his children. A moment of euphoric confusion.) Yes, yes of course. Later I'll tell you . . . *(He takes off his coat and hat and moves toward his old room. Not finding it, he's confused.)* My room? Amalia?

AMALIA: Your room . . .

GENNARO: You got rid of it, too?

AMALIA: You weren't here.

GENNARO: No, no, I wasn't here. Still, it's a shame . . . but, of course, it's nicer this way.

AMEDEO: But tell us, where have you been, Papa?

GENNARO: I don't know. I couldn't tell you if I wanted to. Sit down. *(Puts his coat on a chair.)* Remember the day the Germans told us, "Evacuate! Everybody out in an hour and a half?" Hundreds of people with suitcases and mattresses. I was coming back with ten kilos of apples and four kilos of bread. I'd gone fourteen miles with fourteen kilos on my back. I can't tell you how my back ached. Suddenly on the streets it's, "Run! They're bombing the beach." "To the shelters! The Americans are landing. To the shelters." I kept thinking about you, about the children. Bomb whatever you want, I'm going home. I kept walking with those fourteen kilos, I wasn't going to leave them, eh? Shooting on all sides. It was hell. Machine guns, people dead on the street. I kept running, running — poom, I fell down, all the apples, the bread. All I remember is apples, blood, I'd hit my head.

I wonder who ate all those apples? I kept hearing voices, I wanted to get up, my legs knew I wanted to get up, but the rest of me didn't feel like it. Maybe I'm just in the shelter with all my family around me . . . The sound of a train . . . I could hear it from far away, then it got louder, but I thought, I'm in the shelter, then I opened my eyes to hear better and I say to myself, "It's a train." I could hear the wheels. It *was* a train! A bit of light — on, off, on, off. For how long? Who knows? Then silence. I began to feel space around me, I could move, some light, air, I could breathe. People moving, getting off the train. Me too, Where was I? Who knows. They cleaned my wounds, bandaged me up in an infirmary, in a tent, then a few days later a German sergeant asked me what I did for a living. I thought quick, if I tell him I drive a streetcar he'll say there are no streetcars here, you're useless and *(Demonstrates shooting him.)* parapoom, good-bye.

AMEDEO: Yes, those Germans don't waste time.

GENNARO: I looked around. . . I thought . . . "I dig," I said. "I lift stones." And I lifted some heavy stones, let me tell you. No food, no drink, bombs falling around us. I guess he liked me, because he always came and talked to me. I didn't understand a word, but I kept nodding my head. So three months went by. Then I ran away with some other Neapolitans. What a bunch! One of them said, if they catch us they'll shoot us. "Let them shoot us," I said, "Better to be dead than alive here." It wasn't living, Amalia. And so we walked, from country to country. *(Stops to think about it.)* I rode on top of a cart, on top of a train, I walked. What a sacrilege . . . cities and countries, destroyed, burned. People lost, shot, so much death everywhere. *(He stops, as if seeing it.)* The dead are all the same. Ama', I came back a different man. Remember when I came back from the last war, they found out what was wrong with me? Neurasthenia. I got mad all the time. But after this war, you don't want to hurt anyone. Not anyone, Amalia. *(He bursts into tears.)*

AMALIA: It's all right. There now, Gennarino, it's all right.

AMEDEO: Papa.

GENNARO: *(Mortified, a half smile.)* What can you do? Well, I met a man. We slept in an abandoned barn, I'd go find whatever work I could, then go back to sleep there at night. He never went out . . . at night he talked in his sleep. "Help!" "Here they come!" "Let me go!" He'd leap out of bed. Amalia, he was a Jew.

AMALIA: Poor man.

GENNARO: That poor Christian soul was a Jew. He only told me after about two months. I'd bring him bread and cheese or bread and fruit . . . we'd eat together. One day he was sure I was going to denounce him. He was a wreck, pale eyes popping out of his head. He seemed to have lost his mind. The next morning he woke me up, grabbing my shirt. "You're going to hand me over, aren't you? You want to sell my skin." "No," I said, "I want to go home." He kept crying, "Don't turn me in. Don't do it." A gray-haired man, he had children. He showed me their pictures. What is this world coming to? We'll pay for this someday, Amalia. Crying, "Don't do it, don't do it." I told him, first of all I am a good man. If the Blessed Virgin spares our lives and gets us home, you can come to Naples and everyone will tell you, I am a good man. But he couldn't get it out of his mind. Then we set out again, we crossed borders without even knowing it, we noticed different uniforms. I can't tell you the relief. By the time we separated, we were brothers, I even gave him my address and said "Whatever you need . . . "

AMALIA: Maybe this is his letter.

GENNARO: It's him. Yes. Thank God he got home safe!

(*Starts to reads it aloud, but Amedeo cuts him off, a little irritated.*)

AMEDEO: So, Papa, you had a bad time of it.

GENNARO: Let's not talk about it. I've told you nothing. This is nothing.

AMEDEO: Well, now you're here with us. Don't think about it anymore.

GENNARO: Don't think about it? That's easy to say. Who can forget?

AMEDEO: All right, Papa. The war is over.

GENNARO: You're wrong. You can't have seen what I've seen. The war isn't over.

AMEDEO: Papa, we're doing fine here.

GENNARO: I see you are, I see. I was almost killed so many times. It was Pompeii. But if I died, I wouldn't have seen this beautiful place all fixed up, this furniture, Maria Rosaria all elegant, beautiful, even Amedeo, and you in this dress like a great lady. (*He notices the earrings, the rings on her hands, the necklace, and is momentarily perplexed. Amalia instinctively tries to hide all this wealth.*) Let me see, Ama'. These are diamonds?

AMALIA: Yes, yes, they're diamonds. Diamonds.

(*A long pause. He looks shyly at Maria who slightly lowers her eyes. Now in a firmer tone he asks.*)

GENNARO: Tell me something, Amalia.

AMALIA: What's there to say? We fixed things up. Amedeo works very hard, earns a lot, and I sell a few things.

GENNARO: Do I have to play dead again?

AMALIA: *(Laughs a little too hard at her husband's humorous remark.)* No, of course not, Gennarino.

GENNARO: Don't make me do it again. It was bad luck. Every time I was in danger, I kept seeing those four candles in front of me. It followed me like a curse.

AMALIA: No, it's all different now with the Americans, the English.

GENNARO: I see, they help us, they always said they'd help us. They kept their word. And what do you sell?

AMEDEO: She's in business with Settebellezze.

AMALIA: Yes, we're in business. He comes and goes with his trucks. He's in transport.

GENNARO: Transport. Transport business, and the Americans give you the trucks?

AMALIA: That's right. *(Light irony.)* We tell them we want two trucks and they give them to us.

GENNARO: They were true to their word. And what about you, Amedeo?

AMEDEO: I work with cars. If I see a car in good condition, I sell it. *(To change the subject.)* Maria Rosaria has a surprise for you. She's going to America. She's marrying an American soldier.

(Maria doesn't move. Amalia wants to die. Gennaro is surprised, admiring, and sad. As he speaks he embraces her, she begins to cry, covering her face. He thinks she is sad about leaving her family.)

GENNARO: You? You're going to leave me? You're going over there? And what about your father? Don't cry, my sweetheart, I won't let you go. Papa will make you marry a nice Neapolitan, someone from your own country.

(Enrico enters speaking quickly, then he sees Gennaro and tries to change his tone mid-sentence.)

ENRICO: Ama. Oh . . . my . . . Don Gennaro is here, too!

GENNARO: Greetings, Settebellezze, I've only been here half an hour. I'll tell you. I'll tell you all about it later.

ENRICO: Where have you been?

GENNARO: What can I tell you? It's an *opera*. I hear you and my wife are in the transporting business. Things are going well. Congratulations.

ENRICO: Donna Amalia was telling me only an hour ago that she expected to see you any minute, and here you are. We just have a little business thing we do.

GENNARO: It's going well. Who cares? You are alone. In these terrible times, it's best to stay together, exchange some affection, support each other. It's a sad time. Every country I passed through, you can still hear the cannons, the bombs dropping. Every time I hear a door slam, my blood freezes. I found myself . . .

ENRICO: *(Interrupting.)* It's all right, Don Gennaro, don't think about it anymore. Some friends are coming over for dinner. Forget all about it, have some fun.

GENNARO: Forget it? Are you crazy? The war isn't over.

ENRICO: Have you seen the place, all fixed up?

GENNARO: Nice, very nice.

(Maria Rosaria goes out. The part-time priest enters with a large casserole covered with a big white sheet.)

THE PART-TIME PRIEST: Here's the meat. Don Gennaro! How are you?

GENNARO: You made it, too. I kept wondering if you'd survive the war.

THE PART-TIME PRIEST: We made it. Yes siree, we made it. Miraculously we're still here.

ENRICO: Don Gennaro, here's the roast lamb with potatoes for the special little dinner we're having.

GENNARO: *(Smelling it.)* Oh! Lamb stew with potatoes. There were times when the thought of a stew would have made us go wild. Oh, what we went through. There were times, we were in a ditch in the middle of nowhere, the bombs dropping, three days with no food, no drink, seven people and two corpses blown apart by shrapnel, at a certain point . . .

(The part-time priest is out on the street being handed two more large dishes, which he brings in.)

THE PART-TIME PRIEST: There's also a casserole of peppers, and an eggplant parmigiana.

GENNARO: Good God, a feast! So, as I was saying . . .

(Amalia is tense and nervous, Amedeo checks the clock every few minutes, only Enrico pretends to listen, but obviously his thoughts are elsewhere.)

AMALIA: Later, Gennarino. Later, you can tell us everything. Now it's time to eat.

GENNARO: But I just wanted to say . . .

AMALIA: After dinner. Now, people are coming.

ENRICO: Friends are arriving.

GENNARO: Then I'll go wash my hands and throw some water on my face. I'm covered in dust.

ENRICO: Good.

GENNARO: Then I'll tell you, Don Enrico. The things I saw with my own two eyes would stop your heart, the last war was a joke.

(He exits. Amalia doesn't dare look at Enrico.)

ASSUNTA: I've come to give you a hand, Donna Ama'.

AMALIA: Good, because I don't know where my head is. We have to set the table.

ASSUNTA: You're telling me. *(Amalia takes a tablecloth out of a drawer, gives it to Assunta who starts to set the table. Amedeo helps, they add a small table to the larger one, to make more room for the guests. Then Amedeo goes to the kitchen to get something.)* My aunt is getting dressed. She's wearing a nice new dress. She's making a lot of money, too. I'm not dressing up. I'm in mourning. Donna Ama', I hear that Don Gennaro is back. Is it true? My aunt says he looks terrible. "I wonder how Donna Amalia is doing," she says, "and what Settebellezze will do. Because now it's over for him."

ENRICO: What is?

ASSUNTA: Nothing.

ENRICO: Can't you ever stop talking?

ASSUNTA: Oh well, what can you do.

(Amedeo re-enters. Amalia, irritated by Assunta's talk, goes into the other room. Peppe and Federico enter with other guests, they stop and chat warmly with Enrico. The women are in expensive furs, the men are dressed in dark suits. Lots of showy jewels, lots of bad taste. Then Adelaide enters, also dressed up. Enrico is the obvious star, presents are passed around, some have brought flowers or candies. Enrico looks like the man in charge of their protection and their livelihood.)

PEPPE: Here we are to celebrate you the way you deserve.

ENRICO: Thank you. But this isn't my party. Don Gennaro has come back, this party is for him.

FEDERICO: I heard he was back.

PEPPE: There he is! Don Genna', congratulations.

GENNARO: And to you, Peppe.

(He moves toward the other guests who shake his hand and greet him.)

PEPPE: What have you been doing all this time?

GENNARO: Let's not talk about it. I'm here. It seems like a miracle, but I'm here! What luxury! I'm only sorry I'm not presentable and worthy of your company. This is like the flag of my regiment. If these clothes could talk. Just think, we were in a ditch, bombs falling all around us. *(He stops, hoping for someone's interest, but sees that no one is really listening. A few are nodding their heads, pretending.)* We were three days without food or drink, seven people, two corpses blown apart by shrapnel . . . then . . .

FEDERICO: Don Gennaro, don't think of sad things. We're here to make you forget.

ADELAIDE: You should eat, drink, put on some weight, because you look terrible.

FEDERICO: That's right. Don Genna', tell us about your master plan.

(They all laugh. The part-time priest goes out. Amedeo has finished setting the table, Peppe takes him aside.)

PEPPE: So?

AMEDEO: So nothing.

PEPPE: What do you mean?

AMEDEO: I don't want to land up in jail. Settebellezze warned me, and now my father is back.

PEPPE: What do you mean? This is a no-risk operation. The doctor parks his car right at the top of a hill. I've got a lookout, it's just a matter of minutes.

(They continue to talk sotto voce. Amalia comes back in, wearing a silver fox cape. Maria Rosaria stands off to one side.)

GENNARO: Come and sit, come. Everything here is for you.

AMALIA: Good evening. *(They all answer, "Good evening, Donna Ama'." Many compliments on the food.)* Assunta, tell the part-time priest to start serving. Sit down, everyone.

ADELAIDE: Don Genna', sit down.

GENNARO: Life is really like the movies. I can't believe I'm really here with you. *(He sits.)*

ENRICO: Well, what can you do?

GENNARO: Oh, how we suffered. It wasn't the lack of food, it wasn't the thirst, but the fear of death . . . Can you imagine, there we were in a ditch, grenades, cannons, at a certain point a truck . . .

ENRICO: By the way, excuse me Don Genna' or I'll forget. Federico, there's a truck coming. We'll have to go check it out tomorrow. It even has a permit. If you're interested . . .

FEDERICO: Of course I'm interested. We'll go tomorrow. I'll bring Peppe the Jack.

ENRICO: We only get about ten percent

PEPPE: Yes, it'll be a good deal.

GENNARO: So, there we were in a ditch, grenades falling all around us.

PEPPE: *(Mocking him.)* And the bombs . . . They all say, "Don Genna."

THE PART-TIME PRIEST: Here's the lamb.

PEPPE: Come on, everybody, we're gonna eat.

ASSUNTA: We just want a little peace. To your good health, it's over now.

GENNARO: What are you saying? It's not over.

ENRICO: All right, whatever you say. But let's eat now and not think of trouble.

(Amalia, rolling up the sleeves of her fur, starts to dish out the food. The part-

time priest goes to the next room. Everyone starts to eat, laughing and talk-ing. Gennaro observes, thinks. He gets up.)

GENNARO: Amalia, I'm going in to sit with Rituccia.

ENRICO: What are you doing, Don Genna', where are you going?

(They all call out to him, "Don Genna'.")

GENNARO: I'll go stay with the little one. She's got a high fever.

AMALIA: No, I'll go.

GENNARO: No, no, you stay there. I'm not even hungry and I'm so tired. Stay, it's better this way.

MARIA ROSARIA: I'll come with you, Papa.

(He takes her by the hand and they start to exit, but Adelaide stops them.)

ADELAIDE: Don Genna, I know it doesn't look good. I understand you're still a little frightened. You're still nervous. But everything is fine here. Every-thing's over.

GENNARO: No, you're wrong. The war isn't over. Nothing is over. *(He turns to Maria Rosaria.)* What's wrong?

MARIA ROSARIA: Nothing.

(They go offstage. The half-priest comes on, triumphantly carrying in two big bottles of wine. "Here's the wine." General cries of satisfaction.)

END OF ACT TWO

Act Three

The next day, same as Act Two, it's evening, lights in front of the Madonna are lit. Brigadier Ciappa is seated at the table in the center. Gennaro is walking slowly back and forth behind him. He stops to look out in the street once in a while. After a pause, Ciappa speaks.

CIAPPA: Ever since I met you in your house, I always remembered you with a certain fondness. I passed by here several times while you were away to ask for news of you. Which is why I've come, and I'm sorry to have to tell you this. I have sons myself, three gifts from God. I'm a man of the world. What I mean is, I know the crooks of this world and I know the difference when I meet someone like you . . .

GENNARO: *(Interrupting, but grateful.)* I understand, Brigadier, and I thank you. At another time what you told me about Amedeo would have made me crazy. Who knows what I would have done! But now, what can I do, kick him out of the house? And my daughter and my wife?

CIAPPA: But I haven't told you everything about your son. Tonight, I'm going to arrest him.

GENNARO: Well, he deserves it.

CIAPPA: It's true. We've been watching him and Peppe the Jack for some time now. You wouldn't believe it, Don Genna', people leave their cars, turn their eyes away for a minute, and they're gone. This Peppe has a special talent. He slides under the car, lifts it up with his shoulder, I don't know how he does it. They take the wheels off in two minutes. Tonight, they've got another one planned. If I catch them, they're going to jail.

GENNARO: So, take them to jail.

CIAPPA: You mean I should arrest them?

GENNARO: If you catch them in the act, arrest them.

(Assunta enters.)

ASSUNTA: Is Donna Amalia back?

GENNARO: No

ASSUNTA: When are they coming? The doctor is here, waiting.

THE DOCTOR: *(Enters.)* Has anyone arrived yet?

GENNARO: Not yet, doctor.

THE DOCTOR: Good God, I told you, she's very sick. The fever's not going down.

ADELAIDE: Holy Mother of God!

ASSUNTA: *Ave Maria, gratia plena, Dominus tecum, Benedicta tu in mulieribus . . .*

THE DOCTOR: *(Glaring at the two women.)* It's really serious. Especially because you only remembered to call me at the last minute.

ADELAIDE: Holy Mother of God!

(Assunta starts the Ave Maria all over again.)

THE DOCTOR: These women have such terrible habits.

ASSUNTA: No, it's just that to us the doctor means bad luck.

THE DOCTOR: So then die. But don't talk to me about bad luck. Any minute now that poor child could be dead.

ADELAIDE: Holy Archangel Gabriel, Santa Rita, Santa Christina, save us, save us.

(She starts saying the Ave Maria along with Assunta.)

THE DOCTOR: There's no point in calling on Heaven. Faith is a beautiful thing, but down here, if we don't get the medicine, the little girl will die.

ASSUNTA: You see, we were right.

THE DOCTOR: That we bring bad luck?

ADELAIDE: No, but we can still hope. You don't have the last word.

THE DOCTOR: Yes, I have the last word. Of course we can hope. If we get the medicine, there's a ninety percent chance that the child will live.

ADELAIDE: Holy Mother of God!

(The two women go off praying.)

CIAPPA: Is it really hard to find this medicine?

THE DOCTOR: Hard! Everything is hard to get these days. And at night! Even in the daytime, any medicine costs an arm and a leg. And you can only find it on the black market. Enough. I'll stay a little longer.

GENNARO: Excuse me, doctor.

THE DOCTOR: Nothing, I'll go back to the child.

GENNARO: You can only find it on the black market. When the doctor said, "If you can't find it, the child could die," you should have seen her mother. She ran out of here and now she's chasing all around Naples. Will she find it, who knows? The doctor said, "Only on the black market can you find it." My wife's face turned white.

(Amedeo enters, running.)

AMEDEO: Nothing! Nothing! The two or three pharmacies that were open didn't have it. I went everywhere, door to door. Nothing. They said tomorrow, maybe. It's getting late.

THE PART-TIME PRIEST: Let me sit down. My feet are killing me. Well, I found this, it's medicine.

THE DOCTOR: Let me see. This is for chicken pox.

THE PART-TIME PRIEST: It's no good?

THE DOCTOR: I can't deal with idiots. They drive me crazy.

THE PART-TIME PRIEST: What about this?

THE DOCTOR: This is to dry up the milk of nursing mothers.

THE PART-TIME PRIEST: Really? And this?

THE DOCTOR: It's rubbing alcohol. All of it's useless. Good God, I wrote it down on a piece of paper. If it wasn't the right stuff, why did you bring it?

THE PART-TIME PRIEST: *(Trying to cheer him up.)* Doctor, don't get mad. It's not like before the war when you could get whatever you wanted. You doctors have to be adaptable. Can't you make do with this?

THE DOCTOR: Make do, make do! Leave me alone. Wait. *(He pulls a little note pad out of his pocket and writes.)* Try again. Go to a colleague of mine, see if he's got it. Here's his address.

THE PART-TIME PRIEST: *(Taking the piece of paper.)* Is it far?

THE DOCTOR: You can get there and back in ten minutes. Don't bring me anything useless or I'll throw it in your face.

THE PART-TIME PRIEST: All right.

(The doctor excuses himself and goes back into the room. Amedeo has been circling, looking at Ciappa, at his father, at the clock, at the street. He's agitated. He doesn't leave yet, his mind is elsewhere. Finally, he decides with a half-smile to speak.)

AMEDEO: Maybe Mamma's found it. Maybe she's bringing it now. You just have to be patient. Papa, are you staying here? I'll just go to Torretta.

GENNARO: Maybe you don't need to go. Maybe you don't have to.

AMEDEO: It's important, but I'll be back soon.

GENNARO: You know what I was thinking, Brigadier? That you're always working, even now when you're just sitting here, you're working. *(To Amedeo.)* Are you in a hurry?

AMEDEO: *(Hesitantly.)* No.

GENNARO: I see. Sit down. *(Amedeo sits.)* You're always working because in wartime the delinquents come floating to the top. Smugglers, tricksters, forgers, car thieves. *(Amedeo reacts.)* And remember that day I played dead? You didn't throw me in jail. You understood, people have to live and protect themselves. It takes a lot of courage to sell false documents, to steal trucks, and people have been able to eat because of those trucks that come and go. With war comes poverty and poverty brings hunger. So either because you're poor or hungry or ignorant, people do these things. War destroys everything. But, Brigadier, you don't become a thief because of the war. A thief is born. And you can't say that a thief is Neapolitan or French or English or German. A thief is a thief. He has no mother, no father, no nationality. And there's no room for him in our country. In fact, before the war all the thieves went across the ocean to America to make their fortunes.

AMEDEO: Why are you telling me this, Papa?

GENNARO: Our country doesn't have a good reputation. What can you do? It's a shame. Whenever they hear "Napoletano," they're already suspicious. It's always been that way. When you hear of a great theft that took a lot of cleverness in any other country in the world, the first thing they say is, it must have happened in Naples. Don't you know anything? In Naples, a whole ship loaded with cargo disappeared. Isn't that true, Captain? It's not possible. How can a ship disappear? It's not a handbag. And yet it's true. Logically, if this is true, it means that one Neapolitan pickpocket got together with another pickpocket who wasn't Neapolitan. Or how else could that boat disappear? Trucks, yes. Hundreds of trucks can disappear. So you're a young man. You have to set a good example. When you hear bad things said about your country, you can say, "All right, we have thieves and we have honest people just like in every other country in the world."

CIAPPA: Absolutely.

AMEDEO: Of course. All right, Papa, I'm going.

GENNARO: (Holding back his distress, he speaks as if to say, You deserve it.) Go! (Amedeo starts to go and Gennaro stops him, asking.) Do you have your handkerchief?

AMEDEO: (Reaching in his pocket.) Yes, Papa.

GENNARO: And wear your coat.

AMEDEO: Why, Papa?

GENNARO: Because it may get cold tonight. You may be out late.

AMEDEO: I won't be late. But if you like, I'll take it. I'll be home early, Papa. (Amedeo goes. Gennaro is very sad. A long pause.)

GENNARO: Take care of yourself, Brigadier, and thank you.

CIAPPA: Good night, Don Gennaro. And best wishes for the little girl. (He exits. After a pause, Maria Rosaria enters. She's completely changed. Soberly dressed, she has a strange faraway look. She gets a cup of coffee and leaves. Gennaro looks at her tenderly and sadly. Peppe enters slowly, smoking half a cigarette blissfully.)

PEPPE: Good evening, Don Gennaro. Is Amedeo here?

GENNARO: (Icily.) He just went out.

PEPPE: We have an appointment. I guess he left early. How's the little girl doing?

GENNARO: We'll see.

PEPPE: I don't feel so good either. I've got an ache in my shoulder. I can hardly move.

GENNARO: Your right shoulder?

PEPPE: Yeah.

GENNARO: It's the car.

PEPPE: What?

GENNARO: Your shoulder hurts?

PEPPE: Yes.

GENNARO: Your right shoulder?

PEPPE: Yes sir.

GENNARO: It's the car.

PEPPE: What's the car got to do with it?

GENNARO: Maybe you're driving your car with your shoulder next to the open window.

PEPPE: No, no, that's not it. It's that I'm making a lot of money, Don Genna, but I work too hard. I'm in business with your son, but tonight I'm going to tell him I need a little vacation.

GENNARO: Yes, a little vacation. A couple of years.

PEPPE: A couple of years! That's what I could use. Where no one bothers you. A peaceful place.

GENNARO: Yes, a kind of monastery.

PEPPE: That's right. Something simple, where everything is set up for me. I'm tired of getting out there every day.

GENNARO: A cell.

PEPPE: Exactly. A cell. A nice place where you get your meals every day.

GENNARO: Always at the same time. Where you don't have to worry about what you're going to eat. And someone who watches over you.

PEPPE: Yes. I'd pay him.

GENNARO: Oh, you wouldn't need to. He'd do it out of a sense of duty. A nice window, with bars.

PEPPE: No, I don't like bars on the window.

GENNARO: Well, you have to have them.

PEPPE: Why?

GENNARO: If it's an isolated place, these days, with all the thieves running around, you can't be too careful. A monastery has beautiful iron work. Didn't you want to go to a monastery?

PEPPE: Yes.

GENNARO: Well, then you have to have bars.

PEPPE: Fine, I'll have bars on the window.

GENNARO: Absolutely.

PEPPE: Jesus, I really can't move this shoulder. I'm telling Amedeo tonight.

GENNARO: Just one more push and you can rest all you want.

PEPPE: Right. Good night, Don Genna'.

GENNARO: I'll come visit you when you're in your cell.

PEPPE: Good.

GENNARO: I'll bring you cigarettes.

PEPPE: I'll be expecting you.

GENNARO: I'll be going to see my son. I can see you at the same time.

(*Peppe leaves, a pause, and Enrico enters, coming from the other side of the street. He's tired, a bit agitated, asks with concern about the child.*)

ENRICO: Good evening, how is Rituccia? I met the part-time priest, he told me things haven't changed, she's still got a fever. (*Gennaro is still silent.*) I asked for the medicine. (*He holds up the paper.*) I got the prescription right here. They said, by tomorrow. (*Enrico is thrown by Gennaro's total dismissal of him. He sits slowly. A pause.*) It's so sad, everyone is so sad, especially right now, just as you come home. It's not as if Donna Amalia hasn't been taking care of her. But you know how it is, little children often get these high fevers. Well, we shouldn't worry too much. They can bounce right back. Poor Donna Amalia, she doesn't deserve this. She'd die for her family. While you were away, we all saw how she thought only of them. Anyone who says anything against her is a liar. Don't listen to them. I'm your friend, you can believe me. (*Gennaro looks up to control himself.*) I even tried to give your son some fatherly advice while you were away. I did it with all my heart. (*Gennaro's silence is exasperating. Enrico is almost talking to himself, like a confession.*) A woman alone with no man in the house. You know how it is. They saw me coming and going all the time. What could they have thought? But I give you my word of honor that Donna Amalia respected you and still respects you. You treated me coldly this morning. I noticed, and I've come back to see you and to talk to you. Are we men or beasts? Don Genna', I certainly have to ask you to forgive me. I certainly do. But about Donna Amalia, you can be sure, you can be more than sure. I'm leaving for Calabria tonight, and when you go out at night there, you never know if you come home alive. That's why I wanted to . . . seeing the way you were this morning . . . If I can be helpful to you in any way . . . I wish you well for your little girl and . . . Good night. (*He moves a few more steps. Then, without turning around, he speaks quite moved.*) Again, Don Genna', good-bye.

(*The part-time priest enters.*)

THE PART-TIME PRIEST: Don Genna', I didn't find a thing. I found this box of pills. I'll go show the doctor.

(Amalia enters, frantic, completely changed from the other acts. This is the first time we see her real face, the face of a mother. She's almost old. She has nothing more to hide. She sits by the table.)

AMALIA: Nothing, nothing, nothing. I asked everybody. I went through the whole town. Whoever's got it won't sell it. Don't they have a conscience, trying to raise the price on medicine? Medicine that can save a human being? My daughter has to die. They won't sell it so they can raise the prices. Isn't that monstrous! It's a sin.

(She gets up and goes into the child's room. Gennaro follows her with his eyes. Riccardo enters in a dark raincoat covering his pajamas.)

RICCARDO: Excuse me, good evening. They told me that you need a medicine for the little girl. I think I have it. Is this it?

GENNARO: Please sit down. Doctor, could you come here a minute?

THE DOCTOR: I'm coming. *(Enters.)* What is it?

GENNARO: This man lives right next door. He says he thinks he has the medicine that you asked for. Is this it?

THE DOCTOR: Let me see. Yes, that's it!

RICCARDO: I just happened to have it. Six months ago, my daughter was sick.

THE DOCTOR: What a stroke of luck! Give it to me.

RICCARDO: No, I'd like to give it to Signora Amalia myself.

GENNARO: Ama', come here a minute. Someone wants to see you.

(Amalia enters, followed by the part-time priest. Riccardo speaks with no sense of revenge in his voice.)

RICCARDO: Donna Ama', I have the medicine that you were looking for, for your daughter.

AMALIA: How much do you want for it?

RICCARDO: You'd give me anything for this, wouldn't you? What could you give me? With thousands of lire in my hand I had to beg you for a bit of rice for my daughters. Now you want me to give you this.

AMALIA: But this is medicine.

(Gennaro slowly turns his back on them as if to remove himself from the scene. The part-time priest is busy. He always has something to look for in his pants pocket to keep him uninvolved.)

RICCARDO: I'll bet you've been running through the streets begging. I could say to you, Go ring every doorbell, house by house, street by street, as I had to do, but I won't. Donna Amalia, I just want you to understand that once in a while we have to come knocking on each other's doors. *(Gives the box to the doctor.)* Here. Best wishes for the little girl. Good night.

(Exits. Amalia and the doctor hurry into Rituccia's room. The part-time priest groans.)

GENNARO: Don't you have something to do?

THE DOCTOR: *(Back from Rituccia's room.)* I'm going. We'll have to see if the fever breaks. We have to wait. It will be a long night. I'll be here early in the morning, and I'm sure you'll have good news for me. Good night.

ADELAIDE: Good night

ASSUNTA: Good night

AMALIA: *(Enters. To Gennaro.)* Why are you looking at me? I did what everyone else did. I protected myself. I helped myself. Why don't you speak to me? This morning you just looked at me. You didn't talk. What are you blaming me for? What did they tell you?

GENNARO: You want me to talk? You really want to hear me talk? I'll talk. Hey, part-time, please go away. See you tomorrow morning.

THE PART-TIME PRIEST: Good night

(Gennaro closes the glass door and slowly approaches his wife. He doesn't know where to begin.)

GENNARO: Ama', when I came back from the last war, they couldn't stop talking about it. They wanted to know every detail, all the heroic deeds. They wanted so much, I ended up lying, making up things that had never happened. But now, why doesn't anybody want to talk about it now? First, we didn't want this war. And, second, because you see money and you lose your head. First you started to see a little — a few hundred lire, then a thousand, then millions. And you lost your head. *(He takes a pile of bills and slides them across the table.)* Look, Ama', I can touch it and my heart doesn't pound. Your heart should pound when you touch so much money. What can I say, if I'd stayed here, maybe I would have gone crazy, too. Last night, standing by her sister's bed, Maria Rosaria told me everything that happened to her. What should I do? Throw her out in the street? And you, what should I do? Amedeo's a thief. Our son is a thief. *(He sees Amalia's complete collapse, he is moved.)* I know I should have been here. I should've. Now we have to wait, Ama'. What did the doctor say? We have to wait. It will be a long night.

(He slowly gets up and opens the glass door to get air. Amalia starts to cry as if waking from a bad dream.)

AMALIA: What happened? What happened?

GENNARO: The war, Ama'.

AMALIA: What happened?

(Maria Rosaria enters.)

GENNARO: Mari', heat up some coffee, please.

(Maria lights a spirit lamp under the coffeepot.)

AMALIA: I'd go out in the morning to buy food. Amedeo would take Rituccia to school. I'd come home and cook. What happened? At night, we'd sit around the table and make the sign of the cross before eating. What happened?

(She cries silently. Amedeo enters, slowly.)

AMEDEO: How's Rituccia?

(Gennaro's face lights up.)

GENNARO: We've found the medicine. The doctor did what he could. Now we have to wait. And you? Didn't you go to your appointment?

AMEDEO: No. I couldn't stop thinking about Rituccia. So I didn't go. It seemed wrong.

GENNARO: It was wrong. Give me a kiss. Go stand by her bed. She's got a high fever.

AMEDEO: Yes, Papa.

GENNARO: And if Rituccia's better tomorrow, I'll go with you to the gas company so you can look for work.

AMEDEO: Yes, Papa.

(Maria gives a cup to her father. Gennaro looks at her tenderly and brushes her forehead. He's about to drink his coffee, but he sees Amalia tired and broken.)

GENNARO: Here, have a sip of coffee.

(Amalia accepts gladly, looks up at her husband with questioning eyes as if to say, "How can we go back to what we had before?" Gennaro answers as if he has read her mind.)

We have to wait and see, Ama'. It'll be a long night.

(The lights fade.)

END OF PLAY